INTERPRETING WEIGHT

SOCIAL PROBLEMS AND SOCIAL ISSUES

An Aldine de Gruyter Series of Texts and Monographs

SERIES EDITOR

Joel Best, *Southern Illinois University at Carbondale*

Joel Best (*editor*), **Images of Issues: Typifying Contemporary Social Problems** (Second Edition)

Joel Best (*editor*), **Troubling Children: Studies of Children and Social Problems**

James J. Chriss (*editor*), **Counseling and the Therapeutic State**

della Porta, Donatella and Alberto Vannucci, **Corrupt Exchanges: Actors, Resourses, and Mechanisms of Political Corruption**

Jeff Ferrell and Neil Websdale (*editors*), **Making Trouble: Cultural Constructions of Crime, Deviance, and Control**

Anne E. Figert, **Women and the Ownership of PMS: The Structuring a Psychiatric Disorder**

Mark Fishman and Gray Cavender (*editors*), **Entertaining Crime: Television Reality Programs**

James A. Holstein, **Court-Ordered Insanity: Interpretive Practice and Involuntary Commitment**

James A. Holstein and Gale Miller (*editors*), **Reconsidering Social Constructionism: Debates in Social Problems Theory**

Gale Miller and James A. Holstein (*editors*), **Constructionist Controversies: Issues in Social Problems Theory**

Philip Jenkins, **Intimate Enemies: Moral Panics in Contemporary Great Britain**

Philip Jenkins, **Using Murder: The Social Construction of Serial Homicide**

Valerie Jenness, **Making It Work: The Prostitutes' Rights Movement in Perspective**

Valerie Jenness and Kendal Broad, **Hate Crimes: New Social Movements and the Politics of Violence**

Stuart A. Kirk and Herb Kutchins, **The Selling of *DSM*: The Rhetoric of Science in Psychiatry**

John Lofland, **Social Movement Organizations: Guide to Research on Insurgent Realities**

Donileen R. Loseke, **Thinking About Social Problems: An Introduction to Constructionist Perspectives**

Leslie Margolin, **Goodness Personified: The Emergence of Gifted Children**

Donna Maurer and Jeffery Sobal (*editors*), **Eating Agendas: Food and Nutrition as Social Problems**

Gale Miller, **Becoming Miracle Workers: Language and Meaning in Brief Therapy**

Bernard Paillard, **Notes on the Plague Years: AIDS in Marseilles**

Dorothy Pawluch, **The New Pediatrics: A Profession in Transition**

Erdwin H. Pfuhl and Stuart Henry, **The Deviance Process** (Third Edition)

William B. Sanders, **Gangbangs and Drivebys: Grounded Culture and Juvenile Gang Violence**

Theodore Sasson, **Crime Talk: How Citizens Construct a Social Problem**

Wilbur J. Scott, **The Politics of Readjustment: Vietnam Veterans since the War**

Wilbur J. Scott and Sandra Carson Stanley (*editors*), **Gays and Lesbians in the Military: Issues, Concerns, and Contrasts**

Jeffrey Sobal and Donna Maurer (*editors*), **Weighty Issues: Fatness and Thinnness as Social Problems**

Jeffrey Sobal and Donna Maurer (*editors*), **Interpreting Weight: The Social Management of Fatness and Thinness**

Robert A. Stallings, **Promoting Risk: Constructing the Earthquake Threat**

Frank J. Weed, **Certainty of Justice: Reform in the Crime Victim Movement**

Rhys Williams (*editor*), **Cultural Wars in American Politics: Critical Reviews of a Popular Myth**

INTERPRETING WEIGHT

The Social Management of Fatness and Thinness

Jeffery Sobal and Donna Maurer

Editors

ALDINE DE GRUYTER

New York

About the Editors

Jeffery Sobal is Associate Professor in the Division of Nutritional Sciences at Cornell University, where he teaches about social science analysis of food, eating, and nutrition. His research interests focus on social patterns of obesity, body weight and marriage, and the role of weight in society, particularly stigmatization of obese individuals and medicalization of obesity as a social problem. He co-edited, with Donna Maurer, *Eating Agendas: Food and Nutrition as Social Problems* (Aldine, 1995).

Donna Maurer is a John S. Knight Postdoctoral Fellow in the Writing Program at Cornell University. In 1997, she received her doctorate in sociology from Southern Illinois University-Carbondale, where she won the Outstanding Dissertation Award. She co-edited, with Jeffery Sobal, *Eating Agendas: Food and Nutrition as Social Problems* and is currently completing a book on the North American vegetarian movement.

ALDINE DE GRUYTER
A division of Walter de Gruyter, Inc.
200 Saw Mill River Road
Hawthorne, New York 10532

This publication is printed on acid free paper ∞

Library of Congress Cataloging-in-Publication Data
Interpreting weight : the social management of fatness and thinness /
   Jeffery Sobal and Donna Mauer.
      p.   cm.
   Includes bibliographical references and index.
   ISBN 0-202-30577-5 (alk. paper). — ISBN 0-202-30578-3 (pbk. :
alk. paper)
      1. Obesity—Social aspects.   2. Food—Social aspects.
   3. Nutrition—Social aspects.   I. Sobal, Jeffery, 1950–   .
   II. Maurer, Donna, 1961–   .
   RA645.O23I55   1999
   306.4′61—dc21   99-13617
                                                                                              CIP

Manufactured in the United States of America

10 9 8 7 6 5 4 3 2 1

Contents

Preface   *vii*

PART I   INTRODUCTION

1 The Social Management of Fatness and Thinness
   Donna Maurer and Jeffery Sobal   *3*

PART II   WEIGHT IDENTITIES

2 The Adoption and Management of a "Fat" Identity
   Douglas Degher and Gerald Hughes   *11*

3 Identity Management among Overweight Women:
   Narrative Resistance to Stigma
   Gina Cordell and Carol Rambo Ronai   *29*

4 Fighting Back:
   Reactions and Resistance
   to the Stigma of Obesity
   Leanne Joanisse and Anthony Synnott   *49*

PART III   REDEFINING WEIGHT

5 From "Dieting" to "Healthy Eating":
   An Exploration of Shifting Constructions of
   Eating for Weight Control
   Gwen E. Chapman   *73*

6 Medical Discourse on Body Image:
   Reconceptualizing the Differences between
   Women with and without Eating Disorders
   Susan Haworth-Hoeppner   *89*

7   Weight and Weddings:
     The Social Construction of Beautiful Brides
          Jeffery Sobal, Caron Bove, and Barbara Rauschenbach   *113*

          **PART IV   ORGANIZATIONAL PROCESSES IN
                         WEIGHT MANAGEMENT**

8   Let Go and Let God:
     Religion and the Politics of Surrender
     in Overeaters Anonymous
          Rebecca J. Lester   *139*

9   Fat World/Thin World: "Fat Busters,"
     "Equivocators," "Fat Boosters," and
     the Social Construction of Obesity
          Karen Honeycutt   *165*

10   Creating "Uniformity": The Construction of
     Bodies in Women's Collegiate Cross Country
          Elizabeth Ransom   *183*

          PART V   REINTERPRETING WEIGHT

11   Pounds of Flesh:
     Weight, Gender, and Body Images
          Thomas F. Cash and Robin E. Roy   *209*

12   Re-evaluating the Weight-Centered Approach
     Toward Health:
     The Need for a Paradigm Shift
          Jeanine C. Cogan   *229*

Biographical Sketches of the Contributors   *255*

Index   *259*

Preface

What is "too fat"? What is "too thin"? Interpretations of body weight vary widely across and within cultures. Meeting cultural weight expectations is a major concern for many people because failing to do so may incur dire social consequences, such as difficulty in finding a romantic partner or even finding adequate employment. Attaining an "ideal weight" is a social achievement. Without cultural expectations and sanctions, and without the pressures of social interactions with family, friends, co-workers, and acquaintances, body weight would only be a health issue. While socially constructed standards of acceptable body weight may seem immutable, they are re-created continuously through social interaction. Social interactions can perpetuate or transform social expectations about body weight.

Understanding social constructions of body weight requires insight regarding how people develop and use constructions in their daily lives. While structural conditions and cultural environments make important contributions to weight constructions, the chapters in this book focus on the *social processes* in which people engage while they interpret, negotiate, resist, and transform cultural definitions and expectations. As such, most of the chapters in this volume borrow from and contribute to a symbolic interactionist perspective.

THE SOCIAL CONSTRUCTION OF BODY WEIGHT AND SYMBOLIC INTERACTIONISM

Social constructionist thinking occurs in many forms, with symbolic interactionism as a core theoretical perspective. Symbolic interactionists are concerned with the production of meanings and the creation and social management of selves. In addition, they examine how people construct definitions and preferences in the course of human interaction. This approach contrasts with a "social facts" or objectivist perspective, which focuses on documenting and explaining the existence of social phenomena primarily through quantitative analyses and interpretations (Ritzer 1975).

This brief overview addresses some of the basic concepts used by authors in this volume.

HUMAN AGENCY, MEANING, AND INTERPRETATION

A central concept in symbolic interactionism (as well as in this book) is human agency: each person's potential capacity to make choices and to affect others' actions, despite the constraints imposed by large, pervasive structural realities. While agency can be a problematic theoretical variable (Alexander 1987; Emirbayer and Mische 1998), it is key to symbolic interactionism and other related perspectives (including many forms of social constructionism, social phenomenology, and humanist sociology) because it suggests that human actions are not determined only by social structure. Humans are creative beings fully capable of initiating and carrying out positive social changes.

Exerting agency, however, necessitates an understanding of the social environment, which is discovered through the interpretation of meanings. Meanings do not reside within individuals; they are social phenomena made possible by a common language. "Symbolic interactionism sees meanings as social products, as creations that are formed in and through the defining activities of people as they interact" (Blumer 1969:5). Meanings become solidified through habituated social interaction and often become taken for granted (Berger and Luckmann 1966). Hence, people often act upon these meanings as if they are objectively real. As W. I. Thomas wrote, "If men define situations as real, they are real in their consequences" (1966:301). If people define themselves as "overweight" with reference to a shared cultural ideal, they are likely to act on the basis of this definition, by perhaps dieting, wearing certain clothes, or acting as they believe an "overweight" person should act. When people regard socially constructed meanings as facts, they sustain and perpetuate these meanings as seemingly objective reality.

Shared meanings do not necessarily perpetuate cultural beliefs and standards, however. When people share a social world, they can negotiate joint lines of action that generate new meanings. These emergent meanings can have behavioral consequences. As social meanings about ideal body weight shift, people may interpret their social environments and personal experiences differently. For example, within certain social groups, "fatness" may shift from a pejorative to a neutral term, leading their members to define themselves differently and to act in accordance with these new definitions. Accepting an emergent definition of "fat acceptance" may lead a person to abandon dieting rituals and to focus on personal qualities and characteristics other than body weight.

SELF AND IDENTITY

Symbolic interactionism also deals with the creation and re-creation of the self. "All interactionists . . . agree that self is not an object that has inherent meaning, but is a construct that is given meaning through an actor's choices, mediated by the relationships, situations, and cultures in which she or he is embedded" (Fine 1993:78). The "self" is not innate or static, but an emergent social product created through interacting with others (Charon 1998). Like all other social objects, the self is socially defined; hence one's self is, in part, created by others in the social environment. These social responses contribute to a person's *identity*, how one sees oneself and how others view and categorize one as being a particular *type* of person. While the *self* may include a broad set of perceptions about who one is, one's *identity* tends to be more specifically grounded in socially constructed cultural categories (Cerulo 1997). For example, a person may identify or be identified by others as a fat person or someone with anorexia nervosa.

Cultural consensus develops around the interpretation of specific identities, with some identities preferable to others. For example, being fat in most Western societies is an undesirable, stigmatized identity associated with negative personal characteristics (Sobal 1999). Possessing a stigmatized identity requires social management to lessen the negative responses of others (Goffman 1963). Those with stigmatized identities may engage in behaviors that lessen the magnitude of their negatively perceived characteristic. For example, a culturally defined fat person may dress to diminish the size of her appearance, or may eat less in public to assuage people's negative comments (Zdrodowski 1996).

Self and identity, then, affect people's choices as they present themselves to the world in ways congruent with their self-definitions. People effect presentations of self as they attempt to engage in effective role performances, emphasizing the most desirable aspects of their identities and minimizing the least desirable ones. As people define situations and the attendant social identities of others with whom they interact, they serve as both actors and audiences in a variety of social settings (Cahill 1998). Effective performances are key to managing any social stigma, as social interactions provide opportunities for stigmatized individuals to redefine themselves, both personally and socially.

CONCLUSION

A symbolic interactionist perspective contributes to our understanding of social constructions of body weight because it focuses our attention on the microlevel, interactive, and processual aspects of human life. Social constructions exist within a culture and often are perpetuated by those with economic interests, providing a common set of social meanings that people interpret, respond to, and potentially can transform. A symbolic interactionist perspective provides insight into the various dimensions of these social processes.

Donna Maurer

Jeffery Sobal

REFERENCES

Alexander, J. 1987. *Twenty Lectures: Sociological Theory Since World War II.* New York: Columbia University Press.

Berger, P. L., and T. Luckmann. 1966. *The Social Construction of Reality: A Treatise in the Sociology of Knowledge.* New York: Doubleday.

Blumer, H. 1969. *Symbolic Interactionism: Perspective and Method.* Englewood Cliffs, NJ: Prentice-Hall.

Cahill, Spencer. 1998. "Erving Goffman." Pp. 191–205 in *Symbolic Interactionism: An Introduction, an Interpretation, an Integration,* edited by Joel Charon. Upper Saddle River, NJ: Prentice-Hall.

Cerulo, K. A. 1997. "Identity Construction: New Issues, New Directions." *Annual Review of Sociology* 23:385–409.

Charon, J. 1998. *Symbolic Interactionism: An Introduction, An Interpretation, An Integration.* Upper Saddle River, NJ: Prentice-Hall.

Emirbayer, M., and A. Mische. 1998. "What Is Agency?" *American Journal of Sociology* 104(4):962–1023.

Fine, G. A. 1993. "The Sad Demise, Mysterious Disappearance, and Glorious Triumph of Symbolic Interactionism." *Annual Review of Sociology* 19:61–87.

Goffman, E. 1963. *Stigma: Notes on the Management of Spoiled Identity.* New York: Simon & Schuster.

Ritzer, G. 1975. *Sociology: A Multiple Paradigm Science.* Boston: Allyn & Bacon.

Sobal, J. 1999. "Sociological Analysis of the Stigmatisation of Obesity." Pp. 187–204 in *A Sociology of Food and Nutrition: Introducing the Social Appetite,* edited by J. Germov and L. Williams. Melbourne: Oxford University Press.

Thomas, W. I. 1966. "The Relation of Research to the Social Process." Pp. 289–305 in *W.I. Thomas on Social Organization and Social Personality,* edited by M. Janowitz. Chicago: University of Chicago Press.

Zdrodowski, D. 1996. "Eating Out: The Experience of Eating in Public for the 'Overweight' Woman." *Women's Studies International Forum* 19(6):655–64.

I

INTRODUCTION

1

The Social Management of Fatness and Thinness

DONNA MAURER and JEFFERY SOBAL

People manage their appearance, particularly their weight, in order to make attractive social presentations and obtain positive social reactions. Many strive to manage appearance through weight control because thinness is widely valued and rewarded in contemporary postindustrial societies. Yet how do people construct their weight-related identities and manage them in social situations? How is the ideal presentation of weight shaped by social and cultural contexts? What roles do organizations play in shaping weight ideals? Are reinterpretations of cultural expectations about body weight possible? The chapters in this volume explore these various questions, focusing on the symbolic and interpretive processes involved in managing fatness and thinness. In the following sections, we provide a thematic overview of the chapters in this book.

WEIGHT IDENTITIES

People construct and shape their personal identities through social interaction (Mead 1934). Weight identities are continually open to change. This is particularly evident when someone experiences dramatic weight loss (English 1993). For example, people who lose large amounts of weight undergo a dramatic process of identity change, using informal personal and social rituals to ease the transition and to mark their new status (Rubin, Shmilovitz, and Weiss 1993). This identity change process depends on status cues in the social environment, which are messages that indicate to a person how fat others perceive him or her to be (Degher and Hughes 1991). When external cues do not match a person's internal perception of how he or she appears to others, the person "recognizes" the

3

inappropriateness of the previous identity and constructs a new one. In this volume, Douglas Degher and Gerald Hughes elaborate on the development of a fat identity through the use of internal and external cues, and explain five major ways of coping that people use to minimize the negative effects of possessing a fat identity. People use these coping methods to socially manage their stigmatized identity.

While the social management of the stigma of obesity may focus on the neutralization of negative characteristics associated with the stigma (English 1991), it also may include resistance to the application of a deviant identity or label. Gina Cordell and Carol Rambo Ronai's chapter explains how some stigmatized individuals use narrative resistance to manage their identities and protect themselves from the "external cues" described in the chapter by Degher and Hughes. The authors show how stigmatized individuals, by distancing themselves from people they perceive as fat and the negative attributes associated with them, attempt to resist a deviant identity. In a further analysis of resisting deviant identity, the chapter by Leanne Joanisse and Anthony Synnott also articulates a variety of ways in which large people react to and resist stigmatization, including forms of active, passive, and reflective resistance. The chapters in this section all address the ways stigmatized individuals develop their identities and manage the social reactions of others.

REDEFINING WEIGHT

Weight-related constructions are malleable and shaped by cultural environments, social organizations, experts, and individuals (Fallon 1990). Obesity and eating disorders, for example, are seen as culture-bound syndromes that reflect culture-specific meanings and norms (Ritenbaugh 1982; Swartz 1985). Expectations regarding ideal body weight within a particular culture also depend on a variety of social statuses, including gender, ethnicity, and socioeconomic status (Sobal 1991). Ideal weights and ways of obtaining them are not objective facts, but constructed ideals and prescriptions. The chapters in this section suggest that body weight ideals and ways to achieve them are open to negotiation and reinterpretation. They also point to variations in the ways broader cultural discourses influence interpretive processes.

For many people, especially women, weight control is an ongoing project (Germov and Williams 1996). At any given time, as many as sixty-five million Americans may be dieting, with more than seventeen thousand different weight loss plans from which to choose (Hesse-Biber 1996:39).

Increasingly, however, commercial diet programs seem to be attracting fewer customers (Fraser 1997), while people are engaging in more diffuse weight control practices that may or may not include conventional dieting (Levy and Heaton 1993). In this volume, Gwen E. Chapman analyzes how many people may be shifting from dieting for weight loss to "healthy eating" for weight control. These two discourses on body weight are interrelated, although the "healthy eating" discourse emphasizes permanent lifestyle changes rather than the temporary eating plan promoted by most diets. She proposes that dissatisfaction with the success of conventional diet plans, as well as other discursive shifts within government-sponsored health and nutrition programs and the mass media, have all contributed to an environment in which the "healthy eating" discourse has emerged.

The medical and psychological professions possess a profound capacity to structure the mainstream discourse on fatness and thinness, medicalizing weight and defining the clinical categories for obesity and eating disorders (Sobal 1995). These clinical categories ultimately can affect how diagnosed individuals perceive themselves and the ways they are treated by others. As Susan Haworth-Hoeppner describes in her chapter, medical discourse on eating disorders does not necessarily reflect people's lived experience. While medical discourse sets up a dichotomy between "normal body image" and "abnormal body image" to describe people's self-perceptions, she finds that body image and body satisfaction exist more as a continuum than as dual categories. All of her study participants (clinically defined anorectic, self-defined anorectic, and nonanorectic) expressed degrees of dissatisfaction with their appearance and weight. Her research raises important questions about how medical professionals define normal body image.

Definitions of weight depend on specific cultural contexts. Weight definitions change throughout the life course (Gordon and Tobias 1984), but they are especially evident during life transitions. During these times, our attention to body weight and appearance are especially heightened. Cultural expectations regarding people's weight may change to accommodate changes in their social roles. As people move from one role to another, they often engage in public presentations that mark these transitions. Jeffery Sobal, Caron Bove, and Barbara Rauschenbauch focus on one important social ritual—weddings—to explain how participants (especially brides) construct expectations regarding body weight through three sets of interacting social processes: interpretation and definition; negotiation and management; and performance and presentation. Their chapter draws attention to the influence of cultural expectations on the social processes involved in the construction of body weight.

ORGANIZATIONAL PROCESSES
IN WEIGHT MANAGEMENT

Social organizations provide opportunities to negotiate, interpret, and solidify meanings about weight that exist within the culture. People often seek membership in organizations in order to bond with others who share common experiences. Weight loss organizations, for example, provide various "latent social services" to their members by enabling them to "let off steam," and by providing social support and opportunities to gain practical knowledge about dieting (Allon 1975). These organizations offer their members sets of meanings that they may use to define themselves and others, and they may employ a variety of strategies to motivate their members to lose weight (Laslett and Warren 1975).

Weight-related organizations often provide blueprints for understanding and reconstructing the self. Such organizations may play an important role in the process of "dramatic self-change" (Athens 1995). In this volume, Rebecca J. Lester identifies Overeaters Anonymous (OA) as a "technology of the self" that people may use to reshape their inner lives and describes how the OA recovery process may reinforce cultural values that uphold disordered eating patterns. Lester explains that the philosophy of OA is not focused on changing specific compulsive eating behaviors, but on reforming "sick" selves into "healthy" selves.

While weight-related organizations may offer some unique interpretations of cultural meanings, Karen Honeycutt's chapter suggests that women involved in highly divergent groups with contrasting ideologies—a size acceptance organization and a weight loss organization—as well as women involved in neither group, share some common weight interpretations. As in Haworth-Hoeppner's chapter earlier in this volume, Honeycutt finds that all women in her study, regardless of organizational affiliation, are intensely preoccupied with weight. Her chapter considers the difficulties that organizations may experience when trying to transform dominant cultural expectations about weight.

College athletic teams may not be immediately perceived as weight-related organizations, yet the performance demands upon college athletes often lead them to be highly preoccupied with food and dieting (Brownell, Rodin, and Wilmore 1992; Marquart, Koszewski, and Sobal 1994). In her chapter, Elizabeth Ransom describes how the structure and environment of women's collegiate cross-country track teams lead female athletes to be preoccupied with weight and at risk for developing eating disorders. For many of the women in her study, the desire to appear both feminine and athletic sets up contradictory demands that are difficult to reconcile. Along with the other organizations discussed in this section, college athletic teams provide a set of legitimated meanings that their members are expected to appropriate.

REINTERPRETING WEIGHT

Although current cultural standards of body weight may appear to be immutable, new interpretations of these standards frequently emerge. Certainly, those who have the power to set and shape weight standards can use their capacity to effect new definitions (Sobal 1995), but less influential individuals and small groups also can reinterpret extant definitions and create new ones. For example, as demonstrated in earlier chapters in this volume, weight-stigmatized individuals can resist negative social responses and expectations. The chapters in the final section demonstrate in more detail how reinterpretations of weight are possible at both micro- and macrolevels. Thomas F. Cash and Robin E. Roy explain the concept of body image as a key component of the self and articulate some of the ways a negative body image may be reinterpreted into a more positive one through educational efforts. While people certainly can benefit directly by developing a more positive body image, this positive body image can best be sustained in a cultural environment that accepts people regardless of body size. In the final chapter, Jeanine C. Cogan outlines how people can work toward a shift in the dominant cultural paradigm regarding body weight. As definitions of "ideal weight" change, so can the accompanying social consequences, making it easier for people to maintain a positive body image.

CONCLUSION

All of the chapters in this volume demonstrate the centrality of body weight to people's everyday lives. Various chapters elaborate different concerns about the social management of fatness and thinness, using, developing, and extending important sociological concepts to examine the connections between social interaction, culture, and social structure.

REFERENCES

Allon, N. 1975. "Latent Social Services in Group Dieting." *Social Problems* 23:59–69.

Athens, L. H. 1995. "Dramatic Self Change." *Sociological Quarterly* 36(3):571–86.

Brownell, K. D., J. Rodin, and J. H. Wilmore, eds. 1992. *Eating, Body Weight, and Performance in Athletes: Disorders of Modern Society*. Philadelphia: Lea & Febiger.

Degher, D., and G. Hughes. 1991. "The Identity Change Process: A Field Study of Obesity." *Deviant Behavior* 12:385–401.

English, C. 1991. "Food Is My Best Friend: Self-Justifications and Weight Loss Efforts." *Research in the Sociology of Health Care* 9:335–45.

———. 1993. "Gaining and Losing Weight: Identity Transformations." *Deviant Behavior* 14:227–41.

Fallon, A. 1990. "Culture in the Mirror: Sociocultural Determinants of Body Image." Pp. 80–109 in *Body Images: Development, Deviance, and Change,* edited by T. F. Cash and T. Pruzinsky. New York: Guilford.

Fraser, L. 1997. *Losing It: America's Obsession with Weight and the Industry That Feeds on It.* New York: Dutton.

Germov, J., and L. Williams. 1996. "The Epidemic of Dieting Women: The Need for a Sociological Approach to Food and Nutrition." *Appetite* 27:97–108.

Gordon, J. B., and A. Tobias. 1984. "Fat, Female and the Life Course: The Developmental Years." Pp. 65–92 in *Obesity and the Family,* edited by D. J. Kallen and M. B. Sussman. New York: Haworth.

Hesse-Biber, S. 1996. *Am I Thin Enough Yet? The Cult of Thinness and the Commercialization of Identity.* New York: Oxford University Press.

Laslett, B., and C. A. B. Warren. 1975. "Losing Weight: The Organizational Promotion of Behavior Change." *Social Problems* 23:69–80.

Levy, A. S., and A. W. Heaton. 1993. "Weight Control Practices of U.S. Adults Trying to Lose Weight." *Annals of Internal Medicine* 119:661–66.

Marquart, L. F., W. Koszewski, and J. Sobal. 1994. "Motivations, Risks, and Nutrition Counseling for Weight Loss in Athletes." *Topics in Clinical Nutrition* 10(1):48–57.

Mead, G. H. 1934. *Mind, Self, and Society.* Chicago: University of Chicago Press.

Ritenbaugh, C. 1982. "Obesity as a Culture-Bound Syndrome." *Culture, Medicine and Psychiatry* 6:347–61.

Rubin, N., C. Shmilovitz, and M. Weiss. 1993. "From Fat to Thin: Informal Rites Affirming Identity Change." *Symbolic Interaction* 16(1):1–17.

Sobal, J. 1991. "Obesity and Socioeconomic Status: A Framework for Examining Relationships Between Physical and Social Variables." *Medical Anthropology* 13:231–47.

———. 1995. "The Medicalization and Demedicalization of Obesity." Pp. 67–90 in *Eating Agendas: Food and Nutrition as Social Problems,* edited by D. Maurer and J. Sobal. Hawthorne, NY: Aldine de Gruyter.

Swartz, L. 1985. "Anorexia Nervosa as a Culture-Bound Syndrome." *Social Science and Medicine* 20:725–30.

II

WEIGHT IDENTITIES

2

The Adoption and Management of a "Fat" Identity

DOUGLAS DEGHER and GERALD HUGHES

The interactionist perspective plays an important part in contemporary identity theory. At its core is an emphasis on "process" rather than viewing identity as a static entity. Attention is focused on the interaction between the individual and others and the consequences of this for conceptions of identity.

This chapter examines two crucial issues in the analysis of identity and its relationship to weight management: (1) how people come to think of themselves as "fat" and thereby adopt a "fat" identity; and (2) how individuals cope with the problematic interactions that arise with the adoption of a fat identity. By identity, we refer to the internalization of societal conceptions regarding specific statuses. In this case we focus on obesity. The adoption of a *fat* identity involves the internalization of external and internal status cues that transmit to the individual societal conceptions about being fat. Individuals then use these cues to recognize that they do not possess a "normal" body build. The next step in the process involves "placing" one's self into a more appropriate category. Once placing occurs, the individual must deal with the pejorative aspects of this identity. The second section of this chapter focuses on the techniques and mechanisms obese individuals use to cope with the problematic interactions they confront.

The data in this chapter are drawn from research that was conducted upon members of a national weight reduction organization. Two types of data were collected for this study: field observations performed while attending meetings of a weight control organization, and in-depth interviews of group members. Interviews were conducted with twenty-nine members and yielded more than six hundred pages of typed transcript. This material was coded and subjected to a form of grounded analysis that

11

generated the conceptions of "identity" presented here and in two earlier articles (Degher and Hughes 1991; Hughes and Degher 1993).

"FAT" AS A DEVIANT IDENTITY

Obese individuals possess a "spoiled identity" (Goffman 1963). They suffer both externally from discrimination based upon negative stereotypes, and internally from negative self-concepts.

One of the most significant social consequences of obesity is that it is a condition for which there are many negative stereotypes. Studies of school-age children have consistently found that the overweight child is the least liked, has the fewest friends, and is attributed the greatest number of negative personality characteristics (Dion and Berscheid 1974; Caskey and Felker 1971; Lerner 1969; Lerner and Gellert 1969; Lerner and Schroeder 1971; Penick and Stunkard 1975; Staffieri 1967). The severity of the situation is highlighted by the fact that in studies of children, even obese children accept and often internalize these negative stereotypes (Alexander 1968; Lerner and Gellert 1969, Lerner and Schroeder 1971; Mendelson and White 1985; Penick and Stunkard 1975; Stunkard and Mendelson 1961).

In the area of sexuality, obese individuals, especially obese females, are far less likely to be perceived as desirable sexual partners (Regan 1996). One recent study found that men were less likely to respond to personal advertisements in which the woman was represented as obese than they were when she was represented as having a history of drug addiction (Sitton and Blanchard 1995).

Obese people are not only the subject of negative stereotypes, they also are actively discriminated against in college admissions (Canning and Mayer 1966), pay more for goods and services (Petit 1974), receive prejudicial medical treatment (Maddox, Back, and Liederman 1968; Maddox and Liederman 1969; McArthur and Ross 1997), are treated less promptly by salespersons (Pauley 1989), have higher rates of unemployment (Laslett and Warren 1975), are less likely to be promoted (Baum 1987), and receive lower wages (Register 1990).

In response to the negative externally held stereotypes, most obese individuals have a poor self-concept, suffer from low self-esteem, and have extreme body dissatisfaction (Alexander 1968; Allison et al. 1995; Cahnman 1968; Greenberg and LaPorte 1996; Grilo, Wilfley, Brownell, and Rodin 1994; Grogan and Wainwright 1996; Martin, Housley, and McCoy 1988; Mendelson and White 1985; Pauley 1989; Schumaker, Krejci, and Small 1985; Stein 1987; Striegel-Moore, Schreiber, Pike, Wilfley, and Rodin 1995; Wadden, Foster, and Brownell 1984).

Being labeled "fat" in our society clearly fits Becker's description of a "master status":

> Some statuses in our society, as in others, override all other statuses and have a certain priority. . . . [T]he status deviant (depending on the kind of deviance) is this kind of master status. . . . [O]ne will be identified as a deviant first, before other identifications are made. (1963:33)

Obese people are "fat" first, and only secondarily are seen as possessing ancillary characteristics. The focus of the first part of this chapter is on how individuals develop such a devalued and stigmatized identity.

ADOPTING A FAT IDENTITY: THE IDENTITY CHANGE PROCESS

In conceptualizing how a person adopts a fat identity, it is useful to employ the concept of "career." An important aspect of this career model is career contingencies, which are

> those factors on which mobility from one position to another depends. Career contingencies include both the objective facts of social structure, and changes in the perspectives, motivations, and desires of the individual. (Becker 1963:24)

Thus, the "identity change" process must be viewed on two levels: public (external) and private (internal):

> One value of the concept of career is its two-sidedness. One side is linked to internal matters held dearly and closely, such as image of self and felt identity; the other side concerns official position, jural relations, and style of life and is part of a publicly acceptable institutional complex. (Goffman 1961:127)

On the public level, social statuses exist as part of the public domain. These social statuses are both socially defined and promoted. The social environment not only contains definitions and attendant stereotypes for each status, it also contains information, in the form of *status cues,* about the applicability of that status for the individual.

On the internal level, two distinct cognitive processes must take place for the identity change process to occur: first, the individual must come to recognize that the current status is inappropriate; and second, the individual must locate a new, more appropriate status. In response to the external status cues, the individual comes to internally recognize that the initial status is inappropriate, and locates a new, more appropriate status. Thus, identity change occurs in response to and is mediated through status cues in the social environment.

Status Cues: The External Component

Status cues make up the public or external component of the identity change process. A status cue is some feature of the social environment that contains information about a particular status or status dimension. Status cues provide information about whether or not the individual is "fat," and if so, how "fat."

"Recognizing" and "placing" comprise the internal component of the identity change process and occur in response to and are mediated through the status cues. To fully understand the identity change process, it is necessary to explain the interaction between outer and inner processes (Scheff 1988).

Status cues are transmitted in two ways: actively and passively. Active cues are communicated through interaction. For example, an individual is informed by peers, friends, spouse, etc. that he or she is overweight. The following are typical comments that occurred repeatedly in the interviews in response to the question, How did you know that you were fat?:

> That's when it started. I would say maybe ten or fifteen pounds overweight. I was starting to be called chubby, and being teased in school.

> When my mother would take me shopping, she'd get angry because the clothes that were supposed to be in my age group wouldn't fit me.

A second category of cues might be accurately described as passive. The information in these cues exists within the environment, but the individual must in some way be sensitized to that information. Such passive cues might involve standing on a scale, seeing one's reflection in a mirror, standing next to others, fitting in chairs, or, as frequently mentioned by respondents, the sizing of clothes. The comments below are representative of passive cues.

> I think that it was not being able to wear the clothes that the other kids wore.

> I would see all these ladies come in and they could wear size 11 and 12, and I thought, Why can't I do that? I should be able to do that.

Both active and passive cues serve as mechanisms for communicating an understanding about a specific status. Events occur that force the individual to evaluate conceptions of self.

Recognizing

The term "recognizing" refers to the cognitive process by which an individual becomes aware that a particular status is no longer appropriate. As diagrammed in Figure 2.1, the process assumes the individual's acceptance of some initial status. For obese individuals, the initial status is that of "normal body build." This assumption is based on the observation that none of our interviewees assumed that they were "always fat." Even those who were fat as children could identify the time in their career when they became aware that *they* were "fat." Through the perception of discrepant status cues, the individual comes to recognize that the initial status is inappropriate.[1]

An important point is that the acceptance (or rejection) of a particular status does not occur simply because the individual possesses a set of *objective characteristics*. As a case in point, two people may have similar body builds, and though one may have a self-definition as "fat," the other may not. There appears to be a rather tenuous connection between objective condition and subjective definition. The following comments are supportive of this disjunction.

> I was really, as far as pounds go, very thin, but I had a feeling about myself that I was huge.

> Well, I don't remember ever thinking about it until I was about in eighth grade. But I was looking back at pictures when I was little. I was always chunky, chubby.

This lack of necessary connection between objective condition and subjective definition points to an important and frequently overlooked feature of social statuses: the extent to which they are *self-evident*. Self-evidentiality refers to the degree to which a person, who possesses certain objective status characteristics, is *aware* that a particular status label applies to them.

Some statuses possess a high degree of evidentiality. Gender identification is one of these. We are referring here to the physiological description

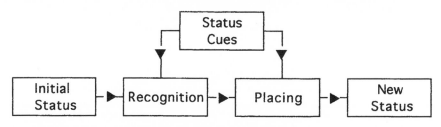

Figure 2.1. Visualization of the identity change process (ICP).

of being male or female. We realize that gender roles are much less self-evident. On the other hand, being beautiful or intelligent is somewhat non-self-evident. This is not to imply that individuals are ignorant of the statuses or the characteristics that they are assigned. A person may know that some people are intelligent, and may apply that designation to others, and yet they may be unaware that the label applies to them.

One idea that emerged quite early from the interviews is that being "fat" is a relatively non-self-evident status. Individuals do not always recognize that "fat" is a description that applies to them. Conversely, a number of individuals thought of themselves as "fat" or "obese," and were objectively "normal." In this case, the existence of objective indicators was insufficient to prevent the individual from adopting a fat identity. The objective condition of being overweight is not sufficient to promote the adoption of a fat identity. This non-self-evidentiality is demonstrated in the following interview excerpts:

> I think that I just thought that I was a little big here and there. I didn't think of it, and I didn't think of myself as looking bad. But you know, I must have.

> I have pictures of me right after the baby was born. I had no idea that I was that fat.

The self-evidentiality of a status is important in the discussion of the identity change process. The less self-evident a status, the more difficult the recognizing process becomes. Further, since recognition occurs in response to status cues, the self-evidentiality of a status will influence the type of cues that play the most prominent role in identity change.

Recognizing, for our subjects, occurred primarily through active cues. When passive cues were involved, they typically involved highly visible and unambiguous cues. In general, the active cues appear to be more potent in forcing the individual's attention to the information that the current status is inappropriate. The predominance of these active cues may be a consequence of the relatively non-self-evident character of the "fat" status. The less self-evident a status, the more likely that the recognizing process will occur through active, rather than passive cues.

Once the individual recognizes the inappropriateness of an initial status, it becomes necessary to locate a more appropriate one. This search for a more appropriate status is referred to as the "placing" process.

Placing

Placing refers to a cognitive process whereby an individual comes to identify an appropriate status from among those available. The number of status categories along a status dimension influences the placing process. A status dimension may contain from two to an infinite number of status categories. If there are only two status-dimensional categories, such as in the case of gender, the placement process is more or less automatic. When an individual recognizes that he or she does not belong in one category, the remaining category becomes the obvious alternative. The more status categories, the more difficult the placing process becomes.

The body build dimension contains an extremely large number of categories. When an individual recognizes that he or she does not possess a "normal" body build, there are innumerable possible alternatives. The knowledge that one's status lies toward the "fat" rather than the "thin" end of the continuum still presents a wide range of choices. In everyday conversation, we hear depictions of these alternatives: Chubby, porky, plump, hefty, full-figured, beer belly, love handles, etc. All are informal descriptions reflecting the myriad categories along the body build dimension:

> I wasn't real fat in my eyes. I don't think. I was just chunky.

> Not fat. I didn't exactly classify it as fat. I just thought, I'm, you know, I am a pudgy lady. I don't think that I have ever called myself fat.

> I have called myself heavy.

Even when individuals adopt a fat identity, they attempt to make distinctions about how "fat" they are. Since being fat is a devalued status, individuals attempt to escape the full weight of the negative attributes, while still acknowledging the nonnormal status. The following response exemplifies this attempt to neutralize the pejorative "fat" status. The practice of differentiating one's status from others becomes vital in managing a fat identity. As one respondent remarked to a question by the interviewer:

> Q. How did you know that you weren't that fat?

> A. Well, comparing myself to others at the time, I didn't really feel that I was that fat. But I knew maybe because they didn't treat me the same way they treated people who were heavier than me. You know, I got teased lightly, but I was still liked by a lot of people, and the people that were heavy weren't.

As is apparent from this excerpt, the individual neutralized self-image by linking "fatness" with the level of teasing by peers.

New Status

The final phase of the identity change process involves the internalization of a negative (deviant) definition of self. For many fat people, accepting a new status brings with it a significant number of personal and pubic changes. Because of the stigmatized and devalued nature of the "fat" stereotype, these individuals are frequently confronted with stressful and emotionally painful social interactions. As this new identity takes hold, it often becomes necessary for individuals to learn mechanisms for managing that identity. This allows individuals to maintain a modicum of self-worth and helps them deal with the negative reactions of others.

Many classic works address the management of the deviant identity. Goffman (1963) described how "stigmatized" individuals attempted to "manage information" about their stigmas in such a manner as to minimize the problematic consequences in dealing with others. Sykes and Matza (1957) analyzed the "techniques of neutralization" used by delinquents to cope with their acquired deviant labels. Bryan (1966) interviewed prostitutes to see how they internalized "occupational ideologies." Lyman and Scott (1970) analyzed two types of "accounts" given by stigmatized individuals to minimize the negative reactions to their condition. Link and his associates (Link 1987; Link, Struening, Cullen, Shrout, and Dohrenwend 1989; Link, Mirotznik, and Cullen 1991) examined three coping strategies used to offset the negative consequences of being labeled mentally ill.

In this section of the chapter, we employ a symbolic interactionist framework to explore the coping strategies used to deal with the devalued and problematic consequences of having internalized an obese identity. While not all behavior is circumscribed by the fact that a person is fat, it is one of the most important factors influencing interactions with others. Since being fat is a devalued and stigmatized status in our society, most of the fat person's interactions are potentially stress producing (Davis 1961; Goffman 1963). Also, obese people are continually confronted with mundane indicators of their devalued condition: clothing that does not fit, chairs that are too small, being unable to engage in certain activities, etc. The information individuals internalize in these situations is almost always stressful. The situation is such that Stunkard (1976) contends that pain is the most characteristic emotion experienced by fat people.

Coping Strategies

During this investigation, five analytically distinct coping strategies emerged. Coping strategies are mechanisms our respondents used to minimize the pejorative characteristics associated with the obese identity. These strategies involve the use of information management techniques, interaction rituals, and internal definitions that allow the obese individual to maintain a modicum of self-respect, and to deflect the negative reactions of others. The names we attached to these strategies were never mentioned by the respondents, but are creations of the authors. We call these strategies (1) avoidance; (2) reaction formation; (3) compensation; (4) compliance; and (5) accounts.

Avoidance

Perhaps the most common coping strategy involves what we call avoidance behavior, which seems to operate in two distinct ways. The first involves the systematic avoidance of situations where being fat is problematic. The individual using avoidance is aware of being obese, but consciously avoids those situations in which being fat is problematic. The second type of avoidance behavior involves blocking or ignoring the condition. Many respondents simply don't think very often about their fatness. Group members reveal their use of the first type of avoidance in the following remarks:

> I hate to look in the mirrors. I hate that. It makes me feel so self-conscious. If I walk into a store, and I see my reflection in the glass, I just look away.

> And when I feel particularly fat, I would just give up swimming because I just didn't like myself after a while.

By avoiding situations that are potentially stress producing, fat individuals are able to minimize some of the negative consequences of being fat.

Perhaps the most common avoidance strategy involves an attempt to ignore the condition. Early in the study a number of conversations and one taped interview were conducted with the lecturer (leader) of the local weight reduction group. During the first interview the lecturer was asked how fat people cope with being fat:

> I think the classic way they cope, for the truly obese person, and I'm talking about people, uh, I'm talking about from eighty pounds up would be a figure, I think that the main way that they cope with it, is by absolutely ignoring it.

One of our respondents confirmed the lecturer's contention by stating:

> I try not to think about being fat very often; when I do I get depressed. It's too painful to think about all the time.

Fat people who disregard their condition are intellectually aware of the fact that they are fat. They simply choose to ignore it. A number of interviewees related that they did not think about being fat most of the time. These comments were likely to arise when the discussion focused on how it was possible to remain fat when there were so many negative consequences. The following is typical of these comments:

> You know, most of the time I am pretty happy. I don't even think about being fat. It is only when something happens, like having to fly, and not being able to fit in the seats and having to ask for a seatbelt extension, that I start to think about it again. If I had to think about it all the time, I think that I would kill myself.

It was easier, many felt, to learn to disregard the fact that they were fat. As mentioned by the lecturer, this strategy was used most prominently by the extremely obese. But many of the less overweight members also reported behaving in this fashion, particularly after a dieting period when they were regaining weight. Most fat people are on diets quite frequently and manage to lose significant amounts of weight. In most cases, however, once the fat person stops dieting the weight is regained. It is during this period of regain that the individual is most likely to display an avoidance strategy.

In most cases, avoidance is an efficient stress management technique. Since our respondents were in a weight reduction organization, it is obvious that this strategy is not one that they employ all the time, but most respondents claimed using it at various times.

Reaction Formation

Another category of coping strategies involves a form of reaction formation. This involves a rejection and even a reversal of societal definitions of appropriate behavior. In this coping strategy, the individual responds to negative input about his/her fat condition by eating more. Some subjects reported it as a spiteful response, others as self-punishing behavior. In any case, this behavior was vocalized repeatedly by group members. The responses below reflect this phenomenon:

> If people told me that I had to lose weight I would gain to spite them. I won't be told. I used to eat to rebel when people told me not to eat.

> When the guys start giving me shit about being fat—telling me that I should diet, my response is "screw you," and I eat all the more.

Reaction formation appeared frequently when an individual was forced into an unavoidable problematic situation. Unlike avoidance behaviors, reaction formation is a sporadic, rather than a habitual coping strategy. It clearly is not a long-term means for dealing with stress, but more of an emergency strategy that the fat person employs when faced with a situation too painful to confront directly.

Compensation

A third coping strategy is compensation. In this strategy, the individual attempts to offset negative consequences of being fat by overachieving in other areas. Many group members reported that they were very active in school and community organizations. By doing more, the fat person is able to achieve a degree of social acceptance that normally would not be accorded a fat person.

> Well, we had a close group of friends that are still friends, that I always felt like I was the biggest. I always felt that I had to be the best cook, the best housekeeper, more mature. I didn't ever feel that I could be frivolous. Well, I just thought I had to prove something. . . . I became an overachiever.

> In every organization I belonged to, I was the head of it at some point, and did this miraculous Messiah job on it. That's one of the ways I coped with my ego.

This particular coping strategy seems to be most prevalent among individuals who had been obese from childhood. Some stigmatized individuals feel they must excel to be marginally accepted socially.

Compliance

A fourth category of coping strategies involves compliance. Compliance takes two specific forms: stereotype and face compliance. In stereotype compliance the fat person attempts to minimize the negative responses from others and maximize acceptance by complying with one or more of the social stereotypes of a "fat" person. In face compliance, the individual agrees to diet to silence demands from significant others, but there is no actual commitment to lose weight.

In stereotype compliance, the most mentioned stereotype is the "jolly fat person." The individual who is willing, even eager, to be the butt of jokes, and who cannot be insulted because problematic interaction is taken as humorous. Fat people, perhaps more than any other group in our society, are expected to degrade themselves and to tolerate any unkind remark, pretending that such remarks are funny. Witness the popularity of contemporary television shows in which fat people are continually abused about their weight. A response from our data exemplifies this type of compliance:

> Q. Okay, now you said that people made fun of this girl who was overweight. What did you think of it? What did you think about her at this time when you saw her? Did you ever make fun of her?

> A. No, I didn't. Um, she was, she took it. She just went along with everybody like it was real funny.

> Q. Did you think that was funny?

> A. At first I did and then after that I didn't when I took a look at myself. Then I didn't think that it was funny at all, that they were teasing her. She laughed, just acted like it was real funny.

Q. Why do you think that she laughed at it?

A. Maybe to keep from getting upset about it, to laugh along with the group instead of crying.

Nearly all of the subjects in the study report similar incidents, either about themselves or about someone close. Being forced to act the "jolly fat person" was discussed frequently in the group meetings. In these discussions many members expressed much pain, resentment, and bitterness about having to put up a jolly facade. One result of being forced into the "jolly" role is the perception of the "normal" as persecutor. Other prevalent stereotypes mentioned by the respondents included the "faithful sidekick" and the "bully"; however, the jolly fat person was by far the most frequently mentioned.

Fat people are frequently confronted with demands from significant others to do something about their weight. These demands can be extremely stressful, especially when the person making the demands is a friend or loved one. A method of coping with these demands is to engage in face compliance. That is, the fat person agrees to diet as a means to silence demands. The individual may even engage in some type of public dieting behavior, although there is no actual commitment to lose weight. Consequently, for most of our respondents who engaged in face compliance, this was not an attempt to exit the fat career. The following comments demonstrate face compliance:

Q. Why did you go that night?

A. Because I finally couldn't take any more of listening to him. My husband paid for me to go to a hypnotist, one who specialized in weight reduction. He gave me a posthypnotic suggestion that would keep me away from food. It never took, but every time Jim (my husband) was around I pretended to hate food. When he left I raided the refrigerator.

Accounts

The fifth coping strategy we call *accounts*. We found two major categories of accounts. The first we call "fat stories,"[2] which are used to explain why the person became fat. The second are "eating stories" and focus on why the individual continues to eat excessively, and thus remains fat. It should be noted that these two strategies were the only ones used universally by all subjects in the study.

"Fat stories" are similar to what Lyman and Scott refer to as "excuses." That is, they are accounts "in which one admits that the act in question is bad, wrong, or inappropriate, but denies full responsibility" (1970:113). The comments below are typical "fat stories":

One of my problems is a hormone problem.

When I first got married I started using birth control pills. We didn't want a child right away. I started to put on weight and have had trouble getting it off.

Last summer, I got back down to 185, and I was just real serious, practically fasted. I was going to the health spa, and then the next day I broke my arm. So really going to the health spa didn't do a whole lot.

Definitely, yeah, because you know, my grandmother, she always told me "you have to eat." Well, she lived through two wars, and she says, "I'm sure you need it because the war will come sometime, and then you will need everything that you have."

No, when we got married, I was real slim. I weighed about 123. After being married to him for a while, I started gaining all this weight, 'cause he's six feet five, and works hard, works at the sawmill, and so he eats so much it makes me gain weight.

Although the characters in the story change, the theme remains the same. The individual is a victim, and being fat is either someone else's fault or the "natural result" of some valued relationship.

Fat people use the second major category of accounts, "eating stories," to explain their continuing "fatness."[3] The eating stories differ from the fat stories in a significant way. Fat stories are almost exclusively what Lyman and Scott (1970) call "excuses," while eating stories are similar to what they call "justifications." The major difference between excuses and justifications lies in the acceptance of responsibility. In the excuse, the person disclaims responsibility for the disapproved behavior. In the justification, the person accepts responsibility for the behavior, but attempts to establish that the behavior is situationally appropriate. Common eating stories involve the recitation of some personal tragedy or disruption:

I got a phone call from my mom, and my grandmother had a heart attack. And I got really upset because I thought this is the time when something is going to happen to her, and I really got upset. And with the tears went the thought of dieting or worrying about myself. I said to my husband, "We could have dinner together and then I'll leave for Phoenix." And I just decided I felt like Burger King.

In the above excerpt, the subject attempts to justify excessive eating by linking its occurrence to a personal tragedy, the critical illness of a grandmother (note that an attempt is made to reinforce the tragedy claim by relating how upsetting the situation was). The eating behavior then becomes permissible rather than unacceptable, since people are permitted and even expected to engage in extreme behavior during times of grief and personal tragedy.

A second type of eating story attempts to invoke obligations to others as a justification for the questioned eating behavior. There appears to be a gender factor in the use of this type of account. Females typically tend to invoke family obligations, while males tend to invoke obligations to entities outside the family:

> I am guilt ridden, I really am, that three of the members of my family are all underweight. And I feel very guilty if there aren't plenty of snacks around for them to snack on.

> Yeah, after I had my children is when it all started piling on, and then we ate. My husband is from the South, and you know, his idea of the perfect meal is cornbread and all that, you know. And, you know, to please him I, that's what I did, you know?

> The last eight weeks of school really got me. I had an organization that we were just forming with fifty people involved. All of the faculty—I just felt the pressure. It all crunched on my head because nobody else would take the ball and roll with it to get this thing going this semester, and so I took over.

The obligation is more important than personal welfare. As a result of personal sacrifice, overload occurs and the only way to continue to function in these situations is to eat.

Our respondents articulated another type of eating story used for identity management that has not been reported by others investigating the use of accounts. This eating story attempted to explain the behavior on the grounds that eating itself was punishing:

> When I eat, I am punishing myself. I don't know why.

> [Well, why don't you stop yourself?] I have thought about that. I think that I am punishing myself.

These accounts are neither excuses nor justifications. In these accounts, the speakers assert that they should not be punished for their eating behavior because eating is itself the punishment.

SUMMARY AND CONCLUSION

This chapter has examined two important issues related to obesity: (1) how individuals come to adopt a fat identity, and (2) the coping strategies used to neutralize that identity.

The adoption of a new identity occurs through cognitive processes of recognizing and placing. Recognizing involves individuals coming to see that a previously assumed identity does not apply to them. Placing involves locating a new, more appropriate identity. Recognizing and placing are triggered by passive and active status cues. These cues exist in the external environment and are either available for interpretation or are transmitted through interaction.

Once a fat identity is internalized, a number of coping strategies are employed to deal with the devalued character of obesity: (1) avoidance (2) compliance, (3) reaction formation, (4) compensation, and (5) accounts. All are used to minimize the structural and interpersonal consequences of being labeled fat. We feel that understanding the relationship between identity and behavior is a logical first step in transforming that behavior.

It is important to understand that the identity change model presented in this chapter is a generic one, and that issues of obesity are transsituational and temporally durable. If obesity were to disappear tomorrow, we believe that our model could be successfully and fruitfully applied to the study of other deviant careers. We also feel that it is important to understand how the coping strategies can be seen as both specific to obesity, and transcending that identity.

NOTES

1. It is possible that the person will perceive the discrepant cues, and will either disattend or reject them, in which case the initial status is retained. The factors regulating such a failure to recognize are important, but are not dealt with in this chapter.

2. The usage of the term here is very similar to the usage made by Cohen (1955) in his discussion of how lower-class delinquent subcultures turn middleclass values on their head. A major difference, however, is that Cohen sees reaction formation as group phenomenon, whereas its usage in the present work is more personal.

3. Fat stories, and the strategy to follow, "eating stories," are specific examples of what Lyman and Scott (1970) call "accounts."

REFERENCES

Alexander, W. R. 1968. "A Study of Body Types, Self Image, and Environmental Adjustment in Freshman College Women." *Dissertation Abstracts* 28, 8A:3048.

Allison, D. B., B. S. Kanders, G. D. Osage, M. S. Faith, S. B. Heymsfield, D. Heber, J. P. Foreyt, R. M. Elashoff, and G. Blackburn. 1995. "Weight-Related Attitudes and Beliefs of Obese African American Women." *Journal of Nutrition Education* 27(1):18–23.

Baum, L. 1987. "Extra Pounds Can Weigh Down Your Career." *Business Week*, 3 August, p. 96.

Becker, H. S. 1963. *Outsiders: Studies in the Sociology of Deviance*. New York: Free Press.

Bryan, J. 1966. "Occupational Ideologies and Individual Attitudes of Call Girls." *Social Problems* 13(4):441–50.

Cahnman, W. J. 1968. "The Stigma of Obesity." *Sociological Quarterly* 9:283–99.

Canning, H., and J. Mayer. 1966. "Obesity: Its Possible Effects on College Acceptance." *New England Journal of Medicine* 275(24):1172–74.

Caskey, S., and D. Felker. 1971. "Social Stereotyping of Female Body Image by Elementary School Age Girls." *Research Quarterly* 42:251–55.

Cohen, A. 1955. *Delinquent Boys: The Culture of the Gang.* New York: MacMillan.

Davis, F. 1961. "Deviance Disavowal: The Management of Strained Interaction." *Social Problems* 9(2):120–32.

Degher, D., and G. Hughes. 1991. "The Identity Change Process: A Field Study of Obesity." *Deviant Behavior* 12:385–401.

Dion, K., and E. Berscheid. 1974. "Physical Attractiveness and Peer Perception Among Children." *Sociometry* 37(1):1–12.

Goffman, E. 1961. *Asylums: Essays on the Social Situation of Mental Patients and Other Inmates.* Garden City, NY: Anchor.

———. 1963. *Stigma: Notes on the Management of Spoiled Identity.* Englewood Cliffs, NJ: Prentice-Hall.

Greenberg, D. R., and D. J. LaPorte. 1996. "Racial Differences in Body Type Preferences of Men and Women." *International Journal of Eating Disorders* 19(3): 275–78.

Grilo, C. M., D. E. Wilfley, K. D. Brownell, and J. Rodin. 1994. "Teasing, Body Image, and Self-Esteem in a Clinical Sample of Obese Women." *Addictive Behaviors* 19(4):443–50.

Grogan, S., and N. Wainwright. 1996. "Growing Up in the Culture of Slenderness: Girls' Experiences of Body Dissatisfaction." *Women's Studies International Forum* 19(6):665–673.

Hughes, G., and D. Degher. 1993. "Coping with a Deviant Identity." *Deviant Behavior* 14:297–315.

Laslett, B., and C. A. B. Warren. 1975. "Losing Weight: The Organizational Promotion of Behavior Change." *Social Problems* 23(1):69–80.

Lerner, R. M. 1969. "The Development of Stereotyped Expectancies of Body Build Behavior Relations." *Child Development* 40(1):137–41.

Lerner, R. M., and E. Gellert. 1969. "Body Build Identification, Preference, and Aversion in Children." *Developmental Psychology* 1:456–62.

Lerner, R. M., and C. Schroeder. 1971. "Physique Identification, Preference, and Aversion in Kindergarten Children." *Developmental Psychology* 5(3):538.

Link, B. G. 1987. "Understanding Labeling Effects In the Area of Mental Disorders: An Assessment of the Effects of Expectations of Rejection." *American Sociological Review* 52:96–112.

Link, B. G., J. Mirotznik, and F. T. Cullen. 1991. "The Effectiveness of Stigma Coping Orientations: Can Negative Consequences of Mental Illness Labeling Be Avoided?" *Journal of Health and Social Behavior* 32:302–20.

Link, B. G., E. Struening, F. T. Cullen, P. E. Shrout, and B. P. Dohrenwend. 1989. "A Modified Labeling Theory Approach to Mental Disorders: An Empirical Assessment." *American Sociological Review* 54:400–23.

Lyman, S., and M. Scott. 1970. *A Sociology of the Absurd*. New York: Appleton-Century-Crofts.

Maddox, G. L., K. W. Back, and V. Liederman. 1968. "Overweight as Social Deviance and Disability." *Journal of Health and Social Behavior* 9(4):287–98.

Maddox, G. L., and V. Liederman. 1969. "Overweight as a Social Disability with Medical Implications." *Journal of Medical Education* 44(3):214–20.

Martin, S., K. Housley, and H. McCoy. 1988. "Self-Esteem of Adolescent Girls as Related to Weight." *Perceptual and Motor Skills* 67:879–84.

McArthur, L. H., and J. Ross. 1997. "Attitudes of Registered Dieticians Toward Personal Overweight and Overweight Clients." *Journal of the American Dietetic Association* 97(1):63–66.

Mendelson, B. K., and D. R. White. 1985. "Development of Self-Body-Esteem in Overweight Youngsters." *Developmental Psychology* 21:90–96.

Pauley, L. L. 1989. "Customer Weight as a Variable in Salespersons' Response Time." *Journal of Social Psychology* 129:713–14.

Penick, S. B., and A. J. Stunkard. 1975. "Newer Concepts of Obesity." Pp. 17–26 in *Overweight and Obesity: Causes, Fallacies, Treatment*, edited by B. Q. Hufen. Provo, UT: Brigham Young University Press.

Petit, D. W. 1974. "The Ills of the Obese." Pp. 84–90 in *Treatment and Management of Obesity*, edited by G. A. Bray and J. E. Bethune. New York: Harper and Row.

Regan, P. C. 1996. "Sexual Outcasts: The Perceived Impact of Body Weight and Gender on Sexuality." *Journal of Applied Social Psychology* 25(20):1803–13.

Register, C. A. 1990. "Wage Effects of Obesity Among Young Workers." *Social Science Quarterly* 71:130–41.

Scheff, T. 1988. "Shame and Conformity: The Deference Emotion System." *American Journal of Sociology* 53:395–406.

Schumaker, J. F., R. C. Krejci, and L. Small. 1985. "Experience of Loneliness by Obese Individuals." *Psychological Reports* 57:1147–54.

Sitton, S., and S. Blanchard. 1995. "Men's Preference in Romantic Partners: Obesity vs. Addiction." *Psychological Reports* 77(3):1185–87.

Staffieri, J. R. 1967. "A Study of Social Stereotypes of Body Image in Children." *Journal of Personality and Social Psychology* 7(1):101–4.

Stein, R. F. 1987. "Comparison of Self-Concept of Non-Obese and Obese University Junior Female Nursing Students." *Adolescence* 22:77–90.

Striegel-Moore, R. H., G. B. Schreiber, K. M. Pike, D. E. Wilfley, and J. Rodin. 1995. "Drive for Thinness in Black and White Pre-Adolescent Girls." *International Journal of Eating Disorders* 18(1):59–69.

Stunkard, A. J. 1976. *The Pain of Obesity*. Palo Alto, CA: Bull.

Stunkard, A. J., and M. Mendelson. 1961. "Obesity and Body Image I: Characteristics of Disturbances in Image of Some Obese Persons." *Journal of the American Dietetic Association* 38:328–31.

Sykes, G., and D. Matza. 1957. "Techniques of Neutralization: A Theory of Delinquency." *American Sociological Review* 23:664–70.

Wadden, T. A., G. D. Foster, and K. D. Brownell. 1984. "Self-Concept in Obese and Normal Weight Children." *Journal of Consulting and Clinical Psychology* 52:1104–5.

3

Identity Management among Overweight Women
Narrative Resistance to Stigma

GINA CORDELL and CAROL RAMBO RONAI

I learned that no matter what anyone says, it really doesn't count if you're smart, kind, funny, sweet, generous, or caring because if you also happen to be heavy, you may find yourself on the receiving end of more cruelty than you even knew existed. (Goodman 1995:ix)

It really hurt my feelings, it hurt me to see that all people saw when they saw me was a fat person, because I felt like they had missed so much because all they could see was a fat person. (Sheila, a thirty-five-year-old professor)

Overweight people are viewed negatively by others (Harris et al. 1991b; Maroney and Golub 1992; Tiggeman and Rothblum 1989). They are considered unlikable (Goodman et al. 1963; Maddox et al. 1968), lazy, sexless, ugly, self-indulgent, and sloppy (Harris et al. 1991a), and are considered to be less competent, less friendly (Lennon 1992), less popular, less likable, less happy, less self-confident, less feminine, less active, weaker, dirtier, and as having less self-discipline than thinner people (DeJong 1993). The overweight are also regarded as physically unhealthy (Chernin 1985; Goodman 1995; Waxler and Liska 1975), emotionally unhealthy (Cash and Hicks 1990; Crocker et al. 1993; LeShan 1979), and unattractive (Cahnman 1968; Maddox et al. 1968; Schroeder 1992; Tisdale 1994). In particular, overweight women are discriminated against more than overweight men (Bellizzi et al. 1989; Harris et al. 1991a; Harris et al. 1991b).

In this chapter we use ten life history interviews with overweight women (ranging in age from twenty-one to fifty-three years old) to explore the concept of narrative resistance. We chose subjects, through snowball sampling, who we or others had heard in passing define themselves as "overweight," eschewing the temptation to define or operationalize such a subjective term. Their education ranged from a high school diploma through a doctoral degree. One woman was African-American and the other nine were white. All of the women in this study claimed that the status of being overweight had a negative impact on their identity.

Sarup states, "When asked about our identity, we start thinking about our life-story: we construct our identity at the same time as we tell our life-story" (1996:15). During a life history interview, the researcher and the research subject simultaneously "negotiate the subject's identity." As a subject relays her life history, at-hand categories and typifications emerge (Berger and Luckmann 1966). These verbal elements, called biographical work (Gubrium et al. 1994), serve to demarcate the structure of her identity. Biographical work "frame[s] and organize[s] one's character and actions, selecting and highlighting the defining aspects of one's past" (ibid.:157). Furthermore, it is "the ongoing effort to integrate accounts of a person's life." A person's life is "continually subject to reinterpretation because it is always the biography-at-hand" (ibid.:156). As a person tells and retells her life story at different times and at different places, the elements of biography change. To analyze biographical work then "is to analyze how a story is organized by the subject rather than treating the story as a final product" (Ronai 1994:197).

Using the life history method, we examined how weight played a role in our subjects' life stories. At the beginning of the interview we did not address the issue of body image. We simply invited each subject to "tell the story of your life." Later in the interview schedule, we included a question, "How do you feel about your body?" for the purpose of prompting those women who had not brought up the topic of body image on their own. Eight of our subjects brought up the issue of weight themselves, while two of the subjects made weight a topic only after the body image prompt. By allowing them the freedom to talk about their lives rather than focusing on their weight at the outset, we believe we were given insight into the terms that were relevant to them and their identity management and construction. From the life history interviews, themes emerged that reflected the various strategies that subjects employed in their identity formation and management, relative to their overweight status.

DISCURSIVE CONSTRAINT AND NARRATIVE RESISTANCE

The unfavorable perceptions of overweight women that permeate society affect how they think of themselves. An overweight woman experiences "discursive constraint" (Ronai 1997:125), in that:

her behavior is constrained by the threat of having a negative category applied to . . . her self. These categories are disseminated throughout society so effectively that they take on a taken-for-granted or given quality. (ibid.)

Through discursive constraint, society controls a person or group of people, such as overweight women, by establishing and perpetuating negative stereotypes that affect their behavior and how they think of themselves. For example, when a mother tells her daughter she is getting "hefty," she is simultaneously offering her a negative category, "hefty," to define herself by and trying to coerce her daughter into losing weight by threatening to think of her as hefty. Calling her hefty is an instance of discursive constraint—literally constraining the discourse that the daughter may apply to her "self."

Embedded within these interviews is evidence that our subjects resist the negative effects of discursive constraint. Subjects actively participate in the construction of their identity by reorganizing the categories made available into alternative conceptions of self. The narrative strategies subjects use to create and manage their own identities and to defy the power of discursive constraint are examples of "narrative resistance" (Ronai 1994). Analysis of the narrative materials of the women we interviewed revealed three types of narrative resistance: exemplars, continuums, and loopholes.

EXEMPLARS: REJECTING DEVIANCE

Narrative resistance involves the creation and use of exemplars. Deviance exemplars are constructed to serve as narrative models "which demarcate identity by setting up a narrative 'straw man' or 'straw woman' to whom one can compare herself" (Ronai 1994:203). Deviance exemplars are concepts that use groups or individuals for the sake of comparison. Exemplars, as they are presented here, are constituted by negative labels that are typically applied to overweight women and that some overweight women choose to categorically reject. Identity emerges narratively by resisting the particular quality or trait the exemplar represents. Exemplars such as physical attractiveness, sexual desirability, and jolliness may be embodied by various comparison groups or individuals and serve as narrative resources for overweight women to resist a deviant identity.

I Am Not Unattractive

As Schroeder states, "[i]ndeed the phrase 'fat and ugly' has practically become a single word for many people" (1992:6). Several of the subjects we interviewed resisted this characterization by describing themselves as attractive, thus rejecting the negative status of "ugly."

When we asked Natalie, a twenty-five-year-old waitress, how she feels about her body, she responded, "I feel OK. I'm overweight now, but I think that I have a good figure. I think that I have a pretty body." She considered herself overweight, yet she affirmed her belief that she is attractive despite her assumption that she is overweight. Natalie recognized that because she is overweight she is likely to be seen as unattractive; however, she eschewed the exemplar of the unattractive overweight woman in favor of labeling herself as pretty.

When we asked how she feels about her body, Lee, a forty-six-year-old university professor, stated:

> Probably for most people the most important thing [that bothers people about being overweight] is the extent to which it influences other people's perception of their attractiveness . . . and I've never had that problem . . . so I can say that, "Yes, I'm overweight, but I must still be reasonably attractive." . . . I just think I could look a lot worse. Maybe I'm really fooling myself here, but I do basically think that with what I have to work with, I've done fairly well.

Lee also acknowledged that overweight people are frequently considered ugly, but, like Natalie, she chose to reject that exemplar through the practice of narrative resistance.

I Am Not Sexually Undesirable

In her seminal book, *Fat is a Feminist Issue,* Susie Orbach lists stereotypes associated with overweight people and states, "To be fat means to wait for the man who will love you despite the fat—the man who will fight through the layers" (1994:33). Similar to being unattractive, the stereotypical notion that overweight women cannot be regarded as sexually desirable represents discursive constraint. Several of the participants indicated that their life experiences differ from this conception, and that men find them sexually desirable.

Sheila explained, "My husband wants a full-figured woman, which is interesting. He likes having a full-figured wife." Her husband's desire for her and his appreciation of her body contradicts the pervasive belief that overweight women are not sexually desirable. The positive identity that Sheila possesses because her husband finds her sexually desirable enables her to withstand the forces of discursive constraint. His discourse is an alternative stock of knowledge from which Sheila draws in the process of constructing her identity. Her husband's discourse is a resource and he is an active co-conspirator in her narrative resistance.

Lynn, a twenty-one-year-old college student, spoke about her boyfriend Brad's appreciation of her body: "I've had positive comments on my body, by people who can recognize. Brad can recognize . . . Brad can talk about my body, and, it's kind of embarrassing, but he can enjoy it." As an overweight woman, Lynn endures many people believing that she cannot be desirable. Her experience with her boyfriend and his desire for her body "in spite of" her being overweight enables Lynn to see herself as sexually desirable and in turn to oppose the elements of discursive constraint. Again, Brad, like Sheila's husband, becomes another co-conspirator in narrative resistance, rejecting the exemplar of sexual unattractiveness.

I Am Not Taken Advantage Of

Orbach states, "To be fat means to have no needs. . . . To be fat means to take care of other's needs. To be fat means never saying 'no'" (1994:33). Several of our subjects narratively resisted the stereotype that overweight people are often exploited.

For example, Shelby, a thirty-four-year-old businesswoman, stated:

> I feel like, when I was little I let people make fun of me because I was overweight, and I let that get to me. . . . I'm a strong person, I don't let people walk over me. . . . I worried what people thought of me, and now I don't care what people think about me. . . . I'm a very strong person. I don't let people walk on me.

Shelby once believed that because she was overweight, she allowed people to ridicule her. Yet she claims she no longer lets people make fun of her, and she does not let herself be taken advantage of. She resists discursive constraint and creates a positive identity for herself by refusing to accept others' derision.

Lynn also described her past tendency to try to please other people: "I was always helpful. I went out of my way to help people, no matter what happened to me." Yet she also spoke of her refusal to be used by other people. When we asked her what she would do differently if she could live her life over, she replied, "I would be a lot braver. . . . [T]he thing I would change the most is that I would not try to please people so they would like me. . . . I don't let anybody run over me now." Lynn describes how she used to attempt to please others but claims that she no longer lets herself be used.

She also discussed her experience in a Bible study group. When the group leader asked her, "What is your wall?" she responded:

> I told these people who were pretty much thin, that my wall was fat, and you could see the grossness of it. It bothered a few of them, but I wasn't going to

allow them to treat me like that. I wasn't going to allow them to dictate what I felt and what I saw. I had a lot of people in my family tell me I could not do things because I was fat, but I went and purposely did them.

Lynn's discourse reveals she is aware that overweight people may be controlled by others and told how to live their lives simply because of their size. By not allowing others to dictate the terms by which she will define her life, Lynn rejects the characterization of overweight people as being easily controlled and exploited, and in turn, resists the effects of discursive constraint and creates a stronger and more positive self-identity.

I Am Not Desperate to Lose Weight and I Do Not Hate My Body

Orbach's comment, "To be fat means having to wait until you are thin to live. . . . To be fat means to be constantly trying to lose weight" (1994:33) illuminates the widely held belief that overweight women are dissatisfied with their bodies, and as a result are always trying to reduce. Some of the women we interviewed reject this manifestation of discursive constraint in favor of having a positive self-image and being satisfied with their bodies.

When we asked Lynn how she feels about her body, she responded, "It's a very weird description, but when I'm alone, and there's nobody else around and I don't have to recognize that I have a lot of rules, I feel very comfortable." Lynn directly referred to discursive constraint as "rules" that dictate that, as an overweight woman, she should not feel comfortable with her body. Yet Lynn managed to resist this form of discursive constraint by describing herself as comfortable.

In talking about how she feels about her body, Sheila stated,

> I feel comfortable, I feel good. . . . And I'm okay, I like being a heavy person, I have no problem being a heavy person. . . . I like being a big person. I really love being a full-figured woman, and the people I find attractive, that I look at and say, "That's a beautiful woman," I find myself looking at full-figured women and saying, "Gosh, she's beautiful."

Sheila does not accept the widely held belief that overweight women should be dissatisfied with their bodies. Her practice of narrative resistance involves her claiming to accept her body as it is, and consequently resisting discursive constraint.

When Sheila was thinner, she did not feel at ease:

> I always say I was a small person with a big person inside of me. I never felt comfortable as a small person, I always felt a little self-conscious. . . . I always felt imprisoned in certain ways as a small person. . . . I always felt trapped, self conscious. . . . I'm comfortable as a big person. . . . I feel more in

charge, more in command. I feel like when I walk into a room people take notice, and not just because I look good, but because they're looking for something . . . they're looking for me to do something. When a big woman walks into a room well-dressed, confident, people are like, "Hmmm, what does she know that we don't know?"

Society dictates that overweight women should want to be thin. Sheila assertively resisted this discourse by stating that her perception of herself is more positive as an overweight person than it was as a thin person.

When we asked Lila, a thirty-five-year-old graduate student, how she felt about her body, she responded, "Fairly comfortable. It's the only one I have. So I'm fairly happy with it. . . . And, even though I feel that other people view my body in a different way than I view myself, I'm comfortable that I can do whatever I want." Lila is aware that, because she is overweight, others may see her body in unfavorable ways. However, through her own identity construction and management, Lila talked about being comfortable with her body, and in doing so, she successfully resisted discursive constraint.

Lee also disclaimed the stereotypical notion that all overweight women are dissatisfied with their bodies and want to lose weight. She stated:

> I say, well yeah, I'd like to lose another thirty pounds, and the reason I don't is that I eat erratically, and when I eat on the run it tends to be junk food, and I don't get enough exercise because it's not as important to me as getting other things done. So I know why it doesn't happen, and I'm just not quite motivated enough to do what I need to do to lose another thirty or fifty pounds. It would be nice, but . . .

Lee verbally articulated that her desire to be thinner does not take precedent over her desire to accomplish other things. The forces of discursive constraint dictated that, because Lee is overweight, she should be concerned with losing weight; however, she refused to accept the negative labels that are characteristically applied to overweight women. She narratively resisted the discursive constraint of the "desperate to lose weight" exemplar.

I Am Not Jolly

For Lynn, managing her identity included resisting the stereotypical notion that overweight people are funny or jolly and self-deprecating (Goodman 1995:141,143): "To be fat means to be outgoing and jovial to make up for what you think are your deficiencies" (Orbach 1994:32). Lynn stated,

> I don't hide it. I don't pretend that I'm not fat. I used to make jokes before anybody else did. But now I don't make jokes and I won't allow anybody

else to make jokes either. I feel disgusted sometimes by overweight people, but not because of their bodies, but because I see their personalities change. I see a lot of servant-type people who are overweight. They want to be happy and they make everybody laugh, and that really grates my nerves. And they have this fakeness about them. Maybe because that's what I go through. Maybe because I used to want to make everybody laugh. And a lot of times fat people, the fat person in the crowd is the person who makes everybody laugh. Sometimes I just want to see them break down and be real, talk about real things.

Lynn is aware that, because she is overweight, society expects her to be funny and make people laugh to compensate for her size. Lynn used strong terms to characterize others—disgust, servant-type people, grates on my nerves, and so forth. Her narrative resistance to this brand of discursive constraint leaves us with a sense that she is not only narratively resisting for herself, but for all overweight people. Her refusal to embrace this particular exemplar in her discourse positions her as an example that others, like herself, should follow.

Grace, a twenty-four-year-old graduate student, also spoke about the role of humor in her identity management:

In the past I've been very sarcastic, like in high school, and I had a reputation for being funny. I think I can be funny now, but it's not one of my defining characteristics like it was then. But I really tried to be funny back then. That was another way I tried to get people to like me. . . . I feel like people didn't like me because I was overweight, and I tried extra hard to make people laugh or put them at ease to make up for the fact that I was so fat.

Grace revealed that she used to try to make people laugh, yet she resists discursive constraint by rejecting the exemplar of the jolly overweight person in the management of her identity.

Sheila also acknowledged the stereotype of the overweight jolly person as an element of discursive constraint. Yet Sheila did not absorb this attribute into her own identity:

I think in several instances people have prejudged me, then when they got to know me realized that, yeah, I may be a full-figured person, but I'm not dumb or silly or however the stereotypes go. You know, people stereotype fat people with so many ugly things.

Whether the exemplar in question is the unattractive overweight person, the sexually undesirable overweight person, the exploited overweight person, or the desperate to lose weight overweight person, each serves as an identity marker to be rejected outright by the subjects in this study. By making claims about who they are not, these subjects created a more favorable identity for themselves. Rejecting the exemplar alters their stocks of knowledge about both themselves and the possibilities for other overweight people. The narrative resistance strategy that we discuss next also uses exemplars, but instead of rejecting deviance outright for the self, the "continuum" distances the self from deviance.

CONTINUUMS: DISTANCING SELF FROM DEVIANCE

Overweight people's narrative resistance strategies often involve the construction of continuums. The mythical ideal body image imposed by society, the media, and the diet industry lies at one end of these subjects' continuums. The deviance exemplar positioned at the other end of their continuum is the overweight person who is the most overweight, and/or someone who represents the most negative aspects that are typically associated with overweight people. The most obvious deviance exemplar would be the fattest person one can imagine or know. The women we interviewed also narratively constructed continuums related to being neat, dressing well, and health.

At Least I'm Not as Fat as She Is

As Orbach states, "To be fat means to compare yourself to every other woman, looking for the ones whose own fat can make you relax" (1994:32). Two of the subjects we interviewed constructed fat continuums on which they compare themselves to others who are overweight in hopes that they will be smaller than the person they are referencing.

Lynn stated, "I used to see a fat person, I'd point to them and ask, 'Do I look like that?'" In constructing her personal fat continuum, Lynn looked at other overweight people and compared herself to them. Because she is overweight, Lynn could not occupy the extreme positive end of her fat continuum, yet she also resisted occupying the position at the extreme negative end of the continuum, which would be held by someone more overweight than she. However, she constructed this continuum in anticipation that she would not be as overweight as the person she compared herself to. If she is thinner than the person she sees, she will be comforted by the distance that she is from that person.

Grace also spoke about constructing her personal fat continuum:

One thing I do is to look at other heavy women and compare myself to them. And I always wonder to myself if I am as big as she is, that woman in the mall, or at school. I'll look at her and wonder if I look as awkward or as uncomfortable as she does. I always feel better when I decide I'm not as fat as they are.

Grace compared herself to other women. She placed women she observed whom she estimated to be more overweight than she was at the negative end of her fat continuum, and distanced herself from those women and the label of overweight. Her use of the fat continuum enabled her to decide that, "Yes, I am fat, but at least I am not as fat as I could be." By sizing up others and deciding that they are more overweight than she is, Grace constructed a positive image of her body and distanced herself from the extreme negative end of her personal fat continuum.

At Least I'm not a Lazy Slob

Sheila commented on her belief that overweight people are stereotypically thought of as being sloppy and not well- dressed:

> I had a lady tell me the other day, I think a lot of times people are kind of scared about the wording, what they say to you, she said, "How should I say it? You're more stylish than many small people I know." Which was kind of funny. It was totally a compliment, and I took it as such, but she wanted to say, "For a fat person you really do dress well, you sure know how to dress and look good." That's really what she wanted to say. . . . It may be the fact that I think I'm cute so I want to dress cute. . . . I'd rather dress up than have on baggy blue jeans and a big T-shirt. I like looking good, you know what I mean?

Sheila constructed a continuum on which the extreme negative end is held by the sloppy and poorly dressed overweight woman as a deviant exemplar. She placed herself apart from women that she viewed as being badly dressed. Sheila saw dressing poorly as a negative characteristic, and the care and pride she takes in dressing well allowed her to distance herself from the negative end of her continuum.

Several of the research subjects placed themselves on this continuum relative to the overweight person who does not dress well or appears to not take very good care of herself physically. Lee stated:

> If I think that somebody is being slothful, I do react to that . . . if I see somebody who's not paying attention to how to make the most of whatever their strengths and limitations are, and I would say that I'd play that to other things too, their intellect, their personality, and to their body.

We asked her if she noticed sloth in people of any size, and she responded:

> I think I do recognize sloth in people of any size, but I think that I probably look twice at people who are overweight, probably because of some personal

identity and my sensibility of it, that a good way to deal with strengths and weaknesses and attractiveness or dis-attractiveness [is to] sort of accept where you are and make the most of it. So I'm probably more inclined to scope out overweight people. I'm sure my attention is attracted to how other people present themselves, presentation of self-type things. I suppose I'm interested in how other overweight people present self, and so yeah, I think I would probably be more likely to label (an overweight person) a sloth.

Overweight women who do not take care of themselves occupy the negative end of Lee's continuum. She viewed not taking care of oneself as a negative attribute, and therefore the negative end of her continuum is occupied by overweight women who don't take care of themselves. Lee judged unkempt overweight women critically, in part so that she would have someone to occupy the negative end of her unkempt continuum, and also because she sensed that their presentation of self could reflect negatively on how other people perceive her.

Claire, a thirty-seven-year-old special education teacher, also stated that overweight people should strive to resist being sloppy or unkempt and should take care with their appearance:

To me, what bothers me, I guess, truthfully, is if you see somebody who is overweight and they don't take care of themselves. You should do the most with what you have, you know what I mean?

Claire revealed her belief that sloppiness and being poorly dressed are undesirable and deviant traits for overweight people and she evoked a "slob" continuum in order to distance herself from overweight people who exhibit these characteristics.

At Least I'm Healthy

Sheila, in talking about her family, stated:

I know that they think this is not good for me. They've always thought being heavy is bad for your health and all that kind of something. I beg to differ. I know a lot of heavy people who are healthy, and I know a lot of skinny people who are awful sick. So I just don't buy into that. I'm just comfortable. I carry my weight. There's nothing I can't do. I walk, I play ball, I do whatever I want to. A lot of people talk about their weight and say they can't breathe and can't walk up a flight of steps. I don't have that problem.

Sheila revealed her belief that overweight people are stereotypically thought of as unhealthy. She practiced narrative resistance by comparing herself to, and distancing herself from, the deviance exemplars of the unhealthy overweight person and the unhealthy skinny person who both occupied positions at the extreme negative end of her continuum.

When we asked Lila how she felt about her body, she responded:

> Fairly comfortable. It's the only one I have. So I'm fairly happy with it, in that I'm healthy and active, and able to go out and play with my dog. Or if I want to go camping, I can go camping, if I want to climb a mountain I can prepare my body to go climb a mountain. And even though I feel that other people view my body in a different way than I view myself, I'm comfortable that I can do whatever I want. And I'm healthy, and that's important.

Lila was aware that other people did not accept her body, yet she formed her identity in response to other people's perceptions of her by speaking of herself positively and describing herself as healthy. Lila distanced herself from the negative end of her health continuum, which is occupied by an amalgam of unhealthy overweight people. Lila identified herself as healthy, and in doing so, she was able to position herself away from the negative end of the continuum she had constructed.

With the combination of exemplars that reject deviance and continuums that distance the self from deviance, it is plain to see how deviance is a narrative resource in constructing identity. Let us now turn our attention to our last type of narrative resistance, the loophole.

LOOPHOLES: EXCEPTING SELF FROM DEVIANCE

Similar to Scott and Lyman's (1968:47) concept of "excuses," loopholes are a form of narrative resistance in which overweight women describe factors that they feel contribute to their being overweight. Scott and Lyman define excuses as

> socially approved vocabularies for mitigating or relieving responsibility when conduct is questioned. . . . Excuses are accounts in which one admits that the act in question is bad, wrong, or inappropriate but denies full responsibility. (ibid.)

These two concepts differ in that excuses are used when a person attempts to relinquish herself from responsibility for an action, while loopholes are formed so that an individual can ease the liability she feels for a particular aspect of her identity, such as being overweight. The women we interviewed used loopholes as a narrative resistance strategy by discussing how past illnesses, their genetically predetermined tendency to be overweight, and how they were socialized all affected their identity management and construction.

... But I Was Sick

Lee addressed how being sick as a child led to her gaining weight:

I started gaining weight when I was in third or fourth grade. The doctor discovered what he called a "potential diabetic situation," as in my blood sugar was high. And he took me off sugar, and I have since come to believe that a lot of this was quackery. He took me off sugar for a year, and then when I could once again have sugar, I cannot remember if I craved it and just really ate myself silly, or if my body was just so out of whack it didn't know how to metabolize it or what, but that's when I started gaining weight.

Lee's identity and her perception of her body was shaped by her belief that her childhood doctor's medical treatment for her was possibly harmful. It is widely believed that overweight people are entirely responsible for their condition (Crocker et al. 1993; English 1991; Maddox et al. 1968). This form of discursive constraint discourages overweight people from acknowledging factors that may have contributed to their being overweight. Lee's discourse on the role that her doctor's instructions had in her gaining weight is an example of narrative resistance. She resisted the pervasive notion that overweight people are always responsible for their situation and improves her self-identity.

Lila also commented on how sickness contributed to her weight gain:

I was a really good swimmer, and really good swimmers are typically not fat.... I had hepatitis when I was fifteen and was very, very, very sick for six months, and put on a hundred pounds because I quit swimming. I couldn't get out of bed. I was very sick. And I never lost it.

Lila claimed that having hepatitis led her to gain weight. Though Lila's sickness may have contributed to her weight gain, the discursive constraint that exists in society dictates that overweight people are totally accountable for being overweight. Again, narrative resistance serves as a loophole for the oppression of discursive constraint.

... But I Have Different Genetics

Claire's practice of narrative resistance involved her stating that her inherited physical build had contributed to her size and shape:

I'm the last of three children. The other two are very physically fit and athletic, and there's me, and I'm overweight. I believe, I truly do believe that we can't change who we are.... I just think I never was meant to be like my sister. I'm the tallest, my feet are much bigger. I have a different build.

Claire maintained that she was genetically predisposed to be her particular size. The genetics loophole eased her responsibility to herself for her body size and shape.

Grace also mentioned inherited physical traits in her management of her identity:

> I'm the tallest person in my family. I'm even taller than my father and grandfather. And I am distributed differently. My middle sister had a baby a year and a half ago, and she's the thinnest she's ever been. And even when she was heavy, she had these tiny hands, and I have big hands. My other sister was always small, little bitty. And my mother has these bird legs. I just think I'm different from other people in my family. I'm heavier, and taller, and stronger. There are lots of things that are different about us, and weight is one of them.

Grace resisted the discursive constraint she experienced as an overweight woman by pointing out that the physical and genetic traits she inherited determined that she would be larger than other people in her family. She accepted that she is overweight, yet she managed her identity by stating her belief that her physical makeup predetermined that she would be larger than other people.

. . . But I Was Poorly Socialized

Sheila, in talking about her childhood, stated:

> I realize too that some of my habits are because of things I learned as a younger person, and so I'm having to rethink my whole life basically right now because one of the things, you know, growing up poor, you don't have a whole lot of money. You aren't allowed to waste food. Whatever was put on your plate, once that plate was blessed, you ate it. And if you didn't, they'd say there are starving children living in Africa or wherever that could have eaten that food, and you never know when you're going to have your next meal, you'd better eat it. And I've lived by that principle. . . . So if my eyes happened to be bigger than my stomach, which a lot of times they would be, I would still eat it because I would feel like, once it's blessed I shouldn't throw God's food out, down the drain or throw it out. That was a real issue for me in my home. And I'm sure it was an issue of control in my home. You couldn't let good food go to waste. We've got too many kids to feed, you can't do that. But I didn't understand it obviously, I brought it all the way through to now even when I don't worry about what we're going to eat.

Sheila felt that the way she was socialized to think about food in her childhood contributed to her size and how she thinks about food today. She incorporated how she was socialized to think about food into her current identity, and in doing so, she resisted discursive constraint by relinquishing some responsibility for her weight.

Grace also claimed that the eating habits she learned in childhood affected her adult eating habits:

> I don't know anything about nutrition. I grew up on McDonald's, and so I don't know how to eat right. It's very hard for me to try to learn. I still have erratic eating habits, and it's hard for me to feel when I'm hungry, physiologically feel it. Sometimes I can't tell if it's hunger or acid reflux or whatever.

Grace attributed her current thoughts about food and her weight to her past socialization, deflecting discursive constraint by abdicating total responsibility for her size. Grace resisted the notion that her being overweight is entirely due to factors within her control.

DISCUSSION AND CONCLUSION

Narrative resistance, engaged in by all ten of our subjects, has been a useful frame for interpreting the discourses of overweight women. By applying a spatial analogy to the terrain of identity, we learn that an overweight woman can categorically contrast her identity with an exemplar, contrast her identity in comparison with others on a continuum, or create a loophole or gap that contrasts her identity with public assumptions about the status of being overweight. We do not suggest that all overweight women engage in narrative resistance. Further research would be necessary with a larger, more varied sample of overweight women to determine if the practice is widespread. However, as we shall see, these concepts do inform us about the implications of discourse for social change.

The relations between overweight women and society can be characterized as domination and resistance. Discursive constraint limits the life chances of overweight women in terms of both their activities and their identity construction. However, the form of domination addressed by this chapter transcends the domination that takes place between society and overweight women. Discursive constraint is a foundation for all forms of domination. People who are stigmatized are objectified as things or categories: thus members of society are not obligated to take their feelings and opinions into consideration. The mass media publicly disparage overweight people, particularly overweight women. As Goffman stated, "We exercise varieties of discrimination through which we effectively, if often unthinkingly, reduce [one's] life chances" (1963:4). Discursive constraint is a form of discrimination.

In response to discursive constraint, everyone, including overweight women, has the option of exercising narrative resistance. Working mothers, for instance, are frequently told they are selfish and should be at home with their children. This form of discursive constraint represents an effort to simultaneously constrain the working mother's behavior (suggesting she should be at home with her children) and her choices for her identity (if you are a mother who works, you must be selfish). After talking with other working mothers, she may conclude she is a good mother even if she works because "at least I spend quality time with my children, unlike other working mothers." By setting up mothers who do not spend time with their children at the deviant end of a continuum and stay-at-home mothers at the positive end, she can, through the use of a deviance exemplar, narratively distance herself from a spoiled identity.

Viewed in this light, narrative resistance is quite ironic in that it serves simultaneously to perpetuate oppressive discourses and to resist them. The working mother in our example appears to accept that it is better to be an at-home mom. To distance herself from the stigma of being a working mom, she oppresses other working moms by setting them up as deviance exemplars.

Likewise, overweight women use negative exemplars to simultaneously resist the attendant stigmas and oppress other overweight women. For example, when Lynn distanced herself from the "jolliness" exemplar, she was criticizing other overweight people who seem too "jolly." Similarly, when Grace informed us: "I always feel better when I decide I'm not as fat as they are," she appeared to accept that it is better not to be "fat." Both women, in distancing themselves from the stigma of being overweight, oppressed other overweight women by setting them up to represent a deviance exemplar.

For Gubrium and Lynott, "Exemplars and their application have a dialectical relationship" (1985:357) between the individual and society. As subjects externalize their various brands of narrative resistance within specific contexts, they are internalized by others to be reproduced at a later date. By passing on these restructured ideas about the status of overweight women, motherhood, or other stigmatized identities, subjects make these alternative discourses available as resources to others for their own personal identity construction as well as to the public. The public, in turn, serves as a site for cultural transmission, circulating the positive narrative resistance exemplars back to subjects as positive identity resources they may draw upon.

In summary, when an overweight woman uses narrative resistance to manage her identity, she resists domination by not allowing herself to be passively swept up in the general public's negative conception of her. Additionally, overweight women actively participate in the restructuring of the stocks of knowledge pertaining to their possible identities. By talking to overweight women and others, they circulate the adjusted, more positive discourses about themselves to the public. For examples of some of the results, one has only to tune in to television and radio talk shows to discover the recently developing positive subculture surrounding overweight women. Expressions such as "Thin is in but fat is where it's at" may be slogans but they contribute to a discourse in which being overweight is not strictly a negative identity.

Likewise, emerging urban dialects that make use of the term *Phat* (pronounced "fat") to denote that something is "cool" or in style also chart new roads across the terrain of being overweight in U.S. society. Grace commented that she saw the term *Phat* in a magazine, and at first she thought they were joking. "Enough already, how much more do we have to take," she stated. When she realized it was not an insult but meant in a positive way, Grace's response was,

> You know it may seem insignificant but it's not. It's the first time that I have seen something about being overweight portrayed in such a positive light. It's almost like that expression "she is the shit" or "she is the bomb," it's meant as ironic, but it actually means something positive. Seeing something like that actually gives me some hope.

Deviance exemplars such as I am not unattractive, I am not sexually undesirable, I am not desperate to lose weight, and I do not hate my body, or the loophole, I have different genetics, are promoted in magazines such as *Big Beautiful Women* (*BBW*) and *Mode*. *Mode*, for instance, encourages overweight women to embrace their size and see their bodies as beautiful. Their format includes profiles of famous "overweight women" such as Rosie O'Donnell, Bette Midler, and Roseanne. Magazines are sites where narrative resistance is circulated by and for overweight women. Additionally, talk shows such as Sally Jessie Raphael, Jenny Jones, and others that feature segments where the focus is on the rights of overweight people, beauty contests for large women, or fashion shows featuring overweight women, are also sites of cultural transmission where narrative resistance can be publicly modeled for other overweight people. Groups such as "chubby chasers," men who seek out relationships specifically with overweight women, also promote more positive images of overweight women.

Several fashion models have emerged in recent years by gaining recognition for their status as "plus-size" models. Emme, a Ford Agency model who is 5-11 and weighs 185 pounds, was selected by *People* magazine as one of the "50 Most Beautiful People in the World." In her motivational book *True Beauty*, Emme (Emme and Paisner 1996:238–39) encourages and models the practice of narrative resistance for her readers:

It has to do with looking beyond your "trouble" spots and discovering aspects of your character or physical traits to cherish and admire. The mirror doesn't lie. Embrace the parts of your body and personality that make you feel good. . . . It has to do with rejecting some of our more commonly held notions of beauty in favor of the ones that make sense. With two kids and two jobs it's impossible to make a fashion statement every time you leave the house. Accept that it's probably foolish to try. But to the one who loves you, you will always look like a page out of the *Victoria's Secret* catalogue. Keep in mind that you can still turn the right heads when it matters most.

While these instances do not represent a giant leap forward in the conception of overweight women by the public or themselves, it must be pointed out that social change is often slow and gradual. In the culture of thinness, any situation in which overweight people are portrayed in a positive light must be counted as a step toward liberation. Each successful instance of narrative resistance, both within and outside the social circles of overweight women, lays a small part of the groundwork necessary to dialectically transform overweight women's social space from something negative to something neutral or perhaps even positive.

ACKNOWLEDGEMENTS

We would like to acknowledge Rabecca Cross, Paul Gahn, and family for their assistance with various stages of this manuscript. We would also like to thank the ten women whose candid, and sometimes painful, revelations gave us insight into the status of being considered "overweight."

REFERENCES

Bellizzi, J. A., M. L. Klassen, and J. J. Belonax. 1989. "Stereotypical Beliefs About Overweight and Smoking and Decision-Making in Assignments to Sales Territories." *Perceptual and Motor Skills* 69:419–29.

Berger, P. L., and T. Luckmann. 1966. *The Social Construction of Reality: A Treatise in the Sociology of Knowledge*. New York: Doubleday.

Cahnman, W. J. 1968. "The Stigma of Obesity." *Sociological Quarterly* 9(3):283–99.

Cash, T. F., and K. L. Hicks. 1990. "Being Fat Versus Thinking Fat: Relationships with Body Image, Eating Behaviors, and Well-Being." *Cognitive Therapy and Research* 14(3):327–41.

Chernin, K. 1985. *The Hungry Self: Women, Eating, and Identity*. New York: Harper & Row.

Crocker, J., B. Cornwell, and B. Major. 1993. "The Stigma of Overweight: Affective Consequences of Attributional Ambiguity." *Journal of Personality and Social Psychology* 64(1):60–70.

DeJong, W. 1993. "Obesity as a Characterological Stigma: The Issue of Responsibility and Judgments of Task Performance." *Psychological Reports* 73:963–70.

Emme and D. Paisner. 1996. *True Beauty: Positive Attitudes and Practical Tips from the World's Leading Plus-Size Model.* New York: Putnam's Sons.

English, C. 1991. "Food Is My Best Friend: Self-Justifications and Weight Loss Efforts." *Research in the Sociology of Health Care* 9:335–45.

Goffman, E. 1963. *Stigma: Notes on the Management of a Spoiled Identity.* Engelwood Cliffs, NJ: Prentice-Hall.

Goodman, N., S. M. Dornbusch, S. A. Richardson, and A. H. Hastorf. 1963. "Variant Reactions to Physical Disabilities." *American Sociological Review* 28:429–35.

Goodman, W. C. 1995. *The Invisible Woman: Confronting Weight Prejudice in America.* Carlsbad, CA: Gurze.

Gubrium, J. F., J. A. Holstein, and D. R. Buckholdt. 1994. *Constructing the Life Course.* Dix Hills, NY: General Hall.

Harris, M. B., L. C. Walters, and S. Waschull. 1991a. "Gender and Ethnic Differences in Obesity-Related Behaviors and Attitudes in a College Sample." *Journal of Applied Social Psychology* 21(19):1545–66.

———. 1991b. "Altering Attitudes and Knowledge About Obesity." *Journal of Social Psychology* 13(6):881–84.

Lennon, W. K. 1992. "Categorization as a Function of Body Type." *Clothing and Textiles Research Journal* 10(2):18–23.

Maddox, G. L., K. W. Back, and V. R. Liederman. 1968. "Overweight as Social Deviance and Disability." *Journal of Health and Social Behavior* 9:287–98.

Maroney, D., and S. Golub. 1992. "Nurses' Attitudes Toward Obese Persons and Certain Ethnic Groups." *Perceptual and Motor Skills* 75:387–91.

Orbach, S. 1994. *Fat Is a Feminist Issue: The Anti-Diet Guide to Permanent Weight Loss.* New York: Berkeley.

Ronai, C. R. 1994. "Narrative Resistance to Deviance: Identity Management Among Strip-Tease Dancers." *Perspectives on Social Problems* 6:195–213.

———. 1997. "Discursive Constraint in the Narrated Identities of Childhood Sex Abuse Survivors." Pp. 123–36 in *Everyday Sexism in the Third Millennium,* edited by C. R. Ronai, B. A. Zsembik, and J. R. Feagin. New York: Routledge.

Sarup, M. 1996. *Identity, Culture, and the Postmodern World.* Athens: University of Georgia Press.

Schroeder, C. R. 1992. *Fat Is Not a Four-Letter Word.* Minneapolis, MN: Chronimed.

Scott, M. B., and S. M. Lyman. 1968. "Accounts." *American Sociological Review* 33:46–62.

Tiggeman, M., and E. D. Rothblum. 1989. "Gender Differences in Social Consequences of Perceived Overweight in the United States and Australia." *Sex Roles* 18(1–2):75–86.

Tisdale, S. 1995. "A Weight That Women Carry." Pp. 15–30 in *Minding the Body: Women Writers on Body and Soul,* edited by P. Foster. New York: Anchor Books, Doubleday.

Waxler, S. H., and E. S. Liska. 1975. "Obesity and Self-Destructive Behavior." Pp. 188–210 in *Self- Destructive Behavior,* edited by A. R. Roberts. Springfield, IL: Charles Thomas.

4

Fighting Back
Reactions and Resistance to the Stigma of Obesity

LEANNE JOANISSE and ANTHONY SYNNOTT

Since the early 1950s, obesity has been claimed by some to be America's foremost health problem (Bennett and Gurin 1982). Considerable research has been conducted on many of the issues relating to matters of obesity and overweight: its prevalence and distribution, its putative causes, the attendant discrimination, the economic and health costs involved in treating obesity, its role in mortality and morbidity, as well as its psychological goals and meanings (Allon 1982; Bouchard 1990; Kuczmarski, Flegal, Campbell, and Johnson 1994; Manson et al. 1995; Orbach 1978; Stunkard 1988; Wolf and Colditz 1994). And, of course, the remedies and solutions to excess weight have also engrossed the lay public's mind. By the turn of the century, it is estimated Americans will have spent $77 billion on the pursuit of weight loss (Rodin 1992:166).

Obesity researchers generally fall into one of two camps (Fraser 1997; Sobal 1995). Medical researchers tend to focus on fatness, view it as pathological, and favor interventions such as diets, drugs, and surgery. The low success rates and hazardous side effects of these treatments are overlooked on the ground that *anything* is justifiable in the management of obesity. More recently, psychological researchers specializing in eating disorders have tended to focus on thinness and to refute the conclusions and recommendations of the medical researchers. They maintain that the solutions are ineffective, expensive, and time-consuming and, moreover, often exacerbate the very problems they are supposed to cure. The former blame fat people as responsible for their size and their subsequent problems; the latter blame the former as responsible for perpetuating the real problem the obese face, which is intolerance and insensitivity: in a word, sizism.

Although this additional paradigm is welcome and useful, the discourse on weight and weight-related matters often does not include the input of fat people themselves. Even the copious studies outlining the tremendous prejudice and discrimination faced by the obese do not rely on firsthand accounts of obese persons; rather, these studies mostly consist of asking higher education samples about their opinions about the obese regarding a particular subject, e.g., employment, marriageability, or esthetics. Consequently, there has been almost no attention paid to how its bearers cope with the virulent stigma that often accompanies this condition. The paucity of research into the life stories of fat people is a brutal illustration of their exclusion and marginalization.

MANAGING STIGMA

In late 1982, an article in an American newspaper featured the tribulations of a high school majorette named Peggy Ward, who had been removed from the school band because she was one and one-half pounds overweight. The article went on to say that Ward was deeply upset by her expulsion and described how she was fighting back. In this case, "fighting back" consisted of fasting for three days in an effort to lose the unwanted twenty-four ounces and rejoin her squad (Jones, Farina, Hastorf, Markus, Miller, and Scott 1984:1). It seems absurd that embarking on a starvation diet can be viewed as defending oneself against arbitrary weight standards but, all too often, altering the body through aggressive interventions has been relentlessly propounded as the best and only means of stigma management available to the obese. This reasoning is based on the logic that sizism can only be avoided by shedding the offending weight—which is popularly assumed to be self-inflicted. Indeed, the medical literature is replete with suggestions that sizism serves as a sufficient motivator for weight loss. The assumption is that fat people are responsible for their own problems in the first place.

It is the offending body that must be changed; not the culture that is offended by it. As Chernin (1981) wryly notes, women living in a fat-phobic culture spend their entire lives in desperate, fruitless efforts to revise their bodies rather than demand that the culture reform its values. The rewards of closely resembling the dominant group are obvious. However, attempts to mold the body have proven to be largely ineffective, as the 95 percent failure rate of diets and other weight-loss techniques attests (Cogan and Rothblum 1992; Garner and Wooley 1991). If weight-loss measures don't work, and obesity is an exceedingly stigmatizing condition with damaging consequences—especially for women—what then are the options for the obese? If transforming the body is relatively impossible, is it more fruitful to transform the current fat-phobic culture?

It is not enough to document sizism and deplore its existence. This chapter attempts to broaden the scope of weight- related studies by examining how obese people cope with the fat phobia so pervasive in North American society. It seeks such understanding through the direct testimony of large persons.

METHOD AND DESCRIPTION OF THE SUBJECTS

We noted that the subject of obesity stigma management has been understudied in North America and, realizing the need for *in vivo* studies, we decided to interview large Canadians about their experiences with sizism from all sources. Since it was our intention to provide our respondents with the opportunity to furnish detailed accounts about their lives, we chose open-ended, semistructured interviews rather than rigidly constructed questionnaires as our method of data collection. We were not only interested in finding out the extent to which obesity is stigmatizing; we also wanted to know, How do the obese cope? How do they manage their stigma? Our goal was to explore the extent to which the stigma of overweight has permeated their lives and to discover the behaviors they have undertaken in response.

For this study, which is part of a larger research project on sizism in contemporary Canadian society, we interviewed twenty-three adults, eleven women and twelve men. Both genders were included because we are interested in ascertaining the part gender plays in the treatment of overweight people. Although fatness is generally viewed as a "woman's problem" (Rothblum 1992; Wooley, Wooley, and Dyrenforth 1979), Millman (1980) predicts that as appearance becomes more of a salient issue to men, they will become increasingly concerned with their weight.

Most of the interviews were conducted by the first author in the spring and summer of 1996 and the summer of 1997. To find our respondents, we proceeded in a snowball fashion, interviewing people living in various cities across Canada. Three of the respondents are leaders in the Canadian size acceptance movement. To ensure confidentiality, all have been assigned pseudonyms.

The informants came from a range of socioeconomic backgrounds, including medical and business professionals, blue-collar workers, clerical workers, and two musicians. Three of the sample members were students and two of the women identified themselves as full-time homemakers. Their ages ranged from twenty-one to sixty-three, with a mean age of thirty-six for the women and forty-two for the men.

Their weights ranged from 196 pounds to 550 pounds, the average being 318 pounds. The percentage above ideal medical weight varied from a low of 32 percent to a high of 179 percent, with a mean of 83 percent for the women and from 31 to 229 percent for the men, the mean being 94 percent. Seven members of the sample were morbidly obese.

Rothblum (1992) charges that weight preoccupation is a peculiarly American obsession. There is reason to believe, however, that Canada shares the United States' concerns with size—not a surprising observation given that country's proximity and its gargantuan influence on our culture. Our level of obesity, at 32 percent of the population, approximates that of the United States (Reeder et al. 1992). Over 80 percent of Canadian women have dieted by the age of eighteen, and 40 percent of nine-year-old girls have already dieted (Sheinin 1990). The *Report of the Task Force on the Treatment of Obesity* (Health and Welfare Canada 1991) estimates that Canadians spend $300 million a year on weight loss attempts. It would appear, then, that Canadians share the American preoccupation with weight to a very large extent.

In these in-depth, semistructured interviews, which averaged one and a half hours in duration, we explored each person's history as a large person, experiences with size discrimination and how they dealt with them, as well as current practices and feelings about their bodies. The respondents discussed the effects of being obese, their self-images, and their consequent behaviors. We have presented their views in two sections. The first documents our informants' difficulties with their families, at school, at work, in romantic relationships, with the medical profession, and with the general public. This first section contextualizes the second, which discusses the main coping mechanisms of our informants: the tactics and strategies and the patterns of reaction and resistance to the stigmatization of obesity.

LIVING OBESE

Family

All but one of the sample were fat as children, and the family was the first environment where they learned they were deviant. Informants were aware at an early age that they were a source of humiliation and disgrace to their parents and a figure of derision and scorn to their siblings and other relatives. They reported being cajoled and threatened into losing weight by their parents. The majority of the women indicated that their mothers criticized them constantly and warned them that "nobody loves a fat girl," although none of the male respondents reported this advice. Many times parental exhortations turned into cruelty and insensitivity. Fathers were more likely than mothers to torment a fat child: "My father told me I was too ugly to be a good prostitute" (Mary Lou). "My father would tell me I was fat and ugly for my own good so that I would be motivated to lose weight" (Rosalind). Fat sons were not spared by their fathers either. Andy reported his father publicly harassed him in a very vicious manner for five years in an attempt to shame him into losing weight. Andy claimed that home offers no respite for fat children, as their parents are likely to share in the cultural aversion to fatness.

School

When the respondents reached school age, they were derided and ostracized by their peers. They were also punched and kicked on many occasions. They pointed out, with outrage, that their teachers often did not intervene to prevent the bullying; more often, the teachers themselves made sarcastic, hurtful remarks: "The teacher told me that she supposed I'd rather stay home and eat cookies" (Debbie). "The teacher referred to me as the fat girl in the front" (Lori). Physical education teachers were singled out as being particularly sadistic toward fat children. Two of the sample members dropped out of school as a result of the constant harassment and abuse.

Loneliness and Isolation

Not surprisingly, the informants who recounted experiences of school ostracization were likely to indicate that they were lonely and isolated. Half the sample, six men and six women, indicated that the school victimization they experienced induced them to become very shy and uncertain of themselves as adolescents. Instead of spending leisure time with friends or participating in extracurricular activities, they stayed home and concentrated on school work or hobbies. This is how Mary Lou described her isolation and its consequences:

> During this period I became very reclusive. I went to very few school dances because nobody ever asked me to dance and I figured I may as well stay home. For my whole teen years I didn't go anywhere except school and home. My school years just passed me by. I was so envious of girls who were openly comfortable with boys. I was envious of the gangs of kids that hung out together after school. I've never been part of a group, I've always been on the outside looking in. Not surprisingly, I have very poor social skills. I just don't know how to interact with people.

Cultural expectations regarding weight and appearance are transmitted to children through the socialization process and have proved to be extraordinarily powerful (Denzin 1979; Dreitzel 1973). The scholarly literature is replete with studies illustrating that hatred of fat starts at an early age (Goodman, Dornbusch, Richardson, and Hastorf 1963; Richardson, Goodman, Hastorf, and Dornbusch 1961; Staffieri 1967; Wooley, Wooley, and Dyrenforth 1980). Fraser (1997:47) describes a poll in which the majority of children replied "getting fat" when queried about their greatest fear. In a study that asked diabetic children if they would prefer to remain diabetic and thin or to become healthy and obese, most preferred the former (Rodin, Silberstein, and Striegel-Moore 1984). Cahnman (1968) sympathizes with young fat people, believing them to be particularly vulnerable because of the uncertainty of their social status as well as the conflicting nature of their emotions. It is difficult for obese children to defend themselves from the humiliation and torment they suffer because they generally have not yet developed coping mechanisms.

Romantic Relationships

Fourteen members of the sample were never married and were not involved in a major relationship at the time of the interview. Two were divorced. The other members of the sample were either married or involved in long-term relationships.

The unmarried participants *all* attributed their single status to their weight, viewing it as an impediment to establishing and maintaining a romantic relationship. They were not only unmarried but remained unattached for long periods at a time. The male respondents reported being frequently rejected by prospective dating partners and expressed feelings of loneliness. Similarly, the females indicated they were rarely asked out on dates, or even complimented, by men. Rather, they had been told that they'd be more attractive if they lost fifty pounds or that a particular man would date them if they weren't "so fat." The women were more likely to report close friendships with men that never evolve into anything more intimate. When queried about this, they demonstrated a remarkable equanimity about this state of affairs, expressing resignation rather than bitterness. They indicated an awareness that physical attractiveness is an important prerequisite for courtship and that their weight precluded them from being considered suitable. Gina explained how men's social prestige is reflected by the attractiveness of their partners:

> In a way I understand them [men]. They don't want an overweight girlfriend because it makes them look bad. A guy would only go out with an overweight girl either because there's something wrong with him or he just wants sex.

When they are involved in a romantic relationship, the participants indicated that they are frequently castigated about their weight and that it is the focus of frequent arguments. It would appear that for many people, dating a fat person is contingent on his or her losing weight; when this does not occur, the partner feels betrayed and disappointed. The two divorced members of the sample both indicated that their failure to lose weight led to the breakdown of their marriages. Rebecca's ex-husband told her that her obese condition was the reason why he had numerous adulterous relationships, and Bill's former wife concluded that his failure to lose weight amounted to a lack of respect for himself, and by extension, for her.

Of the five married members of the sample, four reported that their spouses were obvious in their displeasure about their overweight condition. In particular, the two married women complained that their husbands berated them openly or made cruel remarks cloaked in the guise of humor, especially in the presence of friends. Their husbands consistently refused to recognize their insensitivity; rather, they accused their wives of being thin-skinned. When asked about their reasons for staying in unsatisfactory marriages, both admitted that the primary motive for marrying their husbands—although they didn't love them—was the fear that the opportunity for matrimony might not present itself again. Both these women were threatened with divorce if they did not lose weight, and they were alternately relieved and frightened by this ultimatum: Frightened of being alone the rest of their lives, relieved because at least they wouldn't have to tolerate verbal abuse.

Even those respondents who pronounced themselves as being deeply fulfilled in their careers and friendships expressed anguish about the void in their personal lives: "Fatness has caused devastating effects on my relationships, to the point that I will never have the family I've always wanted—that's the one thing that I've wanted all my life. And I didn't get that" (Ted).

Overweight and obesity have proved to be stumbling blocks to courtship and marriage, especially for women. Vener, Krupka, and Gerard's (1982) subjects said that they would prefer to marry an embezzler, cocaine user, marijuana user, shoplifter, recovering mental patient, and others before they would marry an obese person. The researchers noted that the males expressed greater resistance to the possibility of an obese partner. Similarly, high school students surveyed by Sobal, Nicopoulos, and Lee (1995) indicated an unwillingness to date an overweight person. The males, in particular, were reluctant to consort with a heavy peer. Gortmaker, Must, Perrin, Sobol, and Dietz's (1993) finding that fat women are more likely than their slender peers to remain single is further evidence of male antipathy toward large women as marital partners.

Employment Discrimination

The participants' weight proved to be a serious impediment in job searches. All but one indicated that they had been discriminated against in some measure or other by prospective employers. When Rosalind was looking for a nursing position, she was told she was too fat to fulfill the requirements of the job or that the position had already been filled, even though it continued to be advertised. These experiences were echoed by the majority of the sample. The heavier the respondent, the more difficult it was to find employment. The women, in particular, reported having difficulty in getting hired. A recurring theme was the impression that employers feel that if fat people can't take care of themselves, then they certainly aren't capable of holding a demanding job. As Mary Lou commented, "Things may be tough all over, but it's much, much worse for fat people who are looking for a job."

When the respondents did manage to secure employment, they continued to experience pervasive discrimination. Their colleagues openly sneered at them, and one woman was repeatedly pinched on the arm by a male colleague. Although he never referred to the subject directly, she believed he was expressing contempt about her weight. In general, superiors were rarely convinced that the working environment could be tainted with weight prejudice and they themselves made derogatory comments about the participants' weight. Again, the heavier the respondent, the more likely he or she would report scathing remarks. Curiously, none of the women were told by their bosses that they had to lose weight, although a substantial proportion of the men were admonished to do so. The employees who were more likely to suffer were those who worked in jobs where image was an essential component of their work. In particular, the four participants who worked in the health profession were conscious that they were perceived as being unhealthy themselves and therefore not appropriately representing the health profession. Ted was denied entrance into the Royal College of Physicians on account of his weight. He was told by the chief examiner, "People just don't have to like the way you look in order to fail you." The respondents who work for the public are subjected to insults from clients and patients on a regular basis. Keith, who is a produce clerk, described how difficult it is to be constantly under public scrutiny:

> I've experienced all types of discrimination in the workplace. I had a fellow just a couple of weeks ago, he was sitting down at the front and he was staring at me while I was working. When I ended up close to where he was sitting, he asked me how much food do I have to eat in the course of a day to get to be so fat. These kinds of incidents take place at least every two weeks. When young children come in, the first thing they say is how fat I am. When I make a product suggestion, I get comments like, "Well I can see *you* didn't stay away from the strawberries and cream when you were growing up." It's people trying to be funny at the expense of my feelings.

Rodin (1992) notes that success in most occupations depends on a person's appearance as much as his or her abilities. Predictably, researchers have detected a prevailing stereotype that overweight employees are incompetent and undesirable (Larkin and Pines 1979; Roe and Eickwort 1976; Rothblum, Miller, and Garbutt 1988). The results of Rothblum et al.'s (1990) survey on employment discrimination indicate a strong positive relationship between weight and discrimination. Over 40 percent of the men and 60 percent of the women stated that they had not been hired for a job because of their weight. Over 30 percent indicated that they had been denied promotions or raises. Nearly all had been urged to lose weight. The heavier the respondent, the more likely he or she was to have encountered size-related discrimination in the workplace.

The Medical Profession

Over three-quarters of the sample (eighteen out of twenty-three) related incidents of fat bigotry by health practitioners: the very people who professed to want to help them, and from whom they might have expected compassion, sympathy, and understanding. Consultations with doctors often resulted in their being treated with contempt and ridicule, especially if the visit was concerning attempted weight loss. Physicians made caustic, at times cruel, remarks about the participants' weight and presumed lifestyle, referring to them as "pigs" and "lumps of fat." Not a single respondent reported being assisted in a constructive manner by a physician. When Rebecca expressed her reservations about the hazards of weight-loss surgery, the surgeon's response was, "Well, you people just want to make pigs out of yourselves so this is what's got to be. You're so worried about the mortality rates of this operation, but I'll tell you this: If you don't get the weight off, you're going to die anyway, so what's the difference?"

The females were more likely to recount stories of abusive treatment, not to mention outright bullying, by medical professionals. They routinely received weight loss lectures even when their medical complaints were not weight related, such as bladder infections or nosebleeds, or even a broken arm. They also reported numerous incidents of insults and humiliation. One woman was asked by her gynecologist how many chairs she'd broken in his waiting room that day. Another woman's complaint that her medication made her nauseous was greeted with indifference by her doctor, who remarked that at least that way she'd lose weight. Gina and Mary Lou were warned by their doctors (both male) that fat was not attractive to men.

Even more disturbing was the doctors' tendency to dismiss all ailments as originating from the patient's overweight condition, without the benefit of physical examination or laboratory tests. Some conditions were undiagnosed and untreated for several years as a result of the simplistic perception that weight loss is the panacea to all ills. Lori described how her gynecologist's fat bias played an instrumental role in prolonging the agony of putative infertility:

> After a year, I went to see my gynecologist and told him that I'd been trying to get pregnant but it wasn't happening. He didn't question me about anything else, he just said that if I lost weight, I'd conceive. Well, I lost weight but I still didn't get pregnant. I consulted a second gynecologist who checked both me and my husband out. It turned out that my husband has a low sperm count and I had to get artificially inseminated with his sperm and now we have our daughter. All my reproductive organs work just fine. If the first gynecologist had bothered to run tests on both of us instead of telling me I was too fat to have kids, it could have saved me a lot of worry and frustration. And we would have had our daughter sooner.

These findings are consistent with the literature, which indicates that health professionals constitute an extremely fat-phobic group (Adams, Smith, Wilbur, and Grady 1993; Breytspraak, McGee, Cohen Conger, Whatley, and Moore 1977; Maddox and Liederman 1969; Maiman, Wang, Becker, Finlay, and Simonson 1979; Rand and MacGregor 1990; Rothblum et al. 1990; Young and Powell 1985). The fat bigotry endemic in the medical profession can impede a physician's clinical judgment and this, in turn, can have serious consequences. The counsel "first, do no harm" does not appear to have much salience when the doctor is confronted by a fat patient.

Public Harassment

In a society that considers itself enlightened and politically correct to the point where we are afraid to speak for fear of offending somebody, the experiences of our sample illustrate a commonly held belief that fat people are not worthy of being treated with sensitivity or dignity. While social restraints impede most people from commenting on other aspects of physical appearance, no such barriers exist vis-à-vis fatness. The heavier the respondent, the more likely he or she was to report persecution from strangers. Public harassment ranged from open stares, finger pointing, derisive laughter to verbal taunts. As Ted observed, "Everywhere I go— especially in a shopping mall—people are snickering, especially children. Adolescents too, snickering and hooting and hollering." Keith had been threatened on a number of occasions by groups of young men. In several instances, strangers have openly referred to him as a "big, fat pig."

Also, strangers freely approach the participants with gratuitous stereotypical advice that would purportedly lead to weight loss. And at times they have removed items from various respondents' grocery carts, on the ground that these were too fattening. As outrageous as these acts may seem, our respondents are not alone in being subjected to invasions of privacy and cruelty. The respondents in Rothblum et al.'s (1990) study also revealed that they were both physically and verbally harassed on a regular basis.

By virtue of its visibility, obesity is an exceedingly public condition. It is highly noticeable and often elicits a strong reaction from others as our participants' experiences indicate. On many occasions, advice and admonishment are given on the ground that obesity is unhealthy and the person is merely expressing concern for the fat person's health. Whether or not these motivations are sincere, the magnitude of the loathing prompted by the sight of a severely obese person is extraordinary. As Millman (1980) points out, smoking is an unhealthy activity, yet it does not arouse the same visceral reaction obesity does.

Fat people are unattractively nonconformist and are among what Mankoff (1971) calls achieved deviants; that is, they earn their deviant status on the strength of their own actions. Every culture imposes severe penalties for the failure or refusal of its citizens to conform to its values, and these values include what makes a body "right." In the United States and Canada, the best body is slender and well-toned. It is a commodity greatly sought after by the rest of the population, who are willing to expend effort and experience deprivation in order to attain it. Fat people, on the other hand, freely flaunt their violation of cultural norms and are therefore viewed as deserving of retribution. Goffman (1963) notes that whenever the stigmatized are believed to be the cause of their condition, the prejudicial attitudes are intensified. Bill cogently summarized the rampant fat phobia in North American culture: "We're a society that's running out of people to kick around. It's politically incorrect to make comments about women or different races or whatever—and so it should be. But fat people are fair game."

Our findings indicate that the stigma of obesity infiltrates every area of a person's life: family relationships, social skills, employment opportunities, marriageability, access to health care, and peace in their daily lives. Fat people are abused by their parents, teachers, doctors, employers, colleagues, strangers, and also by their peers, friends, and spouses—sometimes with the best of intentions, sometimes not.

FIGHTING BACK

Our respondents know that fat people serve as society's collective punching bag. Despite the tremendous amount of discrimination the participants endured in all areas of their lives, however, we noted a pro-

nounced spirit of fighting back against tormentors. No instance of fat bigotry goes unchallenged among the overwhelming majority. Indeed, we
noted eight principal methods of reaction and resistance to the stigmatization. The tactics and strategies varied widely, depending on the circum-
stances of the interaction, the temperaments and coping skills of the
informants, and their ages. Broadly, they include methods of passive,
active, and reflective resistance. Passive resistance includes the two types
of reaction that we have called Internalization and Anger: The anger is not
articulated but is the precondition for active resistance. The four tactics of
active resistance are Verbal Assertiveness, Physical Aggressiveness, Flamboyance, and Activism. Self-Acceptance and Enlightenment are two
strategies of reflective resistance, which is neither active nor passive, as
these terms are conventionally understood. Those who engage in reflective resistance do not avoid conflict nor do they initiate it; they have
passed beyond such options, transcend sizism in its various manifesta-
tions, and resist by their confidence in themselves. These typologies are
not mutually exclusive, and they do overlap. Our sample members have
often engaged in more than one of these tactics; but they do tend to specialize in one or two. Each of these types of reaction and resistance is discussed below.

Internalization

Predictably, all the sample members have been internalizers at some
point in their lives. We define *internalizers* as those who agree with the
norms of the majority culture and constantly engage in weight loss
attempts. All have tried weight loss schemes of various sorts and lost
weight, but were unable to maintain it for a sustained amount of time. Not
only was the weight loss short-lived, but the process was often hazardous.
After faithfully following the dictums of Dr. Atkins's diet, one man experienced large amounts of hair loss, severe gingivitis, and ketosis. One
woman developed gallstones and had to have her gallbladder removed
after seven months of the Nutri/System eating plan. Another woman got
scurvy. Five of the sample members were prescribed amphetamines as
children and teenagers and subsequently developed an addiction to them.

All the sample members indicated an awareness of the futility of dieting schemes and voiced suspicions that these ultimately result in making
them fatter. Eighteen of them said that dieting was no longer an integral
part of their lives and that it was easier to accept their weight as a part of
who they were. Instead of restricting their food intake with the sole purpose of losing weight, they now focus on maintaining healthy eating.

The remaining five sample members, three men and two women, are
internalizers. They are eloquent in their distaste for diets but harbor an

intense desire to lose weight. They view their weight as a terrible encumbrance, a prison that prevents them from living their lives to their fullest extent. Rebecca echoed the sentiments of the other internalizers with her description of the limits fatness has placed on her:

> My weight has controlled my life. It really has. It's stopped me from living my life the way I want to. My mind wants to live life just like everybody else—go to the beach, go here, go there, but it's stopped me completely. I've been trapped.

Gina felt similarly constrained by her weight:

> Until I lose weight, I can't go out and socialize with everybody. I'm too self-conscious that they're talking about my weight. I'll get a boyfriend when I lose weight. The way I am now, I could never meet anybody. I'm not someone a guy can present with pride. When I lose weight, it'll be the beginning of a whole new life.

Internalizers are adamant in their belief that their weight is the source of most of their troubles. All rejected the possibility of accepting themselves as fat people; they prefer viewing their weight as a temporary problem that would be eventually solved. *Real* life will commence once they lose weight. In the meantime, their lives are held in abeyance.

Anger

All the sample members expressed anger over their designation as society's more repugnant citizens, but while most display their anger either physically or verbally, three of the women have a tendency to seethe internally rather than defend themselves. While they complained about fat oppression, they indicated a reluctance to stand up to victimizers. When asked why they didn't express their anger openly, all replied that they considered wrath to be an unfeminine trait. Another barrier that may inhibit the desire to express anger is the insistence that the fat person is thin-skinned, unable to withstand lighthearted "teasing."

However, anger can be expressed via other channels. Unlike the internalizers, the angry are not involved in any weight loss schemes. They challenge the common assumption that fatness is a matter of choice and express skepticism that dieting results in permanent weight loss. They may be somewhat unhappy as fat people, but their fatness does not restrict their actions. Also, they question society's conventional standards of attractiveness and the pressures these place on women. It is important to point out that the participants who tend to smolder inwardly are angry with society, not with themselves. Sylvia voices what she cannot articulate to her family:

"Me? I think I'm fine just the way I am. It's everyone else who makes an issue of my weight, not me. I just wish they'd leave me alone."

Verbal Assertion

Most of the participants rely on witty rejoinders to put denigrators in their place. When Arlene is told by a man how fat she is, she sarcastically notes the acuity of his vision. Olivia told a woman who'd made a spiteful remark to her that she just *loved* how she'd dyed her roots brown. David was once told by a stranger that he needed Slimfast, and he was quick to remind that person that *he* needed manners. When Mary Lou hears groups of people snickering and tittering behind her back, she'll go up to them and ask if there's anything they'd like to say to her personally. The laughter quickly stops. Three-quarters of the sample indicated that they regularly offered quick repartee to a negative comment.

Verbal assertion is not limited to witty comebacks to insults; it also involves asserting one's rights. The majority of the men in the sample complain to store managers if the sales associates are rude to them. Six of the women refuse to step on a scale in a doctor's office if it's not warranted. They also do not accept reprimands about their weight.

Also, of those who have been in relationships where their weight was an issue, verbal abuse was simply not tolerated. The abusive partner had a choice: Either stop making insensitive remarks or else the relationship will terminate. As for the married women whose husbands issued them ultimatums that the marriage would end if they didn't lose weight, both told them they could leave. The marriages are still intact and the husbands no longer harangue their wives about their weight. Most of the participants have warned family members to stop making cutting comments or face the penalty of banishment. Olivia described her zero-tolerance policy:

> I haven't let someone make a comment about my weight without repercussion for at least six or seven years, and that includes my family. That includes my parents. Most of all, the message I have for my mother is that I don't have a problem with my weight, you have a problem with my weight. That's something you'll have to deal with. So my weight is an off-limits conversation.

Physical Aggression

Whereas riposte proved to be the ideal method of dealing with harassers for the majority of the sample members, two of the participants have resorted to minor acts of vandalism on occasion and maintain they wouldn't hesitate to do so again. When Mary Lou was told by an ice cream vendor that she needed Slimfast instead, she splattered the ice cream cone all over the counter and refused to pay. She also complained to the manager about his employee's rudeness and was promised swift action. Mary Lou recounted the incident with great pleasure, saying it was deeply satisfying, and that she'd since made a personal resolution to physically confront rude people as often as she could. Keith not only retorts to harassers, but chocolate milk serves as a self-defense mechanism. He recounted, with relish, his enjoyment when he stains the upholstery of the cars of his attackers:

> I'm quite famous for throwing chocolate milk at people. I've had a couple of incidents where people have given me the blowfish cheeks while I'm driving, stuff like that. I just gopped chocolate milk at their car while I was driving. One time, as a fella was passing me, he called me a big, fat slob and making the blowfish cheeks. He had his window rolled down while he was driving alongside me and I tossed a big gulp of chocolate milk in his car. Another time, when I was at the 7-Eleven store, these four punks were laughing at my shorts. . . . When I went outside, I opened a whole two-litre carton of chocolate milk on their front seat. I think that in the last eight years, these gulps with the chocolate milk have happened maybe fifteen times.

Given the prevalence of aggravation to which the respondents are subjected—often on a daily basis—it may be surprising that stories involving physical assault against victimizers were not recounted more often. None revealed a desire to hit aggressors. This reluctance may stem from their childhoods, when their parents counseled them to "just ignore" the children who were teasing them. Also, the more intimidating incidents of taunting and jeering tend to occur when groups of people gather together. The lone fat person is outnumbered and finds it safer to walk away from the scene of intimidation. A lifetime of persecution does not easily inspire a person to defend himself or herself, especially when the message "fat is bad" is propounded from all sides.

Flamboyance

Two of the sample members, David and Arlene, revel in their conspicuousness and emphasize it as much as possible. They display themselves flagrantly by wearing colorful clothing and dying their hair in garish colors. Both of them lost a substantial amount of weight in an earlier period and were profoundly unsettled by the physical transformation, realizing that their slender bodies were aberrant and they were happier being large people. Each insists that the attention they receive is positive and that they enjoy standing apart. David is a self-employed musician and, as he describes, he finds it helpful that people remember him:

> I always kind of figured that I may still be the fattest person in the room, but I'm the fattest person in the room with the best wardrobe, the best haircut, and looking the best I can. They're going to remember me. And I'd rather they remember me for having a diamond-studded waistband as opposed to

a sixty-inch waist. I dye my hair red, like fire engine paint. People will comment on that and I explain that I'm in the entertainment business, I have to stand out from the crowd. And I don't want it to be because I'm big. I want it to be because I'm flamboyant and larger than life. I'm living large here.

This technique of self-flaunting is interesting precisely because it defies the conventional norms of camouflage by wearing loose clothing in dark or muted colors, or taking care which way the stripes run or literally by staying at home as much as possible and fearing to go outside—an evasion technique that we have already seen used by the *internalizers*. This is the opposite. Flamboyance is "in-your-face" self-assertion.

Activism

A fat person who accepts his or her body still lives in a society that is hostile to it. Three of our participants are vocal members of the National Association to Advance Fat Acceptance (NAAFA), the only advocacy group in North America for fat people. NAAFA maintains that human rights should not be contingent on size and is dedicated to eliminating weight prejudice in employment. Sensitizing the medical profession and obtaining full access to public transportation are other concerns. The organization does not recommend weight loss as a means of dealing with fat phobia; rather, it vociferously campaigns against society's perception that fatness is a moral defect.

The three activists who participated in this study are at the forefront of the size acceptance movement in Canada. They appear on talk shows, lecture widely, and write extensively about the need for education and awareness about the problems fat people face. They are cautiously optimistic that fat phobia can be eradicated, pointing out that sexism and racism, which were once openly expressed in our society, are now censured. Ted, one of Canada's most prominent size acceptance activists, has the following advice for fat people:

> For the vast majority of the fat people who will never be thin, I want them to be as healthy as they can be and then get on with their lives. That's what I want. I don't want them to stay awake every night hating themselves; waking up in the morning starving themselves, bingeing themselves to pieces and then feeling guilty by the afternoon and hating themselves at night again. I want them to stop that silly nonsense and get on with life. It's that simple. I want them to feel good about themselves as much as they can and to get on with living.

Self-Acceptance

Verbal and physical defense as well as political activism may constitute the most obvious means of dealing with weight prejudice, but these gestures alone are ineffective. The most salient resource a person can rely on in the fight against sizism is an unconditional acceptance of oneself. As repugnant as fat bigotry is, its most pernicious aspect is not opprobrium, but the internalization of fat oppression and accepting it as rightful and justified. This internalization often leads to feelings of self-loathing, shame and entry into the vicious circle of weight cycling.

The members of the sample who seemed to suffer the least from sizism were not the lowest-weight members, but those who were the most secure within themselves and with what they had to offer as people. Four of the respondents, two men and two women, shrugged off weight prejudice as the fat-phobic's problem, rather than their own. They viewed their bodies as a simple variation in the human population and recognize that not everybody can or even *should* be slender. Unlike the other participants, they felt a sense of ownership and attachment to their bodies, with each voicing the sentiment, "It's just a part of me." Sebastian described his feelings about his body size:

> It's me. It's just been a part of my whole life. It has affected my life, it's a part of who I am. It's a part of everything I do. It's me. And it defines somebody more than just hair color or eye color. It's a part of me.

These self-acceptors are successful in their relationships with intimates. Although they indicated they would not brook shoddy treatment, it is interesting—perhaps revealing—that they complained the least about experiences of sizism. Nor did they display the marked anger and bitterness that was so prevalent among the other sample members. Their contentment illustrates that fatness need not plunge one into the Dantean inferno.

Three of these self-acceptors attributed their inner serenity to the fact that they are deeply spiritual and espouse values of acceptance of themselves and of others, regardless of their appearance and beliefs. Each of them emphasized the importance of loving oneself and the important role it plays in the self-concept. We noted that all four had received unconditional love from at least one significant other when they were growing up, and we believe that this has protected them to a great extent from weight prejudice.

Enlightenment

Two men and one woman indicated that their fortieth birthday was a turning point for them, for it was then that they realized they were holding their lives in abeyance until they lost weight. A lifetime of dieting hadn't made them any thinner, and at the age of forty, they became enlightened to the reality that their lives were being spent waiting for a moment that may never come. Consequently, the best recourse was to accept that they would never be thin, but they could still lead productive, fruitful lives. Most of them cited the antidiet movement, as well as the size acceptance movement, as being very influential in their resolution. Wayne describes his "epiphany":

> I saw the movie *Fat Chance* and I've been tremendously inspired by it. I'm slowly coming to realize that self-acceptance would be the best thing for me because nothing else has worked.

Andy's enlightenment was more reflective, but no less persuasive:

> From the time I was eleven to the time I was forty, I would say weight and obesity has probably consumed 70 percent of my day-to-day thinking. Now, basically, I'm a fifty-year-old man who looks back at all the attempts, all the yo-yoing back and forth, and basically I've resigned myself to always being a big guy. I'm not suffering so much about my weight as I did in the past. I can live with the fact that I'm a heavy man. I think overweight has done its number on me and it's gone its way.

Fat Power

It is worthwhile to note that despite the depth of fat phobia and bigotry in our culture, despite the wide-ranging discrimination against the obese in all the sectors of their lives, all the time, some participants maintained that there were positive aspects to being larger than average. Wayne, a high school teacher, uses his imposing size to establish his authority and maintain discipline in a classroom of unruly students. Arlene, a market research consultant who has been an executive since the mid-1960s, is convinced that she was taken more seriously by her male colleagues because she was nonthreatening, although she admits there were times she deliberately overwhelmed men who were intimidated by her weight, "as my way of keeping the power with me."

Two men mentioned that the trauma of obesity has heightened their awareness of the feelings and sufferings of other people. They consider themselves nonjudgmental and empathetic to those who do not fit the conventional definitions of "normal":

> Overweight has made me a better man. Sometimes you have to go through difficult things in life to become better. Being overweight has made me a better man because I'm now more sensitive, more patient. I'm a good listener, I'm polite. (Allan)

> Because of my life experiences, I look at other people in a different way. I'm very sensitive to other people's feelings. If I see a disfigured person, I don't stare in any strange way. I just smile or acknowledge him or something like that. I don't have any kind of problem with looksism myself. (Keith)

CONCLUSION

Fat people fight back. They resist the contemporary sizism and the hatred, contempt, and disgust that they frequently encounter. They fight back in a variety of ways: Some are quick witted and verbally expressive; some are physically aggressive; some engage in political activism, and the flamboyants emphasize their size with pride: As David said, "I'm living large here!" We think he is living large not only physically but in mind and spirit as well. In these four multimodal methods of active resistance, both individual and collective, surely lie the seeds of social change.

Reflective resistance is also effective and is exercised by those whom we have described as the self-acceptors and the enlightened. The self-acceptors shrug off the stigmatization of obesity as a nonissue. They have a secure sense of their own identity and value built, we believe, on a foundation of love in their families, without the abuse that was the common experience of growing up fat. The enlightened have also come to this stage but usually after the age of forty and after a lifetime of chafing under the burden of their weight. This is the stage at which they have now come to accept both who and where they are: fat people in a fat-phobic society, and they report that they are finally getting on with their lives.

Not everyone can resist, however. It takes time and skill to learn the effective coping mechanisms developed by active and reflective resisters. Some are totally devastated, especially in their youth. The internalizers may internalize the norms of the dominant sizist and fat-phobic society and learn to hate themselves, and then hide from others, failing to learn the usual social skills, unable to relate to others or to develop intimate relations with others. Anger, which is sometimes the next stage, although the chronology is not always clear, provides a channel for individuals to externalize their pain, but they are usually unable—except very occasionally—to express it verbally and physically.

These eight types of reaction and resistance to sizist oppression are important components of personal change and also, to varying degrees, of social change. We should emphasize that these eight styles do not necessarily evolve in any "progressive" sequence. While it is tempting to look for an evolution of tactics, from Internalization to Anger to Verbal Resistance to Physical Resistance to Self-Acceptance, the psychic reality is more complex. First, the modes of active and passive resistance are not necessarily mutually exclusive. Second, people tend to specialize. Third, the self-acceptors, for instance, seem to start that way and stay that way. The enlightened, however, do go through certain stages. Most important, however, one cannot validate any one method as "superior" to another. No doubt some are more effective coping strategies than others; but far be it for outsiders to judge insiders. People adopt the strategies and mechanisms that are most comfortable to them at their own time, and in their own space.

Finally, we interviewed the survivors. Some fat people do not survive, not because of health hazards but because of the social hazards of their lives. Recently, three young people in the United States and England dramatically illustrated their dread of a lifetime of persecution.

In 1994 Brian Head, who had been taunted for years about being overweight, shot himself to death in his classroom in Cherokee, Florida. The fifteen-year-old's last words were, "I can't take it anymore" (*Atlanta Constitution* 1994). Two years later twelve-year-old Samuel Graham was found hanged from a tree in his backyard in the Fort Lauderdale area. His family reported that he'd been terrified of the new school term, knowing that once again he'd be subjected to relentless teasing about his weight (*Montreal Gazette* 1996). Kelly Yeomans of Derby, England, was not only tormented by verbal abuse at the hands of her schoolmates. She also had salt thrown in her food and her clothes flung in the garbage. In the fall of 1997, gangs of neighborhood children screamed insults and pelted her house with stones and blocks of butter and margarine for several consecutive nights. Kelly told her parents that she too "couldn't take it anymore" and took a fatal overdose of painkillers just days later (Lederer 1997). Sizism not only hurts, it kills.

We believe that the more strenuously fat people resist the conventional derogatory definitions, and the more they fight back, in so many different ways, the quicker the norms will change. Meekness may be an admirable virtue, but it is not recommended as an effective method of rapid social change.

REFERENCES

Adams, C., N. J. Smith, D. C. Wilbur, and K. E. Grady. 1993. "The Relationship of Obesity to the Frequency of Pelvic Examinations: Do Physician and Patient Attitudes Make a Difference?" *Women and Health* 20(2):45–57.

Allon, N. 1982. "The Stigma of Overweight in Everyday Life." Pp. 130–74 in *Psychological Aspects of Obesity: A Handbook,* edited by B. B. Wolman. New York: Van Nostrand Reinhold.

Atlanta Constitution. 1994. "Student Kills Himself in Class in Cherokee." 26 March, p. C4.

Bennett, W., and J. Gurin. 1982. *The Dieter's Dilemma: Eating Less and Weighing More.* New York: Basic Books.

Bouchard, C. 1990. "Heredity and the Path to Overweight and Obesity." *Medicine and Science in Sports and Exercise* 23(3):285–91.

Breytspraak, L. M., J. McGee, J. Cohen Conger, J. L. Whatley, and J. T. Moore. 1977. "Sensitizing Medical Students to Impression Formation Processes in the Patient Interview." *Journal of Medical Education* 52:47–54.

Cahnman, W. J. 1968. "The Stigma of Obesity." *Sociological Quarterly* 9(3):283–99.

Chernin, K. 1981. *The Obsession: Reflections on the Tyranny of Slenderness.* New York: Parker and Row.

Cogan, J. C., and E. D. Rothblum. 1992. "Outcomes of Weight-Loss Programs." *Genetic, Social and General Psychology Monographs* 118(4):387–415.

Denzin, N. K. 1979. *Childhood Socialization: Studies in the Development of Language, Social Behavior and Identity.* San Francisco: Jossey-Bass.

Dreitzel, H. P., ed. 1973. "Childhood and Socialization." Pp. 5–26 in *Recent Sociology, No. 5: Childhood and Socialization.* New York: MacMillan.

Fraser, L. 1997. *Losing It: America's Obsession with Weight and the Industry That Feeds on It.* New York: Dutton.

Garner, D. M., and S. C. Wooley. 1991. "Confronting the Failure of Behavioral and Dietary Treatments for Obesity." *Clinical Psychology Review* 11:729–80.

Goffman, E. 1963. *Stigma: Notes on the Management of Spoiled Identity.* New York: Simon and Schuster.

Goodman, N., S. M. Dornbusch, S. A. Richardson, and A. Hastorf. 1963. "Variant Reactions to Physical Disabilities." *American Sociological Review* 28:429–35.

Gortmaker, S. L., A. Must, J. M. Perrin, A. M. Sobol, and W. H. Dietz. 1993. "Social and Economic Consequences of Overweight in Adolescence and Young Adulthood." *New England Journal of Medicine* 329(14):1008–12.

Health and Welfare Canada. 1991. *The Report of the National Task Force on the Treatment of Obesity.* Ottawa: Minister of Supply and Services Canada.

Jones, E. E., A. Farina, A. H. Hastorf, H. Markus, D. T. Miller, and R. A. Scott. 1984. *Social Stigma: The Psychology of Marked Relationships.* New York: W. H. Freeman.

Kuczmarski, R. J., K. M. Flegal, S. M. Campbell, and C. L. Johnson. 1994. "Increasing Prevalence of Overweight Among U.S. Adults: The National Health and Nutrition Examination Surveys: 1960 to 1991." *Journal of the Medical Association* 272(3):205–11.

Larkin, J. C., and H. A. Pines. 1979. "No Fat Persons Need Apply." *Sociology of Work and Occupations* 6(3):312–27.

Lederer, E. M. 1997. "British Teen Takes Fatal Overdose After 'Fatty' Taunts." *Toronto Star* 2 October, p. A22.

Maddox, G. L., and V. Liederman. 1969. "Overweight as a Social Disability with Medical Implications." *Journal of Medical Education* 44(3):214–20.

Maiman, L. A., V. L. Wang, M. H. Becker, J. Finlay, and M. Simonson. 1979. "Attitudes Toward Obesity and the Obese Among Professionals." *Journal of the American Dietetic Association* 74 (March):331–36.

Mankoff, M. 1971. "Societal Reaction and Career Deviance: A Critical Analysis." *Sociological Quarterly* 12:214–18.

Manson, J. E., W. C. Willett, M. J. Stampfer, G. A. Colditz, D. J. Hunter, S. E. Hankinson, C. H. Hennekens, and F. E. Speizer. 1995. "Body Weight and Mortality Among Women." *New England Journal of Medicine* 333(11):677–85.

Millman, M. 1980. *Such a Pretty Face: Being Fat in America.* New York: Norton.

Montreal Gazette. 1996. "He Dreaded Teasing." 27 August, p. B1.

Orbach, S. 1978. *Fat Is a Feminist Issue: The Anti-Diet Guide to Permanent Weight Loss.* New York: Berkley.

Rand, C. S. W., and A. M. C. MacGregor. 1990. "Morbidly Obese Patients' Percep-
    tions of Social Discrimination Before and After Surgery for Obesity." *Southern
    Medical Journal* 83(12):1390–93.
Reeder, B. A., A. Angel, M. Ledoux, S. W. Rabkin, K. Young, L. E. Sweet, and Cana-
    dian Heart Health Survey Research Group. 1992. "Obesity and Its Relation to
    Cardiovascular Disease Factors in Canadian Adults." *Canadian Medical Associ-
    ation Journal* 146:2009–19.
Richardson, S. A., N. Goodman, A. H. Hastorf, and S. M. Dornbusch. 1961. "Cul-
    tural Uniformity in Reaction to Physical Disabilities." *American Sociological
    Review* 26:241–47.
Rodin, J. 1992. *Body Traps*. New York: William Morrow.
Rodin, J., L. Silberstein, and R. Striegel-Moore. 1984. "Women and Weight: A Nor-
    mative Discontent." *Nebraska Symposium on Motivation* 32:267–307.
Roe, D. A., and K. R. Eickwort. 1976. "Relationships Between Obesity and Associ-
    ated Health Factors with Unemployment Among Low-Income Women." *Jour-
    nal of the American Medical Women's Association* 31:193–204.
Rothblum, E. D. 1992. "The Stigma of Women's Weight: Social and Economic Real-
    ities." *Feminism and Psychology* 2(1):61–73.
Rothblum, E. D., P. A. Brand, C. T. Miller, and H. A. Oetjen. 1990. "The Relationship
    Between Obesity, Employment Discrimination and Employment-Related Vic-
    timization." *Journal of Vocational Behavior* 37:251–66.
Rothblum, E. D., C. T. Miller, and B. Garbutt. 1988. "Stereotypes of Obese Female
    Job Applicants." *International Journal of Eating Disorders* 7(1/2):227–83.
Sheinin, R. 1990. "Body Shame." *National Eating Disorders Information Centre Bul-
    letin* 5/5:1.
Sobal, J. 1995. "The Medicalization and Demedicalization of Obesity." Pp. 67–90 in
    Eating Agendas: Food and Nutrition as Social Problems, edited by D. Maurer and
    J. Sobal. Hawthorne, NY: Aldine de Gruyter.
Sobal, J., V. Nicopoulos, and J. Lee. 1995. "Attitudes about Overweight and Dating
    Among Secondary School Students." *International Journal of Obesity* 19:376–81.
Staffieri, J. R. 1967. "A Study of Social Stereotypes of Body Image in Children."
    Journal of Personality and Social Psychology 7(1):101–4.
Stunkard, A. J. 1988. "Some Perspectives on Human Obesity: Its Causes." *Bulletin
    of the New York Academy of Medicine* 64(8):902–23.
Vener, A., L. R. Krupka, and R. J. Gerard. 1982. "Overweight/Obese Patients: An
    Overview." *Practitioner* 226:1102–9.
Wolf, A. M., and G. A. Colditz. 1994. "The Cost of Obesity: The U.S. Perspective."
    PharmoEconomics 5(Suppl. 1):34–37.
Wooley, S. C., O. W. Wooley, and S. Dyrenforth. 1979. "Obesity and Women-II. A
    Neglected Feminist Topic." *Women's Studies International Quarterly* 2:81–92.
——— . 1980. "The Case Against Radical Interventions." *American Journal of Clini-
    cal Nutrition* 33 (February):465–71.
Young, L. M., and B. Powell. 1985. "The Effects of Obesity on the Clinical Judg-
    ments of Mental Health Professionals." *Journal of Health and Social Behavior*
    26(September):233–46.

III

REDEFINING WEIGHT

5

From "Dieting" to "Healthy Eating"

An Exploration of Shifting Constructions of Eating for Weight Control

GWEN E. CHAPMAN

Commentaries on the pursuit of bodily perfection that feature prominently in the lives of many people in contemporary Western culture, especially white middle- and upper-class women, often take body and body image issues as their starting point (Bordo 1993; Frank 1991; Glassner 1992; Hesse-Biber 1996; Székely 1988). These critiques explore the creation and dissemination of ever-changing definitions of the perfect body, the meanings conveyed by different body images, and the ways individuals use the construction of a specific body as a way to construct their self-identity.

In this chapter, I take a somewhat different perspective on the discussion of women's body concerns by starting with one of the core activities in the pursuit of the perfect body: the control of food consumption. My discussion builds on the predominant theme that emerged from a series of research interviews I conducted with women about their dieting experiences. Most of the women explicitly or implicitly differentiated between old beliefs about "dieting" as the way to lose weight and current beliefs in "healthy eating" as a more appropriate approach to weight control. In exploring this shift in what the women believed about how they "should" eat in order to achieve and/or maintain a socially desirable body size, I look at how food and eating practices are produced from the discourses about the body, health, and food that are available in our social environment and, at the same time, shape women's sense of self. I begin with a more detailed description of the women and what they said about food and eating in relation to weight control.

THE WOMEN'S STORIES

I obtained the data presented here through individual interviews with seventeen women who ranged in age from twenty-eight to fifty years. Three informants were students pursuing a second university degree, one worked as a volunteer, and the others had paid employment. All were white and at least ten of the women had a university degree. Eleven lived with male partners, four lived alone, one lived with a friend, and one lived with her parents. Five had young children at home and three had adult children. Their dieting histories ranged from four who said they had never dieted to several who had been on and off diets "practically all their lives."

Each woman participated in a semistructured interview in which she talked about what dieting meant to her, her experiences with dieting, her concerns about body weight and size, and her concerns about food and eating. All interviews were tape-recorded and transcribed. I began the interpretation process by coding the transcripts according to the substantive area being discussed, then sorting the coded transcripts using the Ethnograph (Version 3.0; Qualis Research Associates, Littleton, CO, 1988), a software program designed for qualitative data analysis. In preparing this chapter, I reviewed all interview segments that were coded as "dieting," writing summaries and memos about the emerging patterns and themes throughout the review process.

During the interviews, I asked each woman what the word "diet" meant to her. These were typical responses (the names used to identify women are pseudonyms):

> A bunch of things. Fad diets or just watching what you eat. . . . They're sort of like opposite ends of the dieting spectrum. (Lucie)

> I'm trying to train myself that it's just proper eating and not three chocolate bars a day, but usually cottage cheese and carrots come to mind. (Brenda)

> It used to mean I've got to deny myself. I've got to starve myself. I've got to eat only certain kinds of food and I am going to only do that for this many weeks and I am going to be skinny when I'm finished. Whereas now I have a different attitude. A diet means eating healthy on a long-term basis. Eating the foods that are good for you and not worrying if one day I want to have a cinnamon bun. (Caroline)

This recognition of multiple meanings of dieting was typical of most informants. Some seemed to unconsciously move between different meanings, while others were very clear in differentiating between what dieting used to mean to them and what it meant at the time of the interview. This sense of a shift from "old" ways of thinking about dieting to "new" ways pervaded most interviews. While there were many variations in individual women's definitions, experiences, and examples, there were also many consistencies.

"Old" Ways of Dieting

Most study informants described at least one experience of "going on a diet," and some still practiced old ways of dieting to at least some extent:

> We used to fast one day a week, where we would just have juice. And then the next day we would just have vegetables and then by the end of the week we were eating anything and everything in sight because the next day we were fasting again. (Sandra)

> [With fad diets] usually you feel so deprived that you just don't stop eating for months afterwards. And I find that even Weight Watchers isn't really positive for me—it is really a good diet, I would say it is the best—but you take away a person's control and you don't learn how to have control yourself. Like if you say you can have this, this, this, and this, when that's gone and I don't have to go for my weekly weigh in, I can eat whatever I want and I lose that ability to know what's enough. (Anne)

> I didn't go on a specific diet, but I would tell myself that I was gonna be good starting on Monday. . . . [I'd say] "On Monday, I'm going to behave myself and eat my vegetables" or whatever, and by Wednesday I would be back off. I sort of had this all or none thing. Like if I cheated once, then I would go: "The week's blown. I might as well wait until next week." (Caroline)

The women named a number of specific "diets" that were examples of the old way of dieting. These included published diet plans like the Scarsdale diet, the Atkins diet, the oat bran diet, the grapefruit diet, the drinking man's diet, the banana diet, and the lemon juice cleansing fast. Informants also talked about commercial programs, including Diet Center, Jenny Craig, NutriSystem, and Slim Fast. Various techniques like calorie counting, fasting, eating one meal per day, and using laxatives were also mentioned. The women who had extensive dieting histories tended to have tried a variety of different diets.

> I find I can never go back to a diet. I can never go back because it never works. Like the Scarsdale worked really well but I couldn't do it now. . . . The novelty of following the menu plan wears off pretty quick. . . . I guess Diet Center worked in the fact that they policed you all the time and they gave you these little things that I knew were appetite suppressants of some form, even though it didn't stay on it. Weight Watchers is good. Right now I am doing Slim Fast. (Brenda)

Although the diets included in the "old" ways of dieting category varied in what foods were consumed or eliminated and when food was eaten, they also shared common characteristics. These "fad diets" generally involved following a set menu that the women considered to be a temporary and different way of eating: Dieters would eventually go back to eating the way they had eaten in the past. Increased exercise was sometimes a component of the weight loss regimen, but like changed eating patterns, it was seen as a temporary measure. Finally, fad diets promised quick and substantial weight loss, and were seen as not being very healthy.

When the women described the experience of being on these diets, they often used specific kinds of imagery and metaphorical language. Words like "control," "deprivation," "sacrifice," "restriction," "cheating," and "guilt" were common. For example, Elizabeth described dieting as:

> Restricted food intake. Low calories. Like when you go out with people, you don't drink, you probably don't have desserts, [or] anything high [in] calories. So you got to really watch what you eat. [I feel] deprived a bit.

There are many instances in the interview transcripts of women talking about having to "give up" something like alcohol, sweets, or junk food when they dieted. One woman referred to this as having "to sacrifice food that I like." Some women described themselves as "being good" or "behaving" when they were successfully making the required sacrifices and depriving themselves of the foods they wanted. However, many of them identified specific foods like cookies or ice cream as being their "downfall"—something that would cause them to lose the required control. After eating those foods, they described themselves as having "cheated," having "been bad," and feeling "guilty."

The desired consequence of dieting was, of course, weight loss. Many study participants had been able to lose weight through dieting at various points in their lives. However, there were other, less desirable consequences of dieting as well. The women talked about becoming obsessed about food, and always being conscious of what they were eating. They talked about the feelings of deprivation and guilt mentioned earlier. They talked about dieting taking away their ability to control themselves because they learned to eat according to external rules rather than internal cues of hunger and satiety. The feelings of deprivation, the loss of the ability to follow internal cues, and extreme hunger caused by restrictive eating plans meant that dieting often caused them to overeat. They would feel so hungry or so deprived that they would start eating, and would not be able to stop when the physiological hunger was satisfied. The overeating in turn meant that a final consequence of dieting was weight gain. Some never lost weight to begin with. Others lost, then regained as soon as the diet ended. Several participants talked about how hard this was on their self-esteem. They felt like they were never able to meet their goals and that they were continually failing:

Every time you're dieting, it's like you're telling yourself that you haven't achieved your goal. The years start to go by and you're still on a diet, and it's like you're kind of looking at yourself as if I am a failure. Like I should've had this under control years ago. And why do I have it under control, then all of a sudden I don't have it under control again, and I am always back to dieting. Then you feel like you just want to die. I just see it as being a sort of a bit of a hell you know. (Dallas)

In summary, to these women, old-fashioned fad dieting meant a regulated, restrictive eating plan that caused feelings of deprivation and took away their sense of control over their eating habits. It caused them to monitor their eating behavior, to try to "be good," to feel guilty when they did not behave, and to ultimately feel like a failure when they were unable to achieve or maintain the body they wanted.

Newer Approaches to Weight Control

When some of the study participants talked about their current approach to managing their body weight, their descriptions were quite different from their comments about dieting. For example:

[I'm not on] a strict diet, I'm just watching my food intake. And realizing that I don't need another helping. Or maybe I should have an apple instead. And why do I feel these cravings, you know. Is it the time of the month or am I upset about something? So instead of trying to solve things with food, I'm trying to take a more positive view of it. (Linda)

Reducing the fat content of my diet . . . was the most important thing in order to feel healthier and to get skinnier without going crazy and paying attention and obsessing on food. Just cut out, reduce the fat in your diet which is healthy anyway. [I lost] about five pounds over nine months. Naturally you want to lose whatever you want and get skinny again, instantly. But it doesn't work that way. (Erin)

[To lose weight, I'll] watch what I eat. I'll probably give up wine. . . . And I will stay away from dessert things. But other than that I'll eat what I'd normally eat, but I will exercise and that will be the difference. (Donna)

When informants talked about newer approaches to weight control, they did not talk about following strict eating plans. Instead, they wanted to "just watch what I eat," which meant eating healthy foods like vegetables, fruits, and grains, and reducing fat intake, avoiding desserts, alcohol, junk food, sugar, salt, meats, and fast foods. The goal was to eat three square meals per day and stay away from the "visible no-nos." Unlike the peripheral role exercise played in diets, exercise was seen as integral to the "healthy-lifestyle" plan—some participants felt it was more important for them to embark on a regular active exercise program than to alter their eating habits.

The healthy-lifestyle approach also differed from dieting in being seen as making permanent lifestyle changes rather than going "on" a diet that one would eventually go "off." When I asked Linda if she thought there might be a time in her life when she would not have to be conscious about her weight, she said:

> There might be periods where I feel really good and I'll have a good time and . . . maybe forget about it. But I have found out since I put on this much weight that you always have to be conscious and you always have to be committed to a routine or a schedule. If you go off your schedule that's okay, but don't abandon it.

Another characteristic of the healthy-eating approach was that it involved a psychological component where women would try to assess the reasons for their cravings, as well as listening to their body signals. If a woman did succumb to those cravings and eat something that should have been avoided, she would try to see it as "no big deal," and get back into the routine as soon as possible, rather than looking on it as "blowing" her diet and cause for a binge. In the newer approaches to weight control, weight loss, if it occurred at all, was expected to be gradual and permanent. At the very least, the new plan should allow for weight maintenance. In all, participants viewed the approach as "common sense" and a more positive way of looking at their eating habits.

In contrast to the language of deprivation and sacrifice that dominated their comments about "dieting," the words they used to explain the new approach often involved watchfulness, as in "watching what I eat," and being conscious, as in being health conscious, weight conscious, and conscious of what was going in their bodies. They also talked about the importance of making a commitment to following a healthy lifestyle or making a commitment to their bodies. Donna, for example, admired her younger friends, whom she described as "committed to exercise programs. . . . They are totally committed to their bodies. And they are aware of what they eat." The eating style sought by the women in this study was viewed as proper or sensible eating. Balance was another important concept: Balance within the diet, as well as balance between their food intake and energy expenditure through exercise. As Lucie said: "If food were prepared for me and it was good and healthy and balanced and the right thing, I wouldn't have any trouble with that at all."

Although the study participants tended to refer to their newer approach to weight control as "being healthy" rather than "trying to lose weight," their reasons for embarking on this healthy lifestyle usually involved wanting to fit into their clothes, to look good in a bathing suit, to get skinny, or to keep from getting fat. There was some mention of keeping their arteries healthy or reducing cardiovascular disease risk, but the primary motivation was usually body weight or appearance.

There was little evidence of the healthy lifestyle having much impact on body weight. Although one participant had lost about five pounds by decreasing the fat content of her diet, the loss was recent and it was too early to know if she would lose enough weight to get back into the blue jeans she could wear when she was first married. Other participants tended to talk about the healthy lifestyle as something they *should* do, but were not yet ready to implement. As Ellen put it: "Intellectually we all know what to do, but in our gut, we don't do anything about it."

Overall, then, the women's descriptions of the new healthy-lifestyle approach to weight control differed from their descriptions of the old dieting approach in several significant ways. The new approach emphasized the goal of long-term health (rather than quick weight loss) and the importance of combining proper eating with regular exercise. By providing general guidelines rather than a specific eating plan, the new approach stressed individual responsibility, self-control, and personal decision-making. Women trying to implement the new approach explicitly tried to avoid feeling guilty or becoming obsessed about what they ate. On the other hand, there were also similarities in the two plans: The motivation for embarking on either usually involved the desire to "look good," and women's descriptions of trying to implement either one often involved talking about eating foods they should not be eating, and not eating the foods they should.

A deeper understanding of this changing construction of how one should eat to control one's weight requires more than simply describing the similarities and differences in the approaches. We also need to address questions about why the shift is occurring, what its implications are, and whose interests it serves. Interpreting the different constructions as examples of multiple discourses about eating and the body can help shed light on these questions. In the remainder of this chapter, I will briefly describe some theoretical understandings about nature of discourses, then deconstruct the older and newer discourses about eating for weight control by discussing their discursive characteristics, and conclude by summarizing the implications of the shifting constructions of eating for weight control.

DISCOURSES OF EATING FOR WEIGHT CONTROL

The Nature of Discourses

The centrality of discourses to the operation of social systems has received much attention in poststructural theory, particularly in the work of Michel Foucault (Foucault 1979, 1980, 1996; Weedon 1987). Discourses circulate throughout a social system in the form of spoken and written texts, offering multiple ways to understand or know about an issue. At any given historical moment, a variety of discourses will be in circulation; those used most frequently constitute the dominant way of understanding an issue. Related discourses may be consistent with the dominant discourse and support it, while others may be oppositional discourses that offer people alternative modes of understanding. At different times or in different places, marginal discourses may gain strength and become dominant.

Knowledge or ways of understanding make up only a part of the social role played by discourses. In Foucault's view, discourses are implicated in the circulation of power through society. Instead of seeing power as a repressive force that is held by some people and used to oppress others, Foucault saw power as inherent to all social relationships and enacted through everyday practices. He described how this disciplinary power works through discourses, institutions, and techniques of self-surveillance to produce bodies that direct their energy to the demands of external regulation (Foucault 1979). "Docile bodies" are thus held in the grip of strict disciplinary powers, which impose constraints, prohibitions, and obligations on them.

Finally, discourses also structure how people understand themselves. In some of his last work, Foucault (1988, 1996) discussed the relationships between discourses and "technologies of the self" or the processes people use to create and transform themselves. Because discourses offer multiple ways of understanding phenomena, people have the freedom to use different discourses in different contexts to constitute themselves in different ways.

The Discourse of Dieting

The experiences of "going on a diet" described by the women in this study can be interpreted as examples of a discourse at work by examining the understandings, practices, relations of power, and self-identities inherent to the dieting experience.

The discourse of dieting offers a particular way of understanding body weight as relatively easy to control and change through short-term food restriction. It is widely circulated by a variety of mechanisms including diet businesses, women's magazines, and women's relationships with each other. In settings where this discourse is dominant, talking about and being on diets are seen as normal activities for women. As Linda explained it:

> In my teens, I don't know if I really had to go on a diet or not, but it was like—I won't say expected, but it was not uncommon for my friends to say "Oh yeah, I've got to go on a diet. You know the party is coming up and I've got to look good in the bathing suit." Or "I'm going away and I've got to look good in a bathing suit." So that was always part of the norm.

As suggested by this comment, the diet discourse gains strength through links to related discourses about women's body images. Other writers have discussed in detail the discourse constructing the meanings attributed to the size and appearance of women's bodies (Bartky 1988; Bordo 1993; Coward 1985; Duncan 1994; Germov and Williams 1996, in press; Spitzack 1990). "Looking good" (i.e., thin) has come to be equated with "feeling good" and being seen by others as well as oneself as attractive, competent, and successful. The body image discourse encourages women to engage in various practices to produce a "feminine" body and to gaze on their own bodies with a critical eye, judging themselves as if through the eyes of another viewer.

Like other practices aimed at producing a desired body image, the practices of dieting bear the hallmarks of disciplinary power. Diet plans control women's time, movement, and activities by specifying what must (or must not) be eaten, as well as when, where, and in what form foods should be consumed. Women are never sure when someone will be looking at their bodies, weighing them, or judging what they eat, so they put themselves under continual surveillance and punish themselves when they are "bad." The time and energy that go into this exercise as well as the failure that almost inevitably results ensure that women who diet will not always be able to see themselves as successful, competent people. The diet discourse thus can be seen as serving the interests of a patriarchal social system, keeping women's attention directed toward the production of a docile body and often leaving them feeling that they have failed.

The Healthy-Eating Discourse

The newer approach to weight control described by my study informants is not completely separate from the discourse of dieting. Both discourses, for example, promote an understanding of body weight as controllable through control of food intake, and both assume that the ideal body is slender. However, there are also distinct differences between the discourses, the most prominent of which is probably the emphasis on health. According to the healthy-eating discourse, weight control is needed not only to enhance appearance, but to achieve overall well-being. A healthy (i.e., slender) body is associated with better physical health—living and being active for more years—and with psychological health. A second difference in the discourses is that healthy eating is promoted as a permanent lifestyle change rather than a temporary eating plan. Another distinction between the two approaches is that healthy eating is predominantly a prescriptive approach, emphasizing consumption of certain "healthy" foods, while diets take more of a proscriptive approach, emphasizing elimination of high-calorie, high-fat foods.

The healthy-eating discourse is linked to other discourses that have gained momentum in recent years, including the health promotion and fitness movements. Some of the popularity of health and fitness pursuits can be attributed to scientific evidence relating lifestyle factors to the major diseases of the Western world like cardiovascular disease and cancer (Archer 1996; Hankin 1993; Kris-Etherton and Krummel 1993; Lichtenstein 1996). Studies showing increased morbidity and mortality with increased body weight (Manson et al. 1995; Willett et al. 1995) have fueled social imperatives to maintain a thin body. With regards to diet, nutrition education efforts emphasizing the increased risk of cardiovascular disease associated with high total and saturated fat intakes and the protective effects of diets that are high in fiber, fruits, and vegetables have been translated into popular understandings of foods as either "healthy" or "junk" (Chapman and Maclean 1993; Lupton 1996). Comments made by participants in this study about controlling weight through healthy eating bear marked similarities to comments about healthy eating made by participants in Lupton's (1996) study.

Some sociologists have suggested that the growth of health and fitness movements can also be linked to broader cultural shifts that are occurring in late modernity (Glassner 1992; Shilling 1993). Among other things, modern culture has been characterized by dualistic philosophy that, for example, separates mind from body, male from female, and work from leisure. Modern culture has also involved expectations that advances in science, medicine, and technology will result in progressive societal improvements. (Note that diets, which offer a quick, scientifically based technological fix to the problem of obesity, are consistent with the beliefs of the modern era.) Experience has shown, however, that science and technology may create as many problems as they solve, and that medicine has been unable to cure many of the diseases that currently plague Western countries. Shilling (1993) has suggested that as people have become disillusioned with the ability of science to protect them, they have tended to turn to their bodies as a foundation for a sense of their self-identity. Similarly, Glassner (1992) has described the fitness movement as a postmodern phenomenon, with its reliance on self-creation rather than medicine as the way to health and with its conflation of modernist polarities. In contrast with modern concepts that envision the body as a machine that houses the mind/self, the postmodern body has become inseparable from the self and shaping one's body has become a way to shape one's self. Work and leisure are also not clearly distinct from each other, as fitness enthusiasts spend their leisure time "working out." The movement to healthy eating, then, can be seen as a part of larger cultural constructions of the importance of health and fitness.

The healthy-eating discourse is also supported by growing consensus about the failure and negative effects of dieting. Evaluation research has shown that the long-term success rate of diets is very low: Four years after going off a diet, most dieters will have regained the majority of the weight they lost when they were on the diet (Brownell and Kramer 1989; Kramer, Jeffery, Forster, and Snell 1989). Increased recognition and prevalence of anorexia and bulimia nervosa also have damaged the dieting movement. These eating disorders are characterized by extreme adherence to the practices of dieting, and dieting has been identified as a risk factor for their development (Drewnowski, Yee, Kurth, and Krahn 1994; Patton, Johnson-Sabine, Wood, Mann, and Wakeling 1990). Eating disorders fall within the rubric of psychiatric illness, enhancing dieters' association of negative psychological effects with dieting. Participants in this study, for example, were concerned about becoming obsessed about food when they were dieting, and in another study I conducted about the experience of dieting, female athletes talked about the psychological games and mental drain involved with having to diet in preparation for competitions (Chapman 1997).

In addition to the different understanding of weight control offered by the healthy-eating discourse, this discourse also involved a somewhat different set of practices than those described by the study informants as inherent to dieting. Instead of trying to follow minutely defined routines that dictated what, when, and how much they could eat, the women attempted to implement a more flexible routine. They could choose whatever they wanted to eat from a wide variety of "healthy" foods, and they tried to reduce their intake of the "junk" foods. This routine gave them more of a sense of psychological well-being in that *they* rather than a diet plan were in control of what they could eat. These characteristics of the practices of healthy eating can be interpreted as offering women more freedom and a more positive sense of self than do the practices of dieting.

On the other hand, there was still evidence of a disciplinary power at work in the healthy-eating discourse. There was a clear requirement for self-monitoring, and a dominant image in the women's descriptions of healthy eating was watching themselves eat. Despite its apparent flexibility, the healthy-lifestyle routine often made more demands on the women's time, space, and movement. In addition to always being aware of and assessing what they ate, they now had to find time to work out regularly. "Watching what you eat" can also be seen as more demanding in its permanence. There was no promise of freedom at the end when the women could stop watching themselves. Finally, the participants' sense that while they knew what they *should* be doing but still found it very difficult to implement meant that, as with dieting, the imperative to "watch what you eat" did not always enable them to feel like competent women.

CONCLUSIONS

This chapter has been built around the observation of a shift in the way a group of urban, white, middle-class, educated, Canadian women think about eating for weight control. In contrast to their earlier attempts to lose weight through temporary restrictive diet plans, they had begun to talk about the need to make permanent lifestyle changes that included watching what they eat and regular exercise. When these constructions of eating for weight control are interpreted using discourse analysis, the growing dominance of the healthy-eating discourse can be associated with a variety of other discursive shifts, including biomedical discourses about disease prevention, cultural disillusionment with modernity, and the critique of dieting.

The circulation of these intersecting discourses has been promoted by various social institutions, including government-sponsored health and nutrition education programs; the food, fitness, and fashion industries, which market their products as "healthy"; and mass media articles and advertisements linking eating, health, and body weight (Duncan 1994; Health and Welfare Canada 1989; Keane 1997; United States Department of Agriculture 1995). Even the weight loss industry has assisted in the shift from negative images of restrictive dieting to positive images of healthy eating by promoting the healthfulness of its products (Keane 1997).

Because the notions about eating for weight control described by the participants in this study were shaped by social discourses and institutions, they are not unique to this particular group of women. In fact, similar ideas about dieting have been described by adolescent girls in the United States (Neumark-Sztainer and Story 1998; Nichter, Ritenbaugh, Nichter, Vuckovic, and Aickin 1995). The Australian men and women in Lupton's (1996) study also linked health, eating, and body weight. In contrast, women in Germov and William's (1996, 1999) Australian study appeared to refer only to older notions of restrictive dieting. Their lack of discussion of healthy eating as a way to control weight may be because "watching what you eat" is a style of eating that, like other eating styles, is particularly salient to specific social groups. Professional class women are probably particularly attuned to the healthy-eating discourse because of its connection to the gendered body image discourse described earlier and to the professional class preferences for light, healthy foods (Bourdieu 1984).

Despite the contrasts between the older and newer constructions of eating for weight control, there are similarities between the constructions. The practices associated with both approaches can be interpreted as the workings of a disciplinary power that controls women's time and movement, directing their energies to the production of a docile body. With dieting, there is more external regulation of the women's activities, in that they are following a regimen defined by someone else. With healthy eating, greater self-regulation and self-monitoring is required. Finally, the effects on women's self-identities of the two approaches to weight control also have similarities. Although both offer the women the possibility of creating the kind of bodies/selves they want to be, the difficulty of succeeding with either approach tended to leave them feeling that they were incompetent and unable to have the kind of control they were led to believe they should have over themselves and their bodies.

ACKNOWLEDGMENTS

I would like to acknowledge with thanks the financial assistance of the University of British Columbia Humanities and Social Sciences fund, and the assistance of Dr. Linda McCargar in recruiting the women who participated in this research.

REFERENCES

Archer, M. C. 1996. "Cancer and Diet." Pp. 482–87 in *Present Knowledge in Nutrition*, edited by E. E. Ziegler and L. J. Filer. Washington: International Life Sciences Institute.

Bartky, S. L. 1988. "Foucault, Femininity, and the Modernization of Patriarchal Power." Pp. 61–86 in *Feminism & Foucault: Reflections on Resistance*, edited by I. Diamond and L. Quinby. Boston: Northeastern University Press.

Bordo, S. 1993. *Unbearable Weight: Feminism, Western Culture, and the Body*. Berkeley: University of California Press.

Bourdieu, P. 1984. *Distinction: A Social Critique of the Judgement of Taste*. Cambridge, MA: Harvard University Press.

Brownell, K. D., and F. M. Kramer. 1989. "Behavioral Management of Obesity." *Medical Clinics of North America* 73:185–201.

Chapman, G. E. 1997. "Making Weight: Light-Weight Rowing, Technologies of Power, and Technologies of the Self." *Sociology of Sport Journal* 14:205–23.

Chapman, G. E., and H. Maclean. 1993. "Junk Food and Healthy Food: Meanings of Food in Adolescent Women's Culture." *Journal of Nutrition Education* 25:108–13.

Coward, R. 1985. *Female Desires: How They Are Sought, Bought and Packaged*. New York: Grove.

Drewnowski, A., D. K. Yee, C. L. Kurth, and D. D. Krahn. 1994. "Eating Pathology and DSM-III-R Bulimia Nervosa: A Continuum of Behavior." *American Journal of Psychiatry* 151:1217–19.

Duncan, M. C. 1994. "The Politics of Women's Body Images and Practices: Foucault, the Panopticon, and Shape Magazine." *Journal of Sport & Social Issues* 18:48–65.

Foucault, M. 1979. *Discipline & Punish: The Birth of a Prison*. New York: Random House. [French original published in 1975.]

————. 1980. *Power/Knowledge: Selected Interviews & Other Writings 1972–1977.* New York: Pantheon.

————. 1988. "Technologies of the Self." Pp. 16–49 in *Technologies of the Self: A Seminar with Michel Foucault,* edited by L. H. Martin, H. Gutman, and P. H. Hutton. Amherst: University of Massachusetts Press.

————. 1996. "The Ethics of the Concern for Self as a Practice of Freedom." Pp. 432–49 in *Foucault Live (Interviews, 1961–1984),* edited by S. Lotringer. New York: Semiotext(e).

Frank, A. W. 1991. "For a Sociology of the Body: An Analytical Review." Pp. 36–102 in *The Body: Social Process and Cultural Theory,* edited by M. Featherstone, M. Hepworth, and B. Turner. London: Sage.

Germov, J., and L. Williams. 1996. "The Sexual Division of Dieting: Women's Voices." *Sociological Review* 44:630–47.

————. 1999. "Dieting Women and the Body Panopticon." In *Weighty Issues: Fatness and Thinness as Social Problems,* edited by J. Sobal and D. Maurer. Hawthorne, NY: Aldine De Gruyter.

Glassner, B. 1992. "Fit for Postmodern Selfhood." Pp. 215–43 in *Symbolic Interaction and Cultural Studies,* edited by H. S. Becker and M. M. McCall. Chicago: University of Chicago Press.

Hankin, J. H. 1993. "Role of Nutrition in Women's Health: Diet and Breast Cancer." *Journal of the American Dietetic Association* 93:994–99.

Health and Welfare Canada. 1989. *Nutrition Recommendations . . . A Call for Action.* Ottawa: Ministry of Supply and Services Canada.

Hesse-Biber, S. 1996. *Am I Thin Enough Yet? The Cult of Thinness and the Commercialization of Identity.* New York: Oxford University Press.

Keane, A. 1997. "Too Hard to Swallow? The Palatability of Healthy Eating Advice." Pp. 172–92 in *Food, Health and Identity,* edited by P. Caplan. London: Routledge.

Kramer, F. M., R. W. Jeffery, J. L. Forster, and M. K. Snell. 1989. "Long-Term Follow-Up of Behavioral Treatment for Obesity: Patterns of Weight Regain among Men and Women." *International Journal of Obesity* 13:123–36.

Kris-Etherton, P. M., and D. Krummel. 1993. "Role of Nutrition in the Prevention and Treatment of Coronary Heart Disease in Women." *Journal of the American Dietetic Association* 93:987–93.

Lichtenstein, A. H. 1996. "Atherosclerosis." Pp. 430–37 in *Present Knowledge in Nutrition,* edited by E. E. Ziegler and L. J. Filer. Washington: International Life Sciences Institute.

Lupton, D. 1996. *Food, the Body and the Self.* London: Sage.

Manson, J. E., W. C. Willett, M. J. Stampfer, G. A. Colditz, D. J. Hunter, S. E. Hankinson, C. H. Hennekens, and F. E. Speizer. 1995. "Body Weight and Mortality Among Women." *New England Journal of Medicine* 333:677–85.

Neumark-Sztainer, D., and M. Story. 1998. "Dieting and Binge Eating Among Adolescents: What Do They Really Mean?" *Journal of the American Dietetic Association* 98:446–50.

Nichter, M., C. Ritenbaugh, N. Nichter, N. Vuckovic, and M. Aickin. 1995. "Dieting and 'Watching' Behaviors Among Adolescent Females: Report of a Multimethod Study." *Journal of Adolescent Health* 17:153–62.

Patton, G. C., E. Johnson-Sabine, K. Wood, A. H. Mann, and A. Wakeling. 1990. "Abnormal Eating Attitudes in London Schoolgirls—A Prospective Epidemiological Study: Outcome at Twelve Month Follow-up." *Psychological Medicine* 20:383–94.

Shilling, C. 1993. *The Body and Social Theory.* London: Sage.

Spitzack, C. 1990. *Confessing Excess: Women and the Politics of Body Reduction.* Albany: State University of New York Press.

Székely, E. 1988. *Never Too Thin.* Toronto: Women's Press.

United States Department of Agriculture. 1995. *Nutrition and Your Health: Dietary Guidelines for Americans.* Home and Garden Bulletin Number 232. Washington, D.C.: U.S. Government Printing Office.

Weedon, C. 1987. *Feminist Practice & Poststructuralist Theory.* Oxford: Basil Blackwell.

Willett, W. C., Manson, J. E., Stampfer, M. J., Colditz, G. A., Rosner, B., Speizer, F. E., and Hennekens, C. H. 1995. "Weight, Weight Change, and Coronary Heart Disease in Women." *Journal of the American Medical Association* 273:461–65.

6

Medical Discourse on Body Image

Reconceptualizing the Differences between Women with and without Eating Disorders

SUSAN HAWORTH-HOEPPNER

INTRODUCTION

In recent years, the connection between body image and eating problems has been examined extensively, especially in psychiatric and medical research (Bruch 1962, 1973, 1978, 1982; Gordon 1990; Hsu 1990; le Grange, Tibbs, and Noakes 1994; Striegel-Moore et al. 1990; Thomas and James 1988; Thorton, Leo, and Alberg 1991). The institution of medicine has been particularly influential regarding this connection because it has constructed definitions of what constitutes an "abnormal" or "distorted" body image, and has brought these definitions to bear on the diagnosis and treatment of anorexia nervosa.

Anorexia is defined as an abnormal pattern of food consumption that involves an obsession with thinness and a morbid fear of weight gain (Gordon 1990). Medical literature indicates that it has higher prevalence rates among women than men, and it is particularly prevalent among white females from middle- to upper-class backgrounds (Halmi, Casper, Eckert, Goldberg, and Davis 1979; Herzog and Copeland 1985).[1] The official manual for diagnosing psychiatric illnesses, the DSM IV—which is produced by the American Psychiatric Association (1994)—names four criteria for diagnosing anorexia nervosa:

1. Refusal to maintain body weight at or above a minimally normal weight for age and height (e.g., weight loss leading to maintenance of body weight less than 85% of that expected or failure to make expected weight gain during period of growth leading to body weight less than 85% of that expected).

2. Intense fear of gaining weight or becoming fat, even though underweight.
3. Disturbance in the way in which one's body weight or shape is experienced, undue influence of body weight or shape on self evaluation, or denial
of the seriousness of the current low body weight.
4. In post menarcheal females, amenorrhea, i.e., the absence of at least three
consecutive menstrual cycles. A woman is considered to have amenorrhea if
her periods occur only following hormone, e.g. estrogen, administration.
(ibid.:544–45)

The third criterion, commonly known among clinicians as "distorted
body image," hinges on the concept of "normal body image." This particular aspect of the definition, which draws on a medical notion of body
image, is critical to this discussion.

In this chapter I will explore how the concept of distorted body image,
utilized in medical practice and representing culturally held beliefs about
what constitutes a normal or pathological body image, functions to
uphold the categorical distinction between women with and without eating disorders. Moreover, I will argue that while in some ways anorexics are
substantially different from nonanorexics in their conception of body
image, they also voice similar views. Specifically, women with and without eating disorders share a general dissatisfaction with their bodies, suggesting a continuous rather than a dichotomous phenomenon. In this
chapter, I address the concept of normal body image—as it derives from
and depends upon distorted body image—by examining empirical data
collected from interviews with women who were clinically diagnosed
anorexic, self-labeled anorexic, or nonanorexic. I also discuss the consequences of this body image standard for women's identity issues.

Medical Discourse on Normal Body Image

A definition of normal body image can be obtained from the psychiatric
literature on anorexia nervosa.[2] Normal body image is defined as an
absence of "distorted body image," and operationalized as an overestimation of body size (Hsu and Sobkiewitz 1991), shape (Counts and Adams
1985; Freeman, Thomas, Solyom, and Koopman 1985; Glucksman and
Hirsch 1969; Traub and Orbach 1964), or part (Askevold 1975).[3] Defining
the "normal-bodied" by way of absence results in two categories: those
who do not possess a "distorted body image" are designated "normal"
and those who do are labeled anorexic.[4] Early research in this area supported the conceptual division, reporting that the estimation practices of
"normals" (or controls) clearly distinguished them from anorexics (Slade
and Russell 1973).

Other empirical evidence, however, suggests that there is a blurring of these categories. Numerous studies cite a lack of distinction in the estimates of body shape or size between anorexics and "normals" (Button, Fransella, and Slade 1977; Crisp and Kalucy 1974; Freeman et al. 1985; Garner et al. 1976; Hsu 1982). Quite typically, nonanorexics are reported to overestimate their body size (Freeman et al. 1985), width (Ben-Tovin et al. 1979; Casper et al. 1979), and profile (Counts and Adams 1985) at a rate similar to anorexics. This point is highlighted by Birtchnell, Dolan, and Lacey (1987), who report that among nondisordered women, the subjects most satisfied with their weight are those defined by their study as underweight for their height and age. Moreover, when differences between anorexics and nonanorexics are found, inconsistencies are common (Garner and Garfinkel 1981; Hsu and Sobkiewitz 1991; Slade 1985; Thompson 1987). Overestimation is prevalent not only in clinical samples, but in populations without eating disorders as well (Birtchnell et al. 1987; Dolan, Birtchnell, and Lacey 1987).

Body Image Research among Nonclinical Populations

A theme of dissatisfaction is evident in the research on body image among women without eating problems (Clifford 1971; Davies and Furnham 1986; Dolan 1994; Garner and Kearney-Cooke 1996; Pliner, Chaiken, and Flett 1990; Rodin, Silberstein, and Striegel-Moore 1985). This dissatisfaction is consistent and pervasive, and is plainly evident in women's descriptions of their bodies (Bordo 1993; Cohn and Adler 1992: Jourard and Secourd 1955). Rodin et al. (1985) call it a "normative discontent," an attitude that may be reflected in research findings among female college students, among whom 60 percent indicate dissatisfaction with their body shape (and the lower part of the body in particular [Ben-Tovin and Walker 1991]), and among whom "smallness" is the body profile preferred over all other body sizes (Wooley and Wooley 1980; Wooley, Wooley, and Dyrenforth 1979). This trend is consistent with the findings of Cohn and Adler (1992), who report that among a sample of college students not a single female selected an "ideal figure" that was heavier than her own. They suggest, further, that there is a "consensus" in their data about what constitutes an "ideal" figure for women: *one that represents thinness.*

Bodily Dissatisfaction with Weight

A central element of women's dissatisfaction with their bodies involves a key component of the second diagnostic criterion for anorexia nervosa: "fear of gaining weight or becoming fat" (American Psychiatric Association 1994:540). But "feeling fat" is a common complaint voiced by females of all ages in our society. Beginning in adolescence, females voice more concern about their weight than do males (Wooley and Wooley 1980). They can be underweight for their height and age and still feel the need to lose weight (Birtchnell et al. 1987). For example, in a 1984 convenience sample of 33,000 *Glamour* readers, 75 percent of the respondents indicated that they considered themselves "too fat," even though the researchers determined (by height/weight data) that only 25 percent met the criteria for being overweight, and (ironically) 30 percent met the criteria for being underweight (Wooley and Wooley 1984).

The proportion of females reporting such concerns increases with age. In a study of school age girls, 50 percent of the nine year-olds, 80 percent of the ten- and eleven-year-olds, and 89 percent of the seventeen-year-olds were dieting to lose weight (Owles 1990). Brumberg (1997) observes similar trends among adolescent females: 53 percent of thirteen-year-olds and 78 percent of seventeen-year-olds are dissatisfied with their bodies. Findings from a Swedish study indicate that 50 percent of the fourteen-year-old girls and 70 percent of the eighteen-year-olds reported having "felt fat." When asked about their current status, 25 percent of the fourteen-year-olds and 50 percent of the eighteen-year-olds indicated "feeling fat" at present (Nylander 1971). In comparison, boys are three to seven times less likely to indicate that they "felt fat" than are girls. Similarly, Rosen and Gross (1987) report that 63 percent of the high school girls they surveyed were on a diet, compared with 16.2 percent of the boys. Tiggemann and Rothblum (1988) observe a comparable trend: Regardless of their weight, females indicate that they feel "too fat," whereas males' perceptions of their weights are more accurately connected to standard measures and actual size.

These results are not circumscribed by age. Pliner et al. (1990) report significant differences by gender concerning the importance of weight control: regardless of their age (i.e., ten to seventy-nine), females place more value on weight control than males. The results from a 1992 NIH study indicate that "at any given time, 50 percent of American women are on a weight-loss diet" (cited in Alexander and LaRosa 1994), although only 24 percent are estimated to be overweight (Bray 1987). While weight norms have changed over time (Ritenbaugh 1982)—with some eras representing a fuller figure as the female ideal (Bordo 1993)—modern American women consistently have aspired to weigh less.

THE VIABILITY OF THE CATEGORICAL DISTINCTIONS, ANOREXIC AND NONANOREXIC

The level of dissatisfaction demonstrable in the research on women without eating problems raises questions about the discontinuous nature of the categories of anorexic and nonanorexic. These findings suggest that the designations anorexic and nonanorexic, as derived from the criteria for disturbance in body image, are *not* mutually exclusive categories. They overlap. Rather than representing two discrete sets, homogeneous groups with distinct boundaries, they operate like Venn diagrams.

Additional support for this assertion can be teased out of the medical literature on anorexia. While not directly the focus of current medical research, the commonality in these categories is addressed by Hsu, in his observations concerning dieting behavior: "[T]e boundary between the disorders and 'normal' dieting behavior seems blurred" (1990:4). His report on other research that includes the category "weight preoccupied" acknowledges that the difference in scores between the "weight-preoccupied" and anorexics fails to provide evidence that the categories are "discontinuous." Casper, Halmi, Goldberg, Eckert, and Davis (1979:2) also make this point: "[T]he tendency to overestimate per se cannot be considered a feature unique to anorexia nervosa" (ibid.:6). The finding is reiterated in other research as well (Birtchnell, Lacey, and Harte 1985; Button et al. 1977; Freeman et al. 1985; Slade 1985), most often with the admonition that overestimation is a common characteristic of nonclinical female populations and not "pathognomonic" of anorexia nervosa (Birtchnell et al. 1987; Hsu 1982; Hsu and Sobkiewitz 1991).[5] This lack of distinction may also imply, as Brown (1993) and others (Garner, Olmstead, and Polivy 1983; Way 1995) have suggested, that body image operates on a continuum, with illnesses such as anorexia representing an extreme dimension.

The interests of this study emerge from these prior investigations. They center on the continuous or discontinuous nature of women's dissatisfaction with their bodies, particularly involving the issue of weight. The questions that emanate from this problem clearly hinge upon what constitutes the standard of body image for women in this culture. In other words, what is a "normal body image"? What role does dissatisfaction with the body play in the construction of that standard? Do women with eating disorders embody characteristics that differentiate them from those without? In order to address these questions, I present a qualitative analysis of interviews from women with and without eating disorders who discuss their attitudes and feelings regarding body image.

THE PRESENT STUDY

The data for this study were collected using a purposive sample. Participants were selected using snowball sampling. In-depth interviews were conducted with thirty-two white, middle-class women between the ages of twenty-one and forty-four on the topic of body image and eating disorders. All interviews were tape recorded, at an average length of two hours. Twenty-one of the women in the sample were identified as having an eating disorder, the primary characteristic of which was food restriction.[6] Half of this group had been clinically identified as anorexic by psychiatrists, therapists, or medical doctors; the other half defined themselves as anorexic, but *never had been clinically diagnosed* with an eating disorder. Eleven women identified as not having an eating disorder also were included in the sample. This resulted in three groups that, while mutually exclusive, also form a continuum of responses concerning experiences with and feelings about the body: clinically defined anorexics ($n = 11$), self-defined anorexics ($n = 10$), and nonanorexics ($n = 11$).

The mean age of women in this study was thirty-one years old. The majority were single (59 percent), 34 percent were married, and 6 percent were divorced. Nearly all had spent their childhood in a two-parent household (63 percent), and 81 percent identified that household as middle- or upper-class. Most held a bachelor's degree (63 percent), 22 percent had a master's degree, and most were currently employed (72 percent). Among those who were not, 63 percent were enrolled as students. Only one woman identified herself as a full-time homemaker.

I used grounded theory methods to analyze the data (Glaser and Strauss 1967; Strauss 1987). Three themes emerged in connection with body image: the experience of "feeling fat," the meaning of thinness, and bodily satisfaction. From these themes, I made systematic comparisons between women with and without eating disorders, as well as among the three groups (clinical anorexics, self-defined anorexics, and nonanorexics).

This analysis is organized around the three themes: the first section focuses on the ways women construct "fatness" for themselves; the next segment, the meaning of thinness, centers on the economy of thinness in the culture, and the last section, bodily satisfaction, concentrates on the prevalence of satisfaction and sites of dissatisfaction found among the women in this study. These themes provide the framework within which I address the issue of body image.

FEELING FAT

"Feeling fat" is an experience reported by *all* the women in this study. It is identified, by those with and without eating disorders, as an *ordinary* occurrence. So ordinary is the state of "feeling fat" that it is unanimously described by women in the study as normative for females in the culture. Typical observations made by these women about the pervasiveness of these experience resemble Bridget's (clinical): "I think most women feel fat sometimes, they have a fat day." Katie (nonanorexic) offers a similar view:

"I don't think I've ever been out to lunch or dinner with a woman where she hasn't said 'Ohhh! I can't eat that.' Or, 'Oh, I'm eating too much today.' It's a constant topic of discussion."

In these interviews, explanations offered by women about what "feeling fat" means range from the concrete and physical to the social and psychological. While all women in the study report "feeling fat," their interpretations of its meaning and the extent to which they emphasize it varies by group.

Descriptions from the Nonanorexic Group

Women from the nonanorexic group are most likely to raise the issue of physical discomfort in conjunction with "feeling fat." The majority of women from this group stress this aspect of the experience. Diana's remarks highlight this type of response:

> I guess it means, like, when I go to grab a pair of pants out of the closet and I, they just feel tight, or don't feel right. That's kind of like feeling fat.

"Feeling fat" extends beyond physical discomfort for women in this group; it also encompasses feelings about the self. Many of these women associate "feeling fat" with insecurity or a lack of confidence, and it is frequently linked to issues of control. Some of these women identify "feeling fat" as a kind of strategy they employ to regain control over their thinking, or a way to exert influence over a given situation. This is achieved by rechanneling attention from difficulties at hand to issues about body weight. Diana explains it this way:

> And I don't know, it's like, it almost seems like the feeling fat is a distraction from what I'm thinking about. That I stop thinking about all that's going on in my mind, all that I'm thinking about, and I think about feeling fat.

This type of strategy operates as a temporary diversion that, in the short term, allows a redefinition of the situation; it appears to provide some women, like Diana, with feelings of efficacy.

For others, "feeling fat" is tied to expectations and "personal goals," which are ultimately linked to achievement. For these women, "feeling fat" commonly signals that they have fallen short of those goals, and it articulates that disappointment. Sherrie puts it this way:

> I mean there's a lot of expectations, I think, when I'm feeling that way about things that I should be doing. So maybe there's some guilt there because I'm not doing those things. So, yeah, I think that's probably how I feel when I'm feeling that way.

"Feeling fat," according to several women in this group, is also connected to stressors or life events that are associated with normative aspects of the life cycle. This is especially the case involving life change events linked to independence and change, such as entering college. The college years are most commonly identified as the time in which "feeling fat" originates for these women. For Lisa, a sense of "feeling fat" began then: "I would say in college. Just because I felt, I felt like I was fat." Katie points to a similar experience regarding her first three years in college:

> I did put on weight. And I made adjustments in my lifestyle and it took years, probably three years, before I really felt like, "It's okay to look how I look." But for a while there in college, yeah, that was something that bothered me.

It is perhaps not surprising that women from this group identify the college years as a time when they first experienced "feeling fat." College represents insecurity for many young adults, and many women from this group link it to the necessity of learning to cope.

These are the various ways that nonanorexic women construct and respond to "fatness." For many in this group, the definition of fatness is tailored to individual needs or situations. While "feeling fat" is something these women experience, they repeatedly stress that it does not function to devalue them; in fact, they argue that the experience of "feeling fat" doesn't "change me as a person" or "make me less of a person." This sort of qualification is not made by women from the self-defined and clinical anorexic groups.

Descriptions from the Self-Defined and Clinical Anorexic Groups

Women from the self-defined and clinical groups commonly locate "feeling fat" in a context of self-devaluation. It is frequently used in connection with what Goffman (1963) referred to as a "spoiled identity," and in the interviews this is evident in the references that both self-defined and clinical anorexic women make about themselves: "Feeling fat" means I am not "a good person" or I am "less of a person." It signals a consistency in self-representation (Gross and Stone 1981) that reflects negative sentiments about self-identity. In other words, "feeling fat" is personal evidence of stigma, and it effects permanent damage to the self (Goffman 1963). Bridget, Patty, and Stephanie illustrate the extent to which fatness is deeply discrediting:

> Being fat would like, well, like right now, it's like, I my, if I'm bloated, or find something that's kind of bad—it's like an external reminder that I'm a bad person. (Bridget, clinical)

It meant that I was nobody. That if I was fat, I was just gonna be nobody. (Patty, clinical)

But I think feeling fat or being fat makes me feel, or be, a different person. And I thought, because I'm feeling badly about myself, so I'm not, I don't feel good. (Stephanie, self-defined)

For these women, being "nobody," and feeling "badly" are buttressed by the association of negative physical attributes with the state of "feeling fat." Several women use terms like "ugly," "disgusting," and "huge" in connection with fatness, and extrapolate to other aspects of their identity: "It's not just fat; it's fat, ugly, I hate my hair, I hate my face, I hate everything" (Jeannie, self-defined). In this way, "feeling fat" is a kind of barometer for the self—or, as Jeannie suggests, "everyone's personality for how they feel"—which is interpreted by some women from both the self-defined and clinical groups as a measure of acceptance. For most of these women, however, the experience of "feeling fat" typically signifies rejection, or status as an outsider, reinforcing the association between their construction of fatness and stigma. Cheryl, from the clinical group, describes the connection in this way:

It means feeling like you don't fit in. Feeling out of place enough to stop being in society. Feeling unaccepted, I guess. Feeling like less of a person. There is a lot of pressure to be thin.

This sort of evaluation is important since the perception of stigmatization is clearly influential in shaping attitudes about the self. For example, Kleck and Strenta (1980) point out that individuals who perceive themselves to carry a stigma, perceive others—who are unaware of the stigma—as behaving toward them in negative ways.

Both self-defined and clinical anorexics typically stress constructions of fatness that lend themselves to characterizations of a "spoiled identity." Women from these groups interpret "feeling fat" in the context of personal deficiency, particularly as it is associated with a lack of acceptance by others. These characterizations stand in contrast to those made by nonanorexic women who, while acknowledging the state of "feeling fat" and discussing it in relationship to their identity, do not interpret "feeling fat" as an indicator of "spoiled identity."

THE MEANING OF THINNESS

Physical Attractiveness

One remedy for "feeling fat" that *all* women in the study share is the pursuit of thinness. For a majority, thinness is described as synonymous

with attractiveness. It is articulated as a personal preference and characterized by most women as a normative component of physical success.
Across the three groups, women describe the association between thinness
and attractiveness in a similar manner:

> Well, people tend to find people that are thinner more attractive. (Sue,
> nonanorexic)

> Well, I guess, that people find you attractive. (Stephanie, self-defined
> anorexic)

> Attractiveness. Being more attractive. (Cheryl, clinical anorexic)

For all these women, being thin is perceived to hold certain advantages.
Personally, these benefits translate into positive attention, garnered from
both men and women. This observation is consistently made by a majority of women in the study. Lisa, Stephanie, and Diane's remarks represent
this attitude:

> I mean, more people look at you. More guys want to date you, that type of
> thing. (Lisa, nonanorexic)

> People find you attractive. People want to be around you. (Stephanie, self-
> defined anorexic)

> There's advantages to being thin, being attractive. People like you, they will
> listen to you more, bond better to you. And there are definite advantages.
> (Diane, clinical anorexic)

Personal Attractiveness

The advantage that is afforded by a slender figure extends beyond the
benefits tied to physical attractiveness, and directly involves larger cultural attitudes about thinness. Unanimously, women in this study
acknowledge the role of culture as influential in shaping individual attitudes toward thinness, and they perceive it as instrumental in affecting
behavior. Kathy's (nonanorexic) remarks are characteristic of this belief:

> I mean, the whole society is built on, you know, "thin is in." And if you're
> thin, then you're somebody. And if you're thin, you're gonna get attention.
> If you're thin, you're gonna get dates. And everything else.

Thinness is equated with personal attractiveness, and it embodies a fundamental type of appeal. In this study, thin individuals are characterized
by women from all three groups as "successful," "smart," "active," and
"worth something." Personal success and "work ethic" type qualities are
said to be analogous to a slender body. In fact, positive, nearly *virtuous*
characterizations are made about those who are thin:

Self-discipline. It's associated with an active lifestyle. It's associated with things that it's not directly connected to. It's associated with social advantages. It's associated with, oh, I'm trying to think, I think it's somewhat even associated with background, not directly, but I think that's how it's perceived. (Katie, nonanorexic)

For me, anyway, it's intelligence. A thin person's probably a lot more intelligent, probably a lot more quick-witted. The expressions I'm thinking of are, "on the ball," or "sharper." (Peggy, self-defined anorexic)

You're ambitious, that you care about yourself and about other people. You're quick on your feet, you're quick-minded, you understand things more easily. (Gloria, clinical anorexic)

A similar attitude about thinness is identified by Sobal (1995), regarding constructions of obesity, as well as by Hill and Lundskow (1995) and Edgley and Brissett (1990) in connection with the modern health and fitness movement. In the latter analysis, fitness—which they suggest is commonly linked to slenderness—is evidence of a brand of moral certitude, whereas being physically unfit is conceived of as "moral failure." The association between thinness and health resounds in this study, with over a third of the women from the nonanorexic group making reference to thinness as an indicator of health. Such sentiment is evident in comments such as Katie's, who suggests she'd like to be "thin, like someone who's healthy." Moreover, women from all the groups suggest that thin people are perceived as receiving interpersonal privileges. If one is thin, one is "listened to more," and "people like you" based on your appearance. In fact, most women acknowledge a person's success is linked, in the society, to her weight. Such a sentiment is expressed by Sherrie, a nonanorexic:

Well, you're really successful or you're really worth something if you fall into these [thinness] categories, or you have these characteristics about yourself.

Her remarks are typical of the attitudes held by all the women in this study, and her observation underscores the claim that women across the groups make about thinness: *Personal worth is associated with a slender body.*

Expectations of Thinness

The achievement of thinness or the maintenance of an "ideal weight" seems to represent a goal that some women share, both women with and without eating disorders. In this study, several nonanorexic women and a few clinical anorexic women express this belief. For example, Sherrie, from the nonanorexic group, explains that maintaining a certain weight reflects adherence to personal goals:

And I know that I have a lot of high expectations for myself sometimes. So, I mean, I admit that. But for myself, I wouldn't, I guess I wouldn't be meeting that expectation that I have for myself to, you know, stick at a certain weight. Or try to stay there and watch what I'm eating and stuff. Not only for, like, appearance reasons, but also for health reasons.

For Diane, from the clinical group, thinness represents a similar challenge:

It's just a striving. It's the same thing, the same as any kind of a, it's a goal. It's a goal that I've set up to be physically fit to, I mean, if they would have had the—what is it, the thirty percent fat now, they can calculate the percent fat in your body—I'm sure that I would have set up some specific half-percent goal that I wanted to attain, which was very minimal, and just constantly had that as my goal. Be driven to have that as a goal.

The rewards of this challenge convey a sense of achievement. In fact, striving to meet one's personal goals represents a kind of social maxim; the influence of class on the desire to be thin has been shown to be important, particularly for females from higher socioeconomic backgrounds (Dornbusch, Carlsmuth, Duncan, Gross, Martin, Ritter, and Siegel-Gorelick 1984). Coded into references to accomplishment and hard work, these women name thinness as a goal that is important in the assessment of personal achievement. Sherrie expresses this sentiment as it concerns the attainment of a "slender appearance":

I can also be proud of myself because, you know, I'm meeting that expectation. I'm meeting that goal and it's something I'm working really hard for. (nonanorexic)

Falling short of these goals, or deviating from such expectations, may translate to a personal shortcoming. But this viewpoint is articulated in only a few cases, and exclusively by clinical anorexics. Diane, from this group, expresses her feelings about not maintaining an "ideal" weight: "If you don't meet your goal, you're failing."

Thinness and Self Esteem

Because an individual's weight can provide a gauge for the equilibrium of the self, weight, as it is tied to thinness, can operate as a monitor for self-esteem. In this study, a majority of women with and without eating disorders associate feelings about weight and appearance with feelings about themselves. Women from all the groups generally characterize the relationship in these terms:

I mean, I think a lot of self-esteem is based on—well, I shouldn't say a lot—I mean, I think some of your self-esteem is based on how your perception of yourself as far as appearance goes. And for myself, you know, I like it when I, when my appearance is, you know, somewhat slender. (Sherrie, nonanorexic)

This view is reaffirmed by Marna, a woman from the self-defined group, in an observation about slenderness and self- esteem: Thinness is all about "self-confidence."

Women in this study suggest that thinness functions to enhance self-esteem, while quelling insecurities about the self. One strategy used by some of the women to bolster their self-esteem involves slimming down. This is evident in the interview with Lisa, a nonanorexic, who suggests that feeling good about oneself involves weight reduction: "I must have been feeling really bad about myself, and just felt like I wanted to lose weight." Through appearance, identity announcements are made; however, identity also can be altered through the modification of appearance (Stone 1981). For Lisa and others, weight reduction represents a ploy to transform identity by reformulating appearance, which, consequently, can enhance self- confidence.

In general, adherence to standards of thinness provides women in the study with a kind of comfort or security for the self. This may not be surprising given the importance of the relational aspect of development for females, which places a strong emphasis on approval from others (Striegel-Moore 1993) and, at the same time, on appearance (Pliner et al. 1990). Katie's remarks underscore this observation, as she articulates the relationship between thinness, identity, and social approbation:

> I perceive it as something that would make me more attractive. And attractive is something that I would strive for that reason. Because it's socially acceptable, and it's something that I, I prefer to be that way than otherwise. And because I can be, I choose it. . . . It's like having, you know, a good head of hair or something like that. Sure it's kind of a superficial sort of thing, but if you've got it, if you really had to be honest with yourself, you'd have to say, "Yeah, I like that about me." And, you know, that you like the things about yourself that other people perceive as positive. And that's what it would be. (nonanorexic)

For women in this study, thinness is valued. It enhances feelings about the self that are closely tied to identity. Even in those instances in which the relationship between weight and the self is denied, reducing or being thinner seems to contribute to a sense of continuity regarding conceptions of self. Patty, a woman from the nonanorexic group, suggests as much:

> It doesn't have anything to do with who you are. I don't think that having extra pounds has anything to do with who I am. I would just like to take it off, that's all, because it's not me.

Women will take off extra pounds because those pounds are "not me"; in doing so, they tie identity to an absence of "excess" weight. As a strategy, this idea receives support in the work of Freitas, Kaiser, Chandler, Hall, Kim, and Hammidi (1994) on "identity not": the authors observe that individuals will don clothing that disidentifies them with particular groups (e.g., parents, conservatives, gays). In Patty's case, the absence of "extra pounds" appears to resecure the connection between slenderness and self, underscoring the idea that identity for women is weight- situated.

BODILY SATISFACTION

The complexity of the issues surrounding body image takes shape in discussions of bodily satisfaction. In this study, all women demonstrate some degree of dissatisfaction with their bodies. It is articulated *by each and every woman*, and plays a significant role in the commentary on bodily description, satisfaction, and dissatisfaction.

Dissatisfaction with the Body

Dissatisfaction with body shape or size is apparent across the three groups, and the extent of that dissatisfaction is visible in women's general descriptions of their bodies. A majority of women from all three groups include negative characterizations about their bodies in their self-descriptions. In *all* instances, the central complaint involves body weight. For example, Selena's introduction to her account, in which she gives a description of her body, begins like this:

> OK. I think I'm rather tall, I have long legs which is to my benefit because I can hide a few extra pounds here and there which is good. I feel I have a weight issue around my stomach, thighs, hips kind of area, the only thing I really have a hard time with that will just never go away are my child bearing hips. (nonanorexic)

This type of characterization is quite typical. Most of the women in the study mention body weight in connection with their descriptions, and it represents a prevailing concern. In fact, the issue of weight appears to be so pervasive that even the majority of nonanorexics identify weight or the possibility of gaining weight as a personal worry. Diana's response represents women from this group: "Overall I'm pretty happy with the way my body is, but it's just, like, the extra weight I have around my waist really bothers me." The salience of this remark may be contextualized by the finding that half of the women from the nonanorexic group list thinness as a key attribute (evident in such references as "being thin," "a manageable size," or "no weight problem"). This represents the most common response to the question, "What do you like about your body?" Such an emphasis resounds in Sherrie's response: "And, you know, I don't see myself as overweight at all, so I mean, for the most part, I'm pretty pleased with my weight."

Sites of Dissatisfaction

When the question of bodily dissatisfaction is explored, discussions ensue about *sites* of dissatisfaction with the body. Women who are dissatisfied with their bodies identify either the lower body, or *both* lower and upper, as their "problem" area(s). Most of the women from the self-defined group and many of those from the clinical group—as compared with only some from the nonanorexic group—identify the lower parts of their bodies as the greatest source of dissatisfaction. When asked, "Where, specifically, are you most dissatisfied with your body?" women from the self-defined and clinical groups point to their thighs, stomach, and legs. Sandra and Susan's responses are representative:

> Stomach thinner. And, then, my legs. They have cellulite. I roller skate three times a week, so there are muscles there, but there's, like, fat on the top. (Sandra, clinical)

> I have big thighs. That's like, my major problem with myself. Like, I think I've got, I've got a fat stomach. Um, let's see. Negative things about my body. I feel like I have too much body fat. I feel, like, um, especially with my lower body, you know. (Susan, self-defined)

Women from the nonanorexic group, however, most consistently focus on their stomach as the major source of dissatisfaction with their lower bodies. Sharon's response to inquiries about her dissatisfaction illustrates this:

> My stomach. I don't think it's, I get a little bubble on it, you know. That's about, just, you know, how when your stomach's bloated, you know. It'd be nice to have that [flat] stomach once. I mean, once in my lifetime, I want to have that little muscle rib, little, on my stomach there, you know. You can't ask for everything.

On the other hand, parts of *both* the lower and upper body are specified by a majority of women from the clinical and nonanorexic groups as the major source of bodily dissatisfaction. (This is the case for some women from the self-defined group, but to a much lesser extent.) For women in the clinical group, the largeness of their buttocks and smallness of their breasts are the most commonly identified problems—after thighs, stomach, and legs. When responding to queries about this, Patty (clinical) succinctly suggests, "my butt," and Bridget identifies her "boobs." Bridget elaborates on this response by explaining:

> You know, years it was, just like, "I need breast implants" because then I will be, you know, then I will be beautiful if I—I just thought if I had boobs I would be perfect. (clinical)

This contrasts with responses from the nonanorexic group, in which women most frequently point to hair and complexion—after the stomach—in connection with their discontent. Sherrie's account is illustrative: "I mean, there's certain things that I always, like, stress over, or whatever. Like, my complexion and, you know, my hair, some days."

Differences between Women Concerning Bodily Satisfaction

Despite the similar expressions of dissatisfaction displayed by women across the groups, some important differences emerge. To begin with, nonanorexic women distinguish themselves from the others in the extent to which they discuss their body in positive terms. Sue's description typifies this kind of response for nonanorexics: "Well, I'm five feet, a hundred pounds, pretty slim, and basically physically attractive." Over a third of the women from this group make such affirmations; such responses, however, are rarely made by self-defined anorexics, and never appear in the accounts given by the clinical anorexics. When asked, "What do you like about your body?" some women from the self-defined and clinical groups say "Nothing," or suggest that they "could pick apart every part" (Melissa, self-defined). Still others have difficulty specifying what they *do* like: "Well, I can't say that, but I don't dislike my body. I don't not like it, but I can't focus in on something that I actually could say I like" (Annie, clinical). Moreover, when asked "Currently, how would you characterize your body image?" a majority of nonanorexic women speak in exclusively positive terms (e.g., good or excellent), compared to the majority of women from the self-defined or clinical groups, who describe it as fair or poor.[7]

Beyond these differences, women from the clinical group distinguish themselves from self-defined anorexics by way of description. Clinical anorexics are more apt than self-defined anorexics to cast their bodies in the most negative of terms, referring to themselves as "big as a house," as being a "cow" or a "horse." The use of such descriptors clearly reflects a distortion of body weight, shape, or size. The extremity of responses is visible in Julie's remarks, which embody this group's attitudes toward body image:

> I feel really, I feel fat. I don't feel pretty. When I'm really into the disorder I notice that I look at myself as very fat. I mean, just, like, my legs are huge.

And I've just got, like, fat growing all over me. And I actually see that. You know, like, I could be just sitting there, and my legs, I can just see my leg, and it's, like, this big. I think, "I'm gonna get huge." And that's what I see. But, it's what the disorder sees, it's not what, you know, I should be seeing, because in reality, you know, if my legs were that big, I guess I would be bigger than I am. I don't know. But I see myself as, depending on my day, on my mood, you know. It depends on how things are, how upset I feel. It's usually, I see myself as bigger than I am, I've been told. (clinical)

Such negative sentiments are very suggestive. While it is apparent from the interview data that weight is a concern for all women, the degree to which it overshadows other aspects of identity seems to vary by group. Women from the nonanorexic group demonstrate a consistent dissatisfaction with the body, much like that expressed by women from the self-defined and clinical groups. However, these women also present themselves in positive terms, and in that process relegate "weight" to a less important place in terms of identity. On the other hand, self-defined anorexics and women from the clinical group describe themselves in the most negative of terms, increasing the importance placed on weight. In this way, feelings about the body mark out a continuum of response concerning bodily satisfaction, with the clinical group situated at the extreme end of discontent.

CONCLUSION

For all women in the study, weight is a pervasive concern. It can be characterized as a "normative discontent," a dissatisfaction regarding the body that is not delimited to women with eating disorders. Women across the three groups—clinical anorexics, self-defined anorexics, and nonanorexics—note their desires for change in size or shape, and their abiding concern with weight. Moreover, "feeling fat" is a common experience among women and appears to have implications for self-concept. Women both with and without eating disorders discuss the ways that this state is linked to insecurities about the self and how they use weight reduction as a strategy to combat this condition. However, while both anorexics and nonanorexics identify this experience as normative, only self-defined and clinical anorexics characterize it as an indicator of a "spoiled identity" and associate it with a lack of acceptance by others.

Being thin is widely recognized as a personal asset, tied to larger cultural ideations that link it to physical and personal attractiveness. A thin body elicits attention and brings with it the rewards of affirmation. Consequently, thinness is an ideal shared by all women in this study. At the same time, the benefits of thinness are not perceived by all women as having identical import. Self-defined and clinical anorexics talk about thinness in ways that embody more advantages and that are more far-reaching than they are for women from the nonanorexic group. For women with eating disorders, thinness appears to hold the promise of a corrective for identity.

Nevertheless, all women express some degree of dissatisfaction concerning their bodies and the major complaint involves weight. Women in each group characterize some aspect of their body in negative terms, suggesting that identity for females is weight-situated. However, that displeasure appears to intensify as one moves across the groups; women with eating disorders describe themselves in the most disapproving ways, often not being able to identify anything positive about their appearance. In such discussions, descriptions from the clinical group represent the extremes of that discontent. The data suggest that the incremental nature of dissatisfaction with the body is indicative of a continuum-like effect, with anorexic women representing an intensification and distortion of cultural ideals.

This finding has implications for the standard upon which "normal body image" is based. In order to uphold the viability of the categories anorexic and nonanorexic, one must overlook imprecisions in the definition of "normal body image." One must neglect the fact that women with and without eating disorders, to varying degrees, share a dissatisfaction with the body that has as its central focus the issue of weight or "feeling fat." This is important because the degree of bodily dissatisfaction evident in studies of nonclinical cases, and upon which the ideal of "normal body image" is theoretically constructed, is not directly addressed in the medical research on anorexia. Moreover, the traditional measures used in making assessments of body image often represent inexact methods, focusing on the degree to which people overestimate their body size (Hsu and Sobkiewitz 1991). Consequently, the "normal-bodied" ideal does not recognize the degree of bodily dissatisfaction that exists among the non-eating-disordered population. The data from this study offer new information that reframes that standard and that may help reconceptualize the role of body image in the formation of identity for white, middle-class women.

ACKNOWLEDGEMENT

I Would like to thank Ed Haworth-Hoeppner for his helpful comments.

NOTES

1. Current medical research indicates that the ratio of female to male anorexics is 9:1 (Gordon 1990).

2.   Conceptions of body image are formulated on the basis of perceptual categorization, and therefore height/weight tables are not directly related to normal body image.

3.   Direct references to normal body image do exist; these are derived historically from the neurological literature, where body image was first conceptualized as "body schema" (Head 1920), later modified to include a more expansive psychological dimension, and associated with the development of an ego structure (Fisher and Cleveland 1968). But neither the neurological nor the psychological definition is commonly employed in the psychiatric literature that refers to normal body image.

4.   Two points need to be addressed here. First, the use of absence as a definitive strategy is common in medicine—as in *health* defined as the absence of disease (Mechanic 1978; Mishler 1986)—and it is also characteristic of the way we go about definition. We accomplish this through what Kenneth Burke (1969) calls the "paradox of substance"; this involves defining a word or concept by contextual reference, or by stipulating what the "thing" is not. (Examples include terms like *atheist* or *unemployment*, which depend upon concepts of belief or work). This functional "absence" is not uncommon in our linguistic constructions, and it mirrors a practice found at the level of institutional discourse.

Second, I recognize the contradiction in the use of the terms "anorexic" and "normal," as their very usage facilitates the reproduction of the categories. However, these terms also operate as institutional categories, embedded within medicine—in its discourse and practices—and examining the issues raised in this discussion, which emerge within a medical context, necessitates their usage here.

5.   *Dorland's Illustrated Medical Dictionary* (1988) defines pathognomonic as "specifically distinctive or characteristic of a disease or pathologic condition." The term illustrates the medical profession's concern with "pathology," a concern that extends to the development of a specialized language surrounding illness and disease.

6.   Given the low prevalence rates of anorexia (e.g., 1 to 4 percent) in the population (Garfinkel and Garner 1982; Gordon 1990), it is difficult to find "pure" anorexics. Therefore, in this study women who were clinically diagnosed with either anorexia or bulimia—both of which use disturbance in body image in their clinical definition—have been included in the sample, but with the provision that severe food restriction is a part of that diagnosis. The same holds for the self-defined anorexic category. As such, the term "anorexics" will be used throughout this chapter to represent both anorexics and bulimic-anorexics.

7.   This question was asked using Gergen and Gergen's (1986) measure, a Developmental Narrative of Body Image.

REFERENCES

Alexander, L., and J. LaRosa. 1994. *New Dimensions in Women's Health.* Boston: Jones and Bartlett.

American Psychiatric Association. 1994. *Diagnostic and Statistical Manual of Mental Disorders,* 4th edition. Washington, DC: Author.

Askevold, F. 1975. "Measuring Body Image." *Psychotherapy and Psychosomatics* 27:71–77.

Ben-Tovin, D., and M. K. Walker. 1991. "Women's Body Attitudes: A Review of Measurement Techniques." *International Journal of Eating Disorders* 10(2):155–62.

Birtchnell, S., B. Dolan, and H. Lacey. 1987. "Body image Distortion in Non-Eating Disordered Women." *International Journal of Eating Disorders* 6(3): 385–91.

Birtchnell, S., H. Lacey, and A. Harte. 1985. "Body Image Distortion in Bulimia Nervosa." *British Journal of Psychiatry* 147:408–12.

Bordo, S. 1993. *Unbearable Weight: Feminism, Western Culture, and the Body*. Berkeley: University of California Press.

Bray, G. 1987. "Overweight Is Risking Fate: Definition, Classification, Prevalence and Risks." Pp. 14–28 in *Human Obesity*, edited by R. Wurtman and J. Wurtman. *Annals of the New York Academy of Sciences* 499.

Brown, C. 1993. "The Continuum: Anorexia, Bulimia, and Weight Preoccupation." Pp. 53–68 in *Consuming Passions: Feminist Approaches to Weight Preoccupation and Eating Disorders*, edited by C. Brown and K. Jasper. Toronto, Ontario: Second Story.

Bruch, H. 1962. "Perceptual and Conceptual Disturbances in Anorexia Nervosa." *Psychosomatic Medicine* 24(2):187–94.

———. 1973. *Eating Disorders: Obesity, Anorexia Nervosa, and the Person Within*. New York: Basic Books.

———. 1978. *The Golden Cage: The Enigma of Anorexia Nervosa*. New York: Vintage.

———. 1982. "Anorexia Nervosa: Therapy and Theory." *American Journal of Psychiatry* 139(12):1531–38.

Brumberg, J. J. 1997. *The Body Project: An Intimate History of American Girls*. New York: Random House.

Burke, K. 1969. *A Grammar of Motives*. Berkeley: University of California Press.

Button, E., F. Fransella, and P. Slade. 1977. "A Reappraisal of Body Perception Disturbance in Anorexia Nervosa." *Psychological Medicine* 7:235–43.

Casper, R., K. Halmi, S. Goldberg, E. Eckert, and J. Davis. 1979. "Disturbances in Body Image Estimation as Related to Other Characteristics and Outcome in Anorexia Nervosa." *British Journal of Psychiatry* 134:60–66.

Clifford, E. 1971. "Body Satisfaction in Adolescence." *Perceptual and Motor Skills* 33:119–25.

Cohn, L., and N. Adler. 1992. "Female and Male Perceptions of Ideal Body Shapes: Distorted Views Among Caucasian College Students." *Psychology of Women Quarterly* 16:69–79.

Counts, C., and H. Adams. 1985. "Body Image in Bulimic, Dieting, and Normal Females." *Journal of Psychopathology and Behavioral Assessment* 7(3):289–300.

Crisp, A., and R. Kalucy. 1974. "Aspects of the Perceptual Disorder in Anorexia Nervosa." *British Journal of Medical Psychology* 47:349–61.

Davies, E., and A. Furnham. 1986. "The Dieting and Body Shape Concerns of Adolescent Females." *Journal of Child Psychology and Psychiatry* 27:417–28.

Dolan, B. 1994. "Why Women? Gender Issues and Eating Disorders: Introduction." Pp. 1–11 in *Gender Issues and Eating Disorders*, edited by B. Dolan and I. Gitzinger. London: Athlone.

Dolan, B., S. Birtchnell, and H. Lacey. 1987. "Body Image Distortion in Non-Eating Disordered Women and Men." *Journal of Psychosomatic Research* 31(4):513–20.

Dorland's Illustrated Medical Dictionary. 1988. 27th edition. Philadelphia: W. B. Saunders.

Dornbusch, S., J. Carlsmuth, P. Duncan, R. Gross, J. Martin, P. Ritter, and B. Siegel-Gorelick. 1984. "Sexual Maturation, Social Class, and the Desire to Be Thin." *Developmental and Behavioral Pediatrics* 5(6):305–17.

Edgley, C., and D. Brissett. 1990. "Health Nazis and the Cult of the Perfect Body: Some Polemical Observations." *Symbolic Interaction* 13 (2):257–79.

Fisher, S., and S. Cleveland. 1968. *Body Image and Personality.* New York: Dover.

Freeman, R., C. Thomas, L. Solyom, and R. Koopman. 1985. "Clinical and Personality Correlates of Body Size Overestimation in Anorexia Nervosa and Bulimia Nervosa." *International Journal of Eating Disorders* 4(4):439–56.

Freitas, A., S. Kaiser, J. Chandler, C. Hall, J. W. Kim, and T. Hammidi. 1994. "Appearance Management As Border Construction: Least Favorite Clothing, Group Distancing, and Identity . . . Not!" Paper presented at a conference sponsored by the Midwest Sociological Society, March 13, St. Louis, MO.

Garfinkel, P., and D. Garner. 1982. *Anorexia Nervosa: A Multidimensional Perspective.* New York: Brunner/Mazel.

Garner, D., and P. Garfinkel. 1981. "Body Image in Anorexia Nervosa: Measurement, Theory, and Clinical Implications." *International Journal of Medicine* 11(3): 263–84.

Garner, D. P., Garfinkel, H. Stancer, and H. Moldofsky. 1976. "Body Image Disturbances in Anorexia Nervosa and Obesity." *Psychosomatic Medicine* 38: 327–36.

Garner, D., and A. Kearney-Cooke. 1996. "Body Image 1996." *Psychology Today* (March/April):55–56.

Garner, D., M. Olmstead, and J. Polivy. 1983. "Development and Validation of a Multidimensional Eating Disorder Inventory for Anorexia Nervosa and Bulimia." *International Journal of Eating Disorders* 2(2):15–34.

Gergen, K., and M. Gergen. 1986. "Narrative Form and the Construction of Psychological Science." Pp. 22–44 in *Narrative Psychology: The Storied Nature of Human Conduct,* edited by T. Sarbin. New York: Praeger.

Glaser, B., and A. Strauss. 1967. *The Discovery of Grounded Theory.* Chicago: Aldine.

Glucksman, M., and J. Hirsch. 1969. "The Response of Obese Patients to Weight Reduction." *Psychosomatic Medicine* 31:1–7.

Goffman, E. 1963. *Stigma: Notes on the Management of Spoiled Identity.* Englewood Cliffs, NJ: Prentice Hall.

Gordon, R. 1990. *Anorexia and Bulimia: Anatomy of a Social Epidemic.* Cambridge, MA: Basil Blackwell.

Gross, E., and G. Stone. 1981. "Embarrassment and the Analysis of Role Requirements." Pp. 115–29 in *Social Psychology Through Symbolic Interaction,* 2nd edition, edited by G. Stone and H. Farberman. New York: John Wiley.

Halmi, K., R. Casper, E. Eckert, S. Goldberg, and J. Davis. 1979. "Unique Features Associated with Age of Onset of Anorexia Nervosa." *Psychiatry Research* 1:209–15.

Head, H. 1920. *Studies in Neurology,* vol. 2. London: Hodder and Stoughton.

Herzog, D., and P. Copeland. 1985. "Eating Disorders." *New England Journal of Medicine* 313(5):295–303.

Hill, T., and G. Lundskow. 1995. "All Pain, No Gain: The Protestant Ethic and Female Body Image." Paper presented at the Midwest Sociological Society, April 6–9, Chicago.

Hsu, L. K. G. 1982. "Is There a Disturbance in Body Image in Anorexia Nervosa?" *Journal of Nervous and Mental Disease* 170(5):305–7.

———. 1990. *Eating Disorders*. New York: Guilford.

Hsu, L. K. G. and T. Sobkiewitz. 1991. "Body Image Disturbance: Time to Abandon the Concept of Eating Disorders?" *International Journal of Eating Disorders* 10(1):15–30.

Jourard, S., and P. Secourd. 1955. "Body-Cathexis and the Ideal Female Figure." *Journal of Abnormal and Social Psychology* 50:243–46.

Kleck, R., and A. Strenta. 1980. "Perceptions of the Impact of Negatively Valued Physical Characteristics on Social Interaction." *Journal of Personality and Social Psychology* 39:861–73.

le Grange, D., J. Tibbs, and T. Noakes. 1994. "Implications of a Diagnosis of Anorexia Nervosa in a Ballet School." *International Journal of Eating Disorders* 15(4):369–76.

Mechanic, D. 1978. *Medical Sociology*, 2nd edition. New York: Free Press.

Mishler, E. 1986. *Research Interviewing: Context and Narrative*. Cambridge, MA: Harvard University Press.

Nylander, J. 1971. "The Feeling of Being Fat and Dieting in a School Population: Epidemiologic Interview Investigation." *Acta Sociomedica Scandinavica* 3:17–26.

Owles, J. 1990. "Body Images: How We Feel About How We Look." *Continuing Conversations*. Newsletter, Office for Women's Resources and Services, University of Illinois at Urbana-Champaign, January 1–4.

Pliner, P., S. Chaiken, and G. Flett. 1990. "Gender Differences in Concern with Body Weight and Physical Appearance over the Life Span." *Personality and Social Psychology* 16(2):263–73.

Ritenbaugh, C. 1982. "Obesity as a Culture-Bound Syndrome." *Culture, Medicine and Psychiatry* 6:347–61.

Rodin, J., L. R. Silberstein, and R. H. Striegel-Moore. 1985. "Women and Weight: A Normative Discontent." Pp. 267–307 in *Nebraska Symposium on Motivation 1984: Psychology and Gender*, vol. 32, edited by T. B. Sonderegger. Lincoln: University of Nebraska Press.

Rosen, J., and J. Gross. 1987. "Prevalence of Weight Reducing and Weight Gaining in Adolescent Girls and Boys." *Health Psychology* 6:131–47.

Slade, P. 1985. "A Review of Body-Image Studies in Anorexia Nervosa and Bulimia Nervosa." *Journal of Psychiatric Research* 19(2/3):255–65.

Slade, P., and G. Russell. 1973. "Awareness of Body Dimension in Anorexia Nervosa: Cross-Sectional and Longitudinal Studies." *Psychological Medicine* 3:188–99.

Sobal, J. 1995. "The Medicalization and Demedicalization of Obesity." Pp. 67–90 in *Eating Agendas: Food and Nutrition as Social Problems*, edited by D. Maurer and J. Sobal. Hawthorne, NY: Aldine de Gruyter.

Stone, G. 1981. "Appearance and the Self: A Slightly Revised Version." Pp. 187–202 in *Social Psychology Through Symbolic Interaction,* 2nd edition, edited by G. Stone and H. Farberman. New York: John Wiley.

Strauss, A. 1987. *Qualitative Analysis For Social Scientists.* Cambridge: Cambridge University Press.

Striegel-Moore, R. 1993. "Etiology of Binge Eating: A Developmental Perspective." Pp. 144–72 in *Binge Eating: Nature, Assessment, and Treatment,* edited by C. Fairburn and T. Wilson. New York: Guilford.

Thomas, V., and M. James. 1988. "Body Image, Dieting Tendencies, and Sex Role Traits in Urban Black Women." *Sex Roles* 18(9/10):523–29.

Thompson, K. 1987. "Body Size Distortion in Anorexia Nervosa: Reanalysis and Reconceptualization." *International Journal of Eating Disorders* 6(3):379–84.

Thorton, B., R. Leo, and K. Alberg. 1991. "Gender Role Typing, the Superwoman Ideal, and the Potential for Eating Disorders." *Sex Roles* 25(7/8):469–84.

Tiggemann, M., and E. Rothblum. 1988. "Gender Differences in Social Consequences of Perceived Overweight in the United States and Australia." *Sex Roles* 18(1/2):75–86.

Traub, A., and J. Orbach. 1964. "Psychophysical Studies of Body Image: An Adjustable Body Distorting Mirror." *Archives of General Psychiatry* 11:53–66.

Way, K. 1995. "Never Too Rich . . . or Too Thin: The Role of Stigma in the Social Construction of Anorexia Nervosa." Pp. 91–113 in *Eating Agendas: Food and Nutrition as Social Problems,* edited by D. Maurer and J. Sobal. Hawthorne, NY: Aldine de Gruyter.

Wooley, S. C., and O. W. Wooley. 1980. "Eating Disorders: Obesity and Anorexia." Pp. 135–58 in *Women and Psychotherapy: An Assessment of Research and Practice,* edited by A. Brodsky and R. Hare-Mustin. New York: Guilford.

———. 1984. "Feeling Fat in a Thin Society." *Glamour* (Feb.):198–202.

Wooley, S. C., O. W. Wooley, and S. Dyrenforth. 1979. "Obesity and Women II. A Neglected Feminist Topic." *Women's Studies International Quarterly* 2:81–92.

7

Weight and Weddings
The Social Construction of Beautiful Brides

JEFFERY SOBAL, CARON BOVE, and
BARBARA RAUSCHENBACH

INTRODUCTION

Weddings are events that mark entry into the social roles of husband and wife. As with many other ceremonial occasions, important social norms are invoked and expressed in weddings. Examining weddings as social rituals reveals how individuals embody salient cultural values. This chapter examines how beliefs about fatness and thinness are interpreted on both the societal and individual levels in the processes of preparing for and participating in weddings.

Wedding rituals act as catalysts that focus social norms about weight on individuals as they undergo changes in their social careers at one of the most distinctive events in their lives. Weddings are rites of passage marking the life course transition from being single to being married, which invoke tremendous concern about appearance, including attention to body weight. People's identities change as they enter and leave social roles, and a unique role transition occurs at weddings as women become brides and men become grooms. People often express identity changes through weight management to attain bodies that fit expectations about a new social status.

The roles of bride and groom are temporary and short-lived transitional states between being single and being a husband or wife, beginning at engagement and ending shortly after the wedding. However, because of the great attention paid to individuals in those roles, there is much anticipation of them. The role of the bride especially involves observation and scrutiny in the central spotlight of the wedding. One aspect of preparation for a wedding is dealing with body weight issues.

Both weddings and weight are gendered arenas that are more the realm of women than men. Women care more about weddings, with men focusing on "getting married." Much of the discussion of weight and weddings in this chapter will focus on the bride because weddings focus on brides.

Weddings are special cultural rites that operate on their own separate plane of understanding as rituals set apart from normal social reality. The separation of weddings from usual life in postindustrial societies makes them similar to the transcendent ceremonies that anthropologists describe as suspending perceptions and judgments in traditional cultures. For many people, their wedding will be the most intense cultural ritual they ever experience. When dealing with weddings, frugal people spend tens of thousands of dollars, shy people seek the limelight, and plain people outfit themselves in opulent styles as they suspend their usual habits. Wedding transformations may be extreme, with one woman commenting, "I did not even recognize my friend at her wedding because of her hair, makeup, and gown."

WEDDINGS, WEIGHT, AND CULTURE

Cultural comparisons provide useful contrasts that generate insights about the importance of cultural ideals in events such as weddings (Sobal 1998). Many cultures hold strong values about ideal body shapes, and people often try to change their weight to achieve cultural ideals for a wedding.

Cultural standards about fatness and thinness are located in time and place. Most traditional cultures of the world value fatness as a sign of health and wealth (Anderson, Crawford, Nadeau, and Lindberg 1992; Brown and Konner 1987), and until the late 1800s fatness was admired and sought in the United States (Brumberg 1989; Schwartz 1986; Seid 1989; Stearns 1997). The contemporary concern about obesity has been described as a culture-bound syndrome that is peculiar to postindustrial Western societies (Ritenbaugh 1982).

Some traditional societies have developed fattening rituals to help achieve status for men and fertility for women (Brink 1989, 1995; Guarine 1995). In many societies, fat women are seen as being more likely to bear children, which is a highly valued trait for a good marriage. Institutionalized practices to fatten people before weddings are ritualized attempts to realize idealized cultural images of large body size. "Fattening huts" are used in rituals where young unmarried individuals are isolated, kept inactive, and fed huge amounts of food to gain weight in an attempt to be attractive as marital partners (Brink 1989; Guarine and Koppert 1991; Talbot 1968).

In contemporary postindustrial societies, cultural norms increasingly emphasize the value of slim and "toned" bodies for women and large and muscular bodies for men (Garner, Garfinkel, Schwartz, and Thompson 1980; Wiseman, Gray, Mosimann, and Ahrens 1992; Wolf 1991). People who fit these ideals are valued, and those who do not are rejected. Deviance from body norms is sanctioned by stigmatizing acts that range from subtle rejection and teasing to vicious harassment and discrimination (Sobal 1991, 1999).

Contemporary societies have developed general thinning rituals that encourage achieving thin and toned bodies for women and strong and fit bodies for men. These are used in attempts to attain culturally idealized slim bodies. While body-shaping rituals are employed before weddings, they are not specifically designed for preparation for marriage or wedding rituals. Fattening hut rituals of traditional cultures have functional equivalents in contemporary postindustrial societies, which operate "thinning huts" in the form of spas and weight loss camps; social institutions such as dieting groups, gymnasiums, and fitness centers; and individual rituals such as diets and personal exercise to fit bodies to cultural ideals. The correspondence between these body construction processes in cultures with opposite values about fatness and thinness shows the societal importance of weight, and how weight concerns are heightened prior to weddings.

WEDDINGS IN CONTEMPORARY SOCIETY

Weddings have received surprisingly little attention from social scientists, being an understudied topic except for a handful of anthropological accounts and a few analyses in the marriage and family literature (e.g., Charsley 1991, 1992, 1997; Currie 1993; Edwards 1989; Goodkind 1996; Kendall 1996; Leonard 1980; Reed-Danahay 1996). Weddings are common events that have undergone changes as social rituals and involve considerable personal and social investments.

In the United States, 2,336,000 couples married in 1995 (U.S. Bureau of the Census 1997). Peak marriage months are June, July, and August. Ninety percent of marriages occur among people age fifteen to forty-four, with 7 percent of men and 8 percent of women in that age group marrying each year (National Center for Health Statistics 1994). The median age at first marriage is twenty-four for women and twenty-six for men (U.S. Bureau of the Census 1997). The annual number and rate of marriages is declining as the baby boom cohort ages beyond the peak marriage years.

Not all marriages involve weddings, although most (82 percent) hold religious rather than civil ceremonies and are held in a church or other religious building (Whyte 1990). Weddings incorporate many ceremonial vestiges of past traditions, despite movements toward informality and egalitarianism in other aspects of marriage and other domains of life. In contrast to many traditional societies and past eras, many people today participate in wedding rituals—like throwing rice, jointly cutting the wedding cake, or removing the bride's garter—that they do not understand and about which they cannot explain the meaning or symbolism.

The place of weddings in a person's life course and in the broader society has been changing (Whyte 1990). More people live independently before marriage, with fewer residing with their parents until they marry. Cohabitation before marriage is increasingly practiced and accepted. The number of premarital births is rising. Such structural changes would appear to make weddings seem less important, but they contrast with cultural changes that are making weddings into more significant occasions. Engagements, the public announcements of intention to marry, are increasingly ceremonialized with such events as engagement parties (Whyte 1990). Commercialization and commodification of weddings is occurring as they become more elaborate, more complex, and less casual (Currie 1993). Prewedding rituals like bridal showers and bachelor/bachelorette parties as well as postwedding receptions and honeymoons are increasingly prevalent and elaborate.

Weddings involve large investments of money, time, emotion, and social relations (ibid.). The average cost of a wedding in 1997 was reported to be $19,104, including $7,635 for a reception for an average of 200 guests, $1,311 for photography, $1,016 for rings, $830 for music, $823 for the bride's wedding dress, $756 for flowers, $698 for a rehearsal dinner, as well as many other costs (*Ithaca Journal* 1998). Considerable time is invested in planning and worrying about weddings. The emotional investment in weddings is sufficiently great to label them a stressful life event, parallel with changing jobs or the death of a family member (Holmes and Rahe 1967). Social investments in weddings include asking numerous favors of many people and taking the risk of offending people for not consulting, including, or considering them. Planning weddings often involves reading specialized literature in the form of wedding guidebooks and bridal magazines, and seeking the professional help of wedding planners (Currie 1993). All of these factors emphasize the significance of weddings as key events in contemporary society, and provide a context for considering weight and weddings.

CONSTRUCTION OF WEIGHT AND WEDDINGS

This chapter applies a constructionist theoretical orientation, assuming that people have personal agency with which they actively construct and decide how to deal with weight in relationship to weddings. This perspective assumes that people are not simply pawns driven by larger social structures, and are more than sets of conditioned behaviors that respond to calculations of costs and benefits. The broader concept of social construction can be analytically differentiated into a system of three interwoven and reciprocal processes: (1) interpretation and definition, (2) negotiation and management, and (3) performance and presentation.

Interpretation and definition involve assessing available social information and using it to develop personal models and understandings. People seek and assess mass media messages, folklore, cultural discourses, societal values, and shared schema. They evaluate, classify, and translate this information to apply to their personal situations and preferences. People use these interpretations to define their personal situations and decide how to act within existing contexts. We will examine how people interpret and define social norms and cultural values about both weight and weddings as they construct personal journeys to their weddings and into their marriages.

Negotiation and management involve the creation of personal careers through interrelationships with other people, using strategies and employing resources to accomplish itineraries for action. Social interactions create common meanings that are negotiated and shared between individuals. Personal management uses a variety of strategies to interweave pressures and limitations imposed by relationships and institutions with personal perceptions and desires. We will examine the variations in ways that people deal with others as they decide before their weddings how to "do weight," coping with the expectations of partners, family, friends, and communities as they integrate and engineer their own preferences in managing weight and weight issues before weddings. "Doing weight" involves the creation, accomplishment, and enactment of body weight in a continuing process of reciprocal interactions with others. To do weight is a parallel process to "doing gender" (West and Zimmerman 1987), "doing age" (Laz 1998), and more generally "doing difference" (West and Fenstermacher 1995).

Performance and presentation involve employing various strategies to express weight to others in personal enactments. People exercise social control over themselves and their environment, and attempt to reveal and conceal themselves in the most advantageous way possible using available resources. They personally enact and accomplish weight during interactional processes. We will examine how clothing, photography, and other resources are strategically used to present weight as a part of larger wedding performances that are exhibitions of cultural norms about fatness and thinness.

We gathered evidence for this analysis of weight and weddings from a variety of sources. Long, in-depth ethnographic interviews (Spradley

1979) about weight, diet, and exercise were conducted and audiotaped with twenty-two women and fifteen of their partners shortly before they married, with follow-up interviews of a smaller set of individuals selected from that pool about a year after their wedding. We also conducted additional formal and informal interviews with unmarried and married individuals as well as with people involved in the wedding industry such as bridal shop owners and photographers. We additionally did participant observation (Spradley 1980) at selected bridal fairs and other wedding events. Qualitative content analysis (Weber 1985) of professional and popular literature on weddings and weight provided further data for the analysis. The authors also used introspection (Wallendorf and Brucks 1993) about their personal experiences with their own weddings and those of others for additional supplementary insights.

INTERPRETATION AND DEFINITION OF WEIGHT AND WEDDINGS

Weddings are significant rites of passage, often recognized as one of the most important life events. Brides (and to a much lesser extent grooms) recognize they will be the centers of attention at the wedding ceremony and seek to look their best in light of cultural ideals. This includes interpreting social ideals that emphasize a slim body weight. Various cultural scripts provide a "tool kit" of images and resources (Laz 1998) for doing weight at weddings. The social interpretation process involves gathering and giving meaning to information about wedding ideals and possibilities. A personal definition of weight is constructed to guide people through their journey within the complex of weight and wedding options.

The importance of weddings clearly differs by gender, with the wedding an immensely more important event for the bride than groom. Currie observed, "As 'The bride's day' weddings remain one of the few public occasions where women's roles in the family are celebrated" (1993:419). Women often are socialized to think about weddings beginning at early ages, with ubiquitous dolls such as "Barbie" in wedding attire used to inculcate cultural norms that thin bodies are ideal for weddings. The mass media provide other idealized portraits of weddings, with printed and broadcast news and fiction often touting the wedding as a focal event in a woman's life and typically displaying slim brides as ideals.

A wedding industry has grown up to support the management of weddings as people plan and execute wedding ceremonies. This industry includes a loose coalition of wedding consultants, plus fashion, photography, food, transportation, and travel services. The main routes for directly accessing the wedding industry occur in bridal magazines, bridal newspaper inserts, and bridal fairs, with important access through word-of-mouth in social networks.

Many women would like to lose weight to meet cultural expectations about slimness at their weddings, so an opportunity exists for marketers of weight loss organizations and products to pursue their vested interests with people about to be married. However, overt entrepreneurial activity promoting wedding weight loss appears to be rare. A review of recent bridal magazines revealed few advertisements for weight loss services or products (such as spas or diets), and our assessment of general weight loss advertisements that are ubiquitous in the mass media uncovered few mentions of marriage and weddings.

Exceptions to the lack of public links between weight loss and weddings do occur. A liquid diet food disseminated in television and magazine advertisements that showed before-and-after pictures of a woman with the caption, "Lost 39 lbs. I was getting married. I didn't want to be a fat bride. With Slim Fast, I lost the weight and walked down the aisle in my dream wedding dress." The lack of weight loss industry penetration into the wedding arena may be due to the belief that the general media are so saturated with weight loss advertisements that marketers believe they do not need to provide extra targeting to people getting married, especially if such ventures might appear unseemly, predatory, or exploitative.

Thus, weight loss before weddings appears to be a topic that is not publicly discussed, but rather one that is dealt with in informal, backstage arenas. The lack of overt encouragement for weight loss before weddings may help maintain the conception that every bride is a beautiful bride. Procedures used for dealing with wedding weight draw upon cultural scripts for weight loss that may involve individual, medical, or organizational efforts. Many weight loss efforts in contemporary society are private, shrouded in the shelter of the medical system or hidden from public view in the home. This makes them ideal for constructing beautiful brides by not revealing information about how much (or little) effort a bride invests in changing her weight before the wedding.

The wedding industry has produced many popular books, magazines, newspapers, and even computer sources that provide advice about planning and executing weddings. A review of these revealed little specific consideration of the management of body weight in wedding industry literature. However, two topics about weight are explicitly discussed in bridal books and magazines: Obtaining bridal wear for large women, and ordering appropriately sized gowns that fit different body shapes.

Some larger women are intimidated by a fashion world that emphasizes slimness. One bridal book quoted a bride as saying:

> Since high school I have worn a size 16 dress. When I became engaged, I was frightened to death about going to a bridal shop to try to fit into or possibly

rip a gown. Was I surprised when I discovered that big beautiful brides are in and that bridal salons now carry several larger-size styles in stock that you can actually try on. (Kresse 1994:83)

Several industry sources attempt to reassure larger women that they can obtain attractive gowns. A book stated:

American women are getting larger and bustier, and bridal houses are well aware of that. Look for special bridal fashion shows for the full figured woman and rest assured that an experienced staff in a reputable salon will know how to help every bride look truly beautiful on her wedding day. (Lalli and Dahl 1997:70)

The wedding industry claims that it is dealing with changing body shapes and customer demands and bridal salons are accommodating larger women. One guidebook explained:

Statistics tell us that 40 percent of the women in the United States wear size 14 or larger. Heightened interest in athletics, a less nutritious diet, and larger bone structures of women today are the reasons manufacturers cite for their addition of 'plus size' bridal styles that offer figure-flattering selections. (Kresse 1994:83)

Resource books for large people list dozens of sources for wedding clothing, with gowns up to size 46 and also custom- made dresses (Sullivan 1997). However, while some bridal magazines include advertisements listing the broad range of dress sizes they sell and others have sections featuring gowns for larger women, services for larger women appear to be the exception rather than the rule. Fashion designers traditionally include a wedding gown as the culmination of a runway show, but the gowns are displayed on a typically slim model. The overwhelming number of magazine photographs and bridal displays also use very thin models.

Even though wedding gowns for larger women are available, they may not be equally accessible. One woman reported in an interview:

[S]ociety thinks that you are this way, you should be this way, slim. Because go try looking for a dress in my, the way I look now. It's hard. And you have to pay an extra, you know, two hundred dollars to get a dress. Because they only run your normal sizes. . . . We went out of town somewhere where they cater to bigger women.

In contrast with the acceptance and accommodation of large brides by some sources, others in the wedding industry portray weight loss attempts before weddings as normative. Simultaneously, however, they also provide the pessimistic message that brides-to-be are usually unsuccessful at losing weight. Such discussions of unsuccessful dieting are used to caution against clothing decisions that assume weight loss. One book advised:

> One of the first things women do when they get engaged is go on a diet so they'll be at an ideal weight for the big day. But do not put too much pressure on yourself by buying a dress that's a smaller size than you usually wear. It's a lot easier to take in a larger dress than it is to let out a smaller dress. (Behr 1998:24)

Another source revealed the vested interests of bridal shops in anticipating problems with brides who change weight and in protecting themselves from fitting gowns to women who planned but did not achieve weight loss:

> If you want to lose weight before your wedding (and many brides do), explain that to the shop so they are aware, but order the gown using your present measurements. They can always take a dress in, but letting it out can be more difficult, and sometimes impossible. (Lenderman 1997:135)

Definition of an appropriate wedding weight by a particular person includes future anticipation of records and remembrances of her wedding weight and shape. Weddings are central reference points in a person's life course and often serve as weight references. Many people note and remember what they weighed at their weddings (like similar events such as graduations) and use it as a standard for later comparisons. Sometimes people do this explicitly and formally. One lawyer included a prenuptial contract stipulation that a wife's wedding-day weight would not increase by more than twenty pounds or she would be penalized financially during the marriage (Foderary 1997). Most individuals more subtly continue to recognize their wedding weights in their later years, often etched into their memories and memorialized in photographs.

NEGOTIATION AND MANAGEMENT OF WEIGHT BEFORE WEDDINGS

The joining together of two people in matrimony is a precarious time when couples commit to each other to form a new nuclear family, and officially link themselves into larger networks of family and friends. Although people desire to present themselves in the best possible light to their new kith and kin, tensions and strains may occur. This interactional work is negotiated in progressive stages: first with the partner, then with close family and friends, and finally with those who are more distant. Thus a series of relational circles of weight input and approval are demarcated and negotiated. The extent of family intrusion into the lives of the couple increases as the wedding approaches (Slater 1963).

Weddings are shared events, a time when family and friends prepare together to attempt to jointly construct a successful event. The collective nature of weddings occurs in support for weight management as a give-and-take negotiation process occurs between various individuals. One woman spoke about her mother and others pressuring her to lose weight for her wedding:

> Oh yeah, she always does. I've gotten flack from everybody. Especially try-ing to get the dress because, you know, I'm, what was I? A 20, size 20 and it's hard when you go in the up-sizes. It's hard to get in the up-sizes. It's like they only take it to 18, you know and if I was, lost some more weight, then I could get in the 18 but, oh, it was horrible.

A bride and her close family and friends may provide each other with mutual support, including information that shows the consequences of weight negotiations. People in the bride's social network invoke "success stories" and "horror stories" to help her negotiate decisions about weight issues. One woman explained:

> I've talked to several people who have gained weight and barely have fit into their dresses. . . . They all said, "You'd better order that dress a size larger." And I said, "No," and I wish I did.

A key person in negotiations about weight before weddings is the per-son's future spouse. Some partners favor weight loss. One man proudly described his wife:

> She went to go get fitted for her wedding dress. She got a wedding dress four sizes smaller than what she was at the time. And she said, you know, I'm going to go fit into my wedding dress. And she did.

A woman described how she felt no pressure from her fiance to lose weight for the wedding:

> I really wasn't trying to lose any weight before my wedding. I wasn't actively dieting or anything like that. I mean I was just kind of going with the flow. And I think it's because my husband . . . he's easygoing about it. . . . I think there's some men that are, you know "Honey, you know you're put-ting on a few pounds there." . . . I feel a good level of acceptance about, you know, my appearance and my body.

By contrast, some brides-to-be move through a process of negotiating a shift in focus on weight before the wedding. One woman first noted, "I made a bet with John that before the wedding I'd lose forty more pounds . . . 'cause I know he would like me to get back down to what I was." As the wedding approached she did not lose weight, reporting, "I'm trying, but not being obsessive about it. Because I guess you could say I'm content. I'd love to get back there, but I'm not going to break my back either." When describing her wedding appearance one year later, she emphasized that she had been happy with her weight and that her new husband had shared her new interpretation: "I looked good! I looked great. And he liked it too."

Wedding weight concerns do not just focus on the bride and groom, but also extend to other participants and attendees. One bride-to-be reported: "I work with my sister and we go out to lunch every day together. But since we've been planning the wedding, we've been trying to get the health choice things and everything 'cause she's in my wedding, too." Bridesmaids attend the bride at the wedding and share some attention with the bride, and often work to manage their weight before the wedding. Similar heightening of weight concerns before weddings occurs for parents and other relatives of the bride and groom, although much more so for women than men.

Weight Management Orientations

Management of weight before weddings involves a variety of strategies. Most women (but few men) are concerned about their weight before the wedding. One bridal magazine reported its marketing research about weight, stating that 80 percent of their readers were currently controlling their weight, 79 percent were more motivated to diet than in the past, and nearly half had purchased a physical fitness item within the past year (O'Donoghue 1997).

Our investigations identified five orientations that characterized body weight management before weddings: taking action, vigilant action, postponing action, not taking action, and unusual action. We interviewed and observed people who were characteristic of the first four orientations, and have included the last because it is reported in professional and popular literature.

Taking action is an orientation in which people actively do things to change their weight, employing the strategies of dieting, using or modifying their use of pharmaceutical substances, and exercising. A vigilant action orientation uses weight monitoring and small changes in behavior to maintain weight. In a postponing-action orientation, weight loss is seen as desirable but not currently attainable. A no-action orientation gives no consideration to weight changes. An unusual-action orientation involves nonnormative strategies such as disordered eating or intentional weight gain by overweight individuals. These five orientations will be discussed separately in the following sections although they are not mutually exclusive because some people sequentially use more than one.

Taking Action. One of the common ways of taking action is dieting. Dieting occurs as women "go on a diet" before the wedding to seek slimness for "the big day" and to ensure that they will fit into their wedding gowns. Rodin, Silberstein, and Striegel-Moore (1985) identified weight as a "normative discontent" among American women, and these women exemplified this by trying to change their weight. Many women diet in preparation for their weddings, with varying goals, varying levels of enthusiasm, and varying success. Tactics for dieting before weddings varied widely, and people searched their social networks for solutions to reduce weight.

Some women felt ambivalent about dieting before weddings:

> 'Cause I was on the diet for like six weeks and I lost the ten pounds and I was, I kind of started going off it to see if I could keep eating that way without having to say, "OK, I only get two proteins and three of this." Off it more so I could maybe lose the next ten by just eating better and not have to be on a diet to do it. So lately I've been trying to, I'm still sort of on it but I'm not on it. I'm trying to do OK.

Some dieting women take other risks to lose weight before weddings by using pharmaceutical strategies such as smoking, discontinuing medications, and using weight loss drugs. Smoking was maintained before weddings until weight loss goals were met:

> I can't give that up. Not until after I lose the weight. I want to quit and can quit. I have done, quit. But, I notice that when I do quit, I have a tendency to eat more than when I do smoke. So, I'm not going to quit until I get to where I want to be. . . . I won't, won't even think about quitting now.

One woman stopped taking her birth control pills, deciding:

> Let's just do it this way. Let's see if I can get some weight gone before the wedding. As soon as I get married I'm going to go back on them. Because I'm not taking that chance. But it has helped.

Weight loss drugs are also a tempting shortcut to weight loss, despite cautions by physicians that they are intended for severely obese patients and "not to get into a bikini or wedding dress" (Golden 1997:79).

Exercising is another common way of taking action. People exercise both to lose or maintain weight as well as to "shape," "firm," or even "sculpt" particular body parts (especially those revealed by wedding gowns). Managing weight by emphasizing exercise as much as eating ranged from simply seeking a bit of activity prior to the wedding to engaging in a prewedding exercise "kick." Some women hire personal trainers, even taking the trainers along when shopping for wedding dresses (Henderson 1998). Often the focus among toners is to reduce fat in particular places, and to build and shape muscles in those places.

The back of the arm is seen as a particularly problematic body area exposed by wedding gowns, with even fit women reporting, "I hate my arms" (ibid.). One woman explained in an interview:

> It's just, you know, my arm. I'm worried about my arm showing. . . . You want to look toned and perfect for your, for your wedding. And you want to be your skinniest, I guess. And then after the wedding I'm like, "Who cares, I'm married." There's not all the pressure.

One bridal magazine advised "Declare war on the back of your arms. If the old jiggly-wiggly has you ruling out stunning strapless, sleeveless, or halter wedding gowns, get toned with this new Triceps Kickback exercise" (Seto 1997:40).

Vigilant Action. Vigilant action occurs in women for whom weight already is a continual and salient priority. Vigilant people establish a weight range for themselves as part of their personal identity and maintain their usual attentiveness to any change in their weight as they prepare for their wedding. They take precautions so they do not have to worry about their weight, having heightened attention but not using any extraordinary measures before weddings. Weight monitoring, dietary restraint, and sometimes exercise are deeply ingrained into the lives of vigilant women, and they simply make sure that wedding preparations do not interrupt their usual eating and physical activity patterns. Vigilant people do not let weight become a problem, and take precautions to avoid weight changes beyond their control, even for such unique events as weddings.

One woman always maintained her weight at 135–140 pounds, stating,

> I have a personal goal to be back at a certain weight by my birthday every year. . . . So if I vary by like five pounds or something that's OK because, I mean I've got that year to go up and down a little bit so I don't have to get really freaked out about "dieting," you know.

She did not try to lose weight for her wedding because she was comfortable with her weight anyway, given that it was in her acceptable range: "I was within five pounds the whole year pretty much."

Postponing Action.   Postponing action occurs when people choose to wait until after the wedding to attempt to change their bodies. Women who engaged in postponing desired to lose weight, but had decided to defer any concrete actions until after the wedding and honeymoon were over and they were established in their new marital roles. Most were overwhelmed with wedding preparations and foresaw their new, calmer identities as wives as being more congruent with dealing with weight issues.

Some women postponed attention to weight loss during the period of suspended attention to virtually all nonwedding issues as they planned and prepared for their wedding: "It was just, it was really, really crazy trying to, you know, plan the wedding and stuff like that. We were just stressed, you know, just like 'We'll worry about it later, we'll worry about it later.'" Others prioritized their commitments and saw weight as an issue they would face in their later marital role: "I've kind of decided in my life that there are some things I need to get over with right now, like buying this house and getting married before I'm going to start dwelling on that." Several men gained weight during rapid courtships, but felt that it was hopeless to try to decrease their weight before the wedding.

Not Taking Action.   Not taking action about weight before weddings occurs among most men and some women who either do not worry about their weights or are reassured by their partner that they need not worry. One woman reported:

> He made me very aware of the fact that he was marrying me for me and not for me being a size 2 or a size 12, you know. I didn't feel any overpowering need to [lose weight] and my mom was like, "You know, you really don't need to," so. . . . Everybody that I've talked to as a woman, have tried to lose weight before their wedding cause they want to look their best on their wedding day. And, I mean I was getting married to the man I love so I figured I looked my best anyways.

Concern about weight at the wedding simply was not a relevant consideration for most men, a number of whom wanted to gain weight and muscle unrelated to the wedding.

Unusual Action.   Unusual actions, mentioned in the literature but not by people we interviewed, include disordered eating and intentional weight gain. Disordered eating prior to a wedding occurs when someone psychopathologically deals with weight. A case report (Woodside, Shekter-Wolfson, Brandes, and Lackstrom 1993:72) of what may be termed "wedding anorexia nervosa" describes a woman with preexisting anorexia nervosa who initiated rigid dieting and vomiting the day after she became engaged, losing considerable weight as her wedding approached. On her wedding day she experienced pain from several months of constipation that was so severe as to require hospitalization. Such extreme behavior is probably rare even among the few percent of the population afflicted with anorexia nervosa or bulimia nervosa (American Psychiatric Association 1994; Hoek 1993).

Intentional gaining of weight occurs for individuals who seek to increase their weight before weddings. A small subculture of male fat admirers (or FAs, as they are identified within their subculture) are "chubby chasers," who view extremely obese women as very attractive (Goode 1983). Women who are going to marry an FA strive to maintain or even increase their weight for the wedding. Social circles surrounding FAs also provide opportunities for large women to meet and marry men who are "feeders," desiring their partners to gain weight and assisting them in increasing their weight (including before their weddings).

Contextual Factors. In addition to the weight management orientations and strategies just described, we also identified two contextual factors—stress and socializing—that had the potential to influence weight management. People saw stress and socializing as complicating factors that needed to be strategized about to successfully deal with weight issues. Tactics and approaches were developed to avoid the consequences of strains and pressures that are specific to weddings as well as the increased obligatory eating involved in prewedding social events. These conditions were viewed as "traps" that brides-to-be could fall into without their awareness. Stories about avoiding these pitfalls were shared by friends and family and also mentioned in bridal magazines and books in an effort to help brides successfully manage these situations in their prewedding weight careers.

Stress occurred when people were so overwhelmed by planning and preparing for a wedding that they experienced unanticipated weight changes. Some stressed people lose weight when they do not desire to do so, while others gain. A wedding book warns prospective brides that many brides gain or lose ten to fifteen pounds before a wedding due to stress (Blum and Kaiser 1997:52). One bride explained:

> They ended up letting the dress out an inch so I could wear it! I shouldn't laugh cause it's not funny, but it is funny . . . . I find that if, if I'm a little bit stressed I eat everything that's not nailed down. Even if I don't like it, I'll eat it.

Another woman had learned from her sister's prewedding experience:

> I want to make sure that, well, my one sister gained like twenty pounds before her wedding and couldn't fit in her dress. So, I'm like, that's like my biggest fear.

Once a women buys her gown, fears about weight loss are as salient as those for weight gain: "I can't lose a lot 'cause they won't be able to take in the dress that much and still make it look good either."

Socializing occurs as people become involved in prewedding activities that lead to unanticipated weight gain (or loss). Bridal parties, showers, office lunches, and dinners with families and friends provide festivities that the bride and groom are obligated to attend. These food events carry expectations and temptations to eat specially obtained and prepared ceremonial foods, many of which are extremely high in calories. One woman reported a three-pound weight gain the week before her wedding. Another described a sister's socializing experiences and prewedding weight in great detail:

> And my other sister, you know, was really bent on looking, having lost weight and keeping it off for her wedding. I think she still gained like the week before, she still gained like a couple pounds back because of the nervous[ness] and having to go out to dinner . . . and the luncheons and, cause we, all of her sisters brought her out, we brought her out for lunch in like a bachelorette luncheon where we all just got together, her last lunch-with-her-sisters type deal while she was single and we brought her out to a big Chinese lunch. And then some of her in-laws brought her out that week for lunch, because his parents got separated, they're both remarried so two separate dinners that she went to there . . . so I know she gained back a couple pounds before her wedding day but it wasn't, you know . . . it wasn't like my other sister gained major poundage.

Others who are "talkers" rather than "eaters" are so busy socializing that they eat less in prewedding festivities.

Weight management before weddings may occur at the last minute or begin well ahead of the event. "Bridal magazines suggest starting anything up to six months before the wedding with diets and exercise to lose weight, firm muscles, and improve skin and hair" (Leonard 1980:130). Stories about friend's experiences are used to communicate the importance of timing in managing weight, as described by one woman:

> I know my best friend . . . was very self-conscious when she got married. I know she went to a weight clinic to lose weight before she got married. I mean, he asked to marry her, and she said, you know, she made the date like almost a year [later] so that she could lose weight.

The actual purchase of a wedding gown demarcates a crucial weight event in the preparation for the wedding, placing limits on future weight gains and losses. It also forces a woman to confront her weight directly, as she compares styles, selects sizes, and gazes at herself in a full-length mirror. Some women obtain their dresses months before the wedding and repeatedly try them on to be sure they fit: "Oh yeah, I try it on every other once in a while, I just tried it on last week, just to make sure it still fits." Other women wait until the last possible moment, continually hoping to lose more weight before committing to their purchase.

Postwedding honeymoons provide additional motivation for weight loss and maintenance beyond the wedding itself. Honeymooners often travel to places where bathing suits are worn:

> [W]e're going on our honeymoon to Florida and we want to, you know, look halfway decent in shorts and a T-shirt or, you know whatever I decide to wear, swimsuit, so when we're on a beach or Disney that, you know, I don't look like a beached whale out there. . . . My thinking now is that I want to look good in my wedding dress, and I want to look good on the beach and that's my thinking at this point. That's why I'm exercising and eating a lot better.

Weight control for weddings is not exclusively an issue for women, although the image of a slim bride is a more salient cultural norm than that of a thin groom. Men in general more often use exercise than dieting to lose weight (Serdula, Williamson, Anda, Levy, Heaton, and Byers 1994), and this applies to men before weddings. One man wanted to manage his weight for his wedding, especially for the photographs in which he would be standing next to his muscular younger brother:

> I think it'll probably come down a little bit. I probably will run, exercise a little bit . . . and when I run I do push- ups and sit-ups before and after I run, push-ups, sit-ups, and pull-ups. . . . I want to thin out a little bit. Actually I have to stand next to my brother who's gotten taller and bigger.

Brides and grooms draw upon social interpretations and personal definitions of weight as they negotiate management strategies to deal with their bodies as they prepare for their wedding. This section examined the ways people deal with others in their relational circle and the variety of tactics they use to deal with weight before the wedding. Finally, when the actual wedding occurs, weight needs to be enacted for the event.

PERFORMANCE AND PRESENTATION OF WEIGHT AT WEDDINGS

At the wedding event itself further strategies are used to "do" weight. People put on performances as they present themselves to the world, strategically selecting and manipulating the impressions they seek to create (Goffman 1959, 1963). Particularly at formal ceremonial events such as weddings, people try to display themselves in the best possible light.

Performances and presentations of weight occur in weddings using clothing, space, and other resources to reveal thinness and conceal fatness at the
wedding, and using professional photographers to manipulate the way
body sizes and shapes are recorded at weddings. One bride explained:

> With the wedding, I think it's just the stress that everything's got to be per-
> fect. You're trying to get the wedding perfect so you feel that you have to be
> perfect. You're the one people look at all day. . . . In a wedding you're the one
> who everybody stands up and watches walk down the aisle. You've got that
> pressure. I mean you're trying to get your nails done, your hair done, your
> makeup done. Of course you want to look your best and be as skinny as you
> can be.

Wedding clothing is a focal point in the preparation for presentation at
the wedding event. A major purpose of the wedding gown is to make a
bride look beautiful by accentuating her most attractive points and con-
cealing attributes that she views as less appealing (Leonard 1980). One
woman stated:

> I want to look, you know, perfect in my dress. . . . So I bought a dress that, I
> mean it looked excellent when I tried it on. It made me look really great, it
> made me look tall, you know, everything that, you know, you want a wed-
> ding dress to make you look right.

Women spend considerable time and effort choosing and modifying
wedding gowns to best emphasize their size and shape. Bridal books claim
that "there is a wedding dress to flatter every figure," "waistlines can be
minimized with slimming shapes . . . camouflaging the figure dilemma"
(McBride-Mellinger 1993:115). Presentation of beautiful brides is enacted
through the selection of the gown itself, the use of accessories, and in the
employment of other clothing such as undergarments to manage the way
brides present their weight. Couturiers work to construct beautiful brides
by using their skills to "transform, conceal, and celebrate the feminine
form" (ibid.). Men are less invested in managing their weight presentations through clothing, but do employ cummerbunds to flatten their stom-
achs and padded shoulders to emphasize their muscles.

Weddings are such important life events that they are widely discussed
by people who are not actually present, and permanent records of the
events will be displayed long into the future. Wedding photography (and
more recently videography) is the major strategy for visually communicating about weddings beyond the immediate audience at the actual
event. Wedding photography is used to construct beautiful brides on film,
with professional wedding photographers employed and trusted to present people in their best light (Lewis 1994). Professional photographers

have developed strategies to manage their subjects' presentation of their weight, with camera angles, lighting, and posing used to create stylized pictures that portray the weights of people at weddings in socially desirable ways. For example, professional wedding photographers coach brides to hold their chins high in an S-shaped pose to stretch their necks to avoid appearances of "double chins" (ibid.).

Photographs taken at weddings immortalize the appearance of brides and grooms. These photographs communicate much information to others about appearance and status (Mazur 1993). Thone (1997) describes how women show their wedding photographs to others as an example of when they lost weight and looked slim. One affianced woman proclaimed, "Sure, it's family and friends, but there's 200 of them out there, and this is the memory they're going to keep of you, frozen in time" (Henderson 1998). Another woman observed, "She knew these pictures were going to be around forever, the picture is going to be you." The fear of appearing fat on film is a prominent influence on brides-to-be, as one woman reported:

You're going to have those wedding pictures for the rest of your life. And you want to show people beautiful pictures. And if you don't think that you look really good, you know, they're not beautiful pictures any more. You know, you don't want to show them to people because, you know, you're heavy, you don't look good.

Spatial manipulation of weight presentations includes control over the access and distance of the bride and groom to observers, the use of lighting to selectively reveal or conceal visibility, and the management of privacy as people prepare to be presented before the wedding event. Wedding ceremonies involve both frontstage and backstage areas (Goffman 1959), with more carefully attended frontstage performances that avoid revealing unwanted views of body shapes and weight.

Performance and presentation invoke the interpretations and definitions of weight that brides and grooms established as they negotiated and managed their weights in preparation for the wedding. "Doing weight" at the wedding event used clothing and spatial control to attempt to enact weight in a favorable manner. This includes special enactments of weight in the form of wedding photographs that will be observed in the future by the wedding participants as well as others.

CONCLUSION: CONSTRUCTION OF WEIGHT AND WEDDINGS

Weddings provide a unique window for examining the social construction of body weight in contemporary society. The heightened focus on appearance, particularly for the bride, in anticipation of and during the wedding ritual, provides a touchstone for considering the complex and sometimes ambivalent cultural values about fatness and thinness. Many women have to deal with the mixed messages that brides should be thin, but that all brides are beautiful. This chapter suggests that weight is socially constructed, involving a system of interpretation and definition of social values, negotiation and management using multiple orientations and strategies, and performance and presentation of weight for weddings. These processes operate together as individuals establish and execute plans for dealing with weight and weddings.

Many factors suggest that weddings should create intense pressures to conform to idealized social appearance norms that emphasize extreme slimness, encouraging people to seek to be thin, if only temporarily. However, few people interviewed for this project took the path of extreme dieting to fit cultural ideals of slimness. Instead, people constructed a variety of routes to deal with weight for their weddings.

Explanations for the diversity of rather than consensus in dealing with weight for weddings include variations in wedding stress, partner's concern about weight, and self-efficacy for weight loss. Many people were concerned about weight but simply elected to not "do" weight loss for the wedding. Experience in passing through other life transition ceremonies for social functions (proms, etc.), religious events (church initiation ceremonies, etc.), and socioeconomic transitions (graduations, etc.) may diminish the significance of weddings. Alternative wedding forms make some weddings less important and less ceremonial, such as informal or less religious weddings that de-emphasize and give less priority to weight. Higher weights may be more acceptable for brides and grooms today than in the past, especially with the rising age at first marriage, the growing number of remarriages that contribute to more mature (and probably heavier) people in weddings, the influence of the size acceptance movement, and the increase in the prevalence of high body weights in the United States.

Wedding and weight issues warrant recognition as important social and cultural phenomena, deserving increased attention in the future. The prevalence and intensity of emphasis on weight before and at weddings have yet to be well understood. It is also not clear whether the consequences of taking various pathways in constructing weight at weddings are important for future weight careers after marriage.

ACKNOWLEDGMENTS

This analysis is part of a larger project examining the relationship between marriage and body weight supported by a grant from the

National Institutes of Health, titled "Marital Status, Marital Satisfaction, and Obesity." The authors thank Carol Devine and Donna Maurer for helpful comments.

REFERENCES

American Psychiatric Association. 1994. *Diagnostic and Statistical Manual of Mental Disorders*, 4th ed. Washington, DC: Author.

Anderson, J. L., C. B. Crawford, J. Nadeau, and T. Lindberg. 1992. "Was the Duchess of Windsor Right? A Cross-Cultural Review of Socioecology of Female Body Shape." *Ethnology and Sociobiology* 13:197–227.

Behr, M. 1998. *The Beautiful Bride*. New York: Perigree.

Blum, M., and L. F. Kaiser. 1997. *Weddings for Dummies*. Foster City, CA: IDG.

Brink, P. J. 1989. "The Fattening Room Among the Annang of Nigeria." *Medical Anthropology* 12:131–43.

——— . 1995. "Fertility and Fat: The Annang Fattening Room." Pp. 71–85 in *Social Aspects of Obesity*, edited by I. Guarine and N. J. Pollock. New York: Gordon and Breach.

Brown, P. J., and M. Konner. 1987. "An Anthropological Perspective on Obesity." *Annals of the New York Academy of Sciences* 499:29–46.

Brumberg, J. J. 1989. *Fasting Girls: The History of Anorexia Nervosa*. Cambridge, MA: Harvard University Press.

Charsley, S. R. 1991. *Rites of Marrying: The Wedding Industry in Scotland*. Manchester: Manchester University Press.

——— . 1992. *Wedding Cakes and Cultural History*. New York: Routledge.

——— . 1997. "Marriages, Weddings, and their Cakes." Pp. 50–70 in *Food, Health and Identity*, edited by P. Caplan. New York: Routledge.

Currie, D. H. 1993. "'Here Comes the Bride:' The Making of a 'Modern Traditional' Wedding in Western Culture." *Journal of Comparative Family Studies* 24(3): 403–21.

Edwards, W. 1989. *Modern Japan Through Its Weddings: Gender, Person, and Society in Ritual Portrayal*. Stanford, CA: Stanford University Press.

Foderary, L. W. 1997. "Prenuptial Contracts Find New Popularity." *New York Times*, 21 August.

Garner, D. M., P. E. Garfinkel, D. Schwartz, and M. Thompson. 1980. "Cultural Expectations of Thinness in Women." *Psychological Reports* 47:483–91.

Goffman, E. 1959. *The Presentation of Self in Everyday Life*. Garden City, NY: Doubleday.

——— . 1963. *Behavior in Public Places*. New York: Free Press.

Golden, F. 1997. "Who's to Blame for Redux and Fenfluramine?" *Time* 29, September, p. 79.

Goode, E. 1983. "The Fat Admirer." *Deviant Behavior* 4(2):175–202.

Goodkind, D. 1996. "State Agendas, Local Sentiments: Vietnamese Wedding Practices amidst Socialist Transformations." *Social Forces* 75(2):717–42.

Guarine, I. 1995. "Sociocultural Aspects of the Male Fattening Sessions among the Massa of Northern Cameroon." Pp. 45–70 in *Social Aspects of Obesity*, edited by I. Guarine and N. J. Pollock. New York: Gordon and Breach.

Guarine, I., and G. J. A. Koppert. 1991. "Guru-Fattening Sessions among the Massa." *Ecology of Food and Nutrition* 25:1–28.

Henderson, S. 1998. "Get Me to the Gym on Time: Brides Are Making Sure That What They Show Is Shapely." *New York Times* 1 March, Section 9, p. 1.

Hoek, H. W. 1993. "Review of the Epidemiological Studies of Eating Disorders." *International Review of Psychiatry* 5:61–74.

Holmes, T. H., and R. H. Rahe. 1967. "The Social Readjustment Rating Scale." *Journal of Psychosomatic Research* 11:213–18.

Ithaca Journal. 1998. "Average Wedding Tab Tops $19,000." 29 January, p. 7A.

Kendall, L. 1996. *Getting Married in Korea: Of Gender, Morality, and Modernity.* Berkeley: University of California Press.

Kresse, S. 1994. *Secrets of Successful Brides: Brides Share Their Wedding Wisdom and How They Did It.* New York: St. Martin's.

Lalli, C. G., and S. H. Dahl. 1997. *Modern Bride: Complete Wedding Planner.* New York: John Wiley and Sons.

Laz, C. 1998. "Act Your Age." *Sociological Forum* 13:85–113.

Lenderman, T. 1997. *The Complete Idiot's Guide to the Perfect Wedding,* 2nd edition. New York: Alpha.

Leonard, D. 1980. *Sex and Generation: A Study of Courtship and Weddings.* New York: Tavistock.

Lewis, C. W. 1994. *Working the Ritual: Wedding Photography as Social Process.* Unpublished Ph.D. dissertation, University of Minnesota, Minneapolis.

Mazur, A. 1993. "Signs of Status in Bridal Portraits." *Sociological Forum* 8(2):273–83.

McBride-Mellinger, M. 1993. *The Wedding Dress.* New York: Random House.

National Center for Health Statistics. 1994. *Annual Summary of Births, Marriages, Divorces, and Deaths: United States, 1993.* Monthly Vital Statistics Report, Volume 42, No. 13. Hyattsville, MD: Public Health Service.

O'Donoghue, D. 1997. "The Bridal Beauty Customer . . . Who Is She and What Does She Want to Know?" *Drug and Cosmetic Industry* 160(5):84–88.

Reed-Danahay, D. 1996. "Champagne and Chocolate: 'Taste' and Inversion in a French Wedding Ritual." *American Anthropologist* 98(4):750–61.

Ritenbaugh, C. 1982. "Obesity as a Culture-Bound Syndrome." *Culture, Medicine, and Psychiatry* 6:347–61.

Rodin, J., L. R. Silberstein, and R. H. Striegel-Moore. 1985. "Women and Weight: A Normative Discontent." Pp. 267–307 in *Nebraska Symposium on Motivation: Psychology and Gender,* edited by T. B. Sonderegger. Lincoln: University of Nebraska Press.

Schwartz, H. 1986. *Never Satisfied: A Cultural History of Diets, Fantasies, and Fat.* New York: Free Press.

Seid, R. P. 1989. *Never Too Thin: Why Women Are at War with Their Bodies.* Englewood Cliffs, NJ: Prentice Hall.

Serdula, M. K., D. F. Williamson, R. F. Anda, A. Levy, A. Heaton, and T. Byers. 1994. "Weight Control Practices in Adults: Results of a Multistate Telephone Survey." *American Journal of Public Health* 84:1821–24.

Seto, L. 1997. "Your Body: Upper-Arm Attack." *Bridal Guide* (May/June):40.

Slater, P. 1963. "On Social Regression." *American Sociological Review* 28(3):339–64.

Sobal, J. 1991. "Obesity and Nutritional Sociology: A Model for Coping with the Stigma of Obesity." *Clinical Sociology Review* 9:125–41.

————. 1998. "Cultural Comparison Research Designs in Food, Eating, and Nutrition." *Food Quality and Preference* 9(6):187–204.

————. 1999. "Sociological Analysis of the Stigmatisation of Obesity." Pp. 187–204 in *A Sociology of Food and Nutrition: Introducing the Social Appetite,* edited by J. Germov and L. Williams. Melbourne: Oxford University Press.

Spradley, J. P. 1979. *The Ethnographic Interview*. New York: Holt.

————. 1980. *Participant Observation*. New York: Holt.

Stearns, P. 1997. *Fat History: Bodies and Beauty in the Modern West*. New York: New York University Press.

Sullivan, J. 1997. *Size Wise: A Catalog of More Than 1000 Resources for Living with Confidence and Comfort at Any Size*. New York: Avon.

Talbot, D. A. 1968. *Woman's Mysteries of a Primitive People: The Ibibios of Southern Nigeria*. London: Frank Cass.

Thone, R. R. 1997. *Fat—A Fate Worse than Death? Women, Weight, and Appearance*. New York: Hawthorne.

U.S. Bureau of the Census. 1997. *Statistical Abstract of the United States: 1997,* 117th edition. Washington, DC: U.S. Government Printing Office.

Wallendorf, M., and M. Brucks. 1993. "Introspection in Consumer Research: Implementation and Implications." *Journal of Consumer Research* 20:339–59.

Weber, R. P. 1985. *Basic Content Analysis*. Newbury Park, CA: Sage.

West, C., and S. Fenstermacher. 1995. "Doing Difference." *Gender and Society* 9:8–37.

West, C., and D. H. Zimmerman. 1987. "Doing Gender." *Gender and Society* 1:125–51.

Whyte, M. K. 1990. *Dating, Mating, and Marriage*. Hawthorne, NY: Aldine de Gruyter.

Wiseman, C., J. J. Gray, J. E. Mosimann, and A. H. Ahrens. 1992. "Cultural Expectations of Thinness in Women: An Update." *International Journal of Eating Disorders* 11:85–89.

Wolf, N. 1991. *The Beauty Myth: How Images of Beauty Are Used Against Women*. New York: William Morrow.

Woodside, D. B., L. F. Shekter-Wolfson, J. S. Brandes, and J. B. Lackstrom. 1993. *Eating Disorders and Marriage: The Couple in Focus*. New York: Brunner/Mazel.

IV

ORGANIZATIONAL PROCESSES IN WEIGHT MANAGEMENT

8

Let Go and Let God

Religion and the Politics of Surrender in Overeaters Anonymous

REBECCA J. LESTER

In *Conversations with Anorexics,* Hilde Bruch (1988), one of the most respected experts on anorexia nervosa in American medical history, chides an emaciated patient for her "childish thinking and resistance" when the client expresses anxiety about her developing female body and the expectations tied to female sexuality. "Why not accept normal healthy womanhood?" Bruch challenges: "What do you really have to give up in order to get well?" (ibid.:121). The answers to these questions touch the very heart of the eating-disordered woman's struggle. What, indeed, must she "give up" to get "well"? What is this "normal healthy womanhood" that Bruch's client is so reluctant to accept? And what does this have to do with her relationship to food?

Notions of what constitutes mental "health" and "illness" are notoriously proficient vehicles for the communication of a society's values and moral dictates about what it means to be a "good" person in our culture—a good woman, a good man, a good African-American, a good heterosexual, a good wife or mother, a good citizen (cf. Bittner 1980; Broverman, Draguns, Phillips, and Caudill 1970; Busfield 1996; Caplan 1985; Chesler 1989; Chin-Shong 1968; Crocetti, Spiro, and Siassi 1974; Fink and Tasman 1992; Fleming and Manvell 1985; Foucault 1988a, 1988b, 1988c; Gamwell and Tomes 1995; Kirk and Kutchins 1992; Lerman 1996; Mezzich 1996; Pfohl 1978; Radden 1985; Seeman 1995). Our accepted understandings of "proper" mental and emotional states both reflect and legitimate a myriad of cultural features regarding relationships of power and dominance, affection and sexuality, altruism and self-promotion, and the like.

The moral dimension to perceptions of mental illness is particularly evident in the diagnosis and treatment of eating disorders, which, by their

139

very natures, tap into powerful cultural beliefs about consumption and self-restraint, passion and control, femininity and strength, and, of course, beauty and acceptance. In her ground-breaking work, Orbach (1978) argued that eating disorders arise out of women's struggles to make sense of conflicting notions of womanhood in our culture, which tell women we are "liberated" while at the same time communicating to us in a more covert way that, in order to be successful as women, we must conform to a strict model of physical beauty. Compulsive eating, Orbach argues, is symptomatic of this paradox and may be read as an act of rebellion against these controls. Wolf (1991) explored this in the context of myths of beauty, suggesting that images of female beauty (thinness) continue to dominate the cultural landscape, and have indeed become even more restrictive as women have made gains in the workplace and in the area of women's rights. Wolf theorizes that this is not coincidental, but rather articulates our culture's deep-seated anxieties over what it means for women to succeed in what has traditionally been a man's world. Eating disorders, she suggests, encapsulate this tension as it is experienced by individual women, who manifest their ambivalence about their success through the unyielding punishment of their bodies in the service of an elusive cultural ideal of feminine beauty. Bordo (1993) takes a more philosophical approach, linking these concerns to core Western cultural values that dichotomize the mind and the body, gendering the former as male and the latter as female. This leads, Bordo argues, to significant tensions for women, who are told that, to be valued by our society, they must deny their femaleness and strive for the ideal of disembodied (male) intellect. One very explicit response to this situation, says Bordo, is the development of anorexia nervosa, where a young woman attempts to literally "starve out" her female body in the pursuit of a self unencumbered by (feminine) physicality.[1]

Even those who don't accept the feminist-cultural interpretation of eating disorders generally agree that these illnesses rest on issues of gender, control, and power. The traditional psychoanalytic approach and its contemporary adaptations, for example, hold that eating disorders emerge from sexual conflicts and anxieties about moving from girlhood to womanhood (cf. Bruch 1973, 1978, 1988; Coles 1988; Levenkron 1981; Mogul 1989; Schneider 1995; Zerbe 1992, 1993). Others argue that eating disorders stem from faulty relationships with the mother (Chernin 1985) or the father (Maine 1991), both disturbing a young woman's sense of herself as "female." Those such as Brumberg (1989), who adopt a more historical-functionalist approach, suggest that food and eating may become the language of distress for individuals who are restricted in their domains of control to the domestic sphere.[2]

In other words, it seems that, regardless of theoretical position, experts in the field generally accept that eating disorders are overdetermined illnesses and are perhaps unusually rich in their embodiment (both literal and figurative) of the societal values and moral evaluations of fin-de-siècle America. Given this, we might expect that the accepted treatments of these illnesses likewise speak to key cultural values about what makes the anorexic, bulimic, or compulsive overeater "sick" and how best to make her "well."

In this chapter I will consider what has in the past two decades become perhaps the most popular, transformative—and morally charged—philosophy in eating disorders treatment since the advent of psychoanalysis: That of the "twelve steps" as articulated in the self-help program of Overeaters Anonymous (OA).[3] Here, I will examine OA as a technology of the self, a means of stylizing the self in a particular way. OA is, I suggest, a rather singular kind of self-program, in that it links the moral and cultural "hot points" of eating disorders (sex, power, control, morality, etc.) and the cultural/moral "hot points" of traditions of asceticism, control, discipline, and purity, which are foundational to American culture and pervade its institutions and cultural productions, and which have regained prominence in the late twentieth century. I will focus on how these issues are bundled in powerful ways in the OA program by focusing on the moral/religious substrata of the twelve-step philosophy as it relates to compulsive eating in OA and the function of this paradigm in constructing the "proper" OA subject. My key concern will be with drawing out the implications of this for understandings of OA's definitions of "healthy" versus "sick" selves as culturally loaded templates for ways of being. I will suggest that this has particular consequences for women struggling with eating disorders and the concerns of control, gender, power, and sexuality that accompany them, and that these consequences are yet to be fully recognized. A closer consideration of these issues speaks, I believe, to what may be the significant "costs" of recovery in this program.

This chapter is meant to be an exploratory foray into these issues—more of a work in progress rather than a report of ethnographic findings. The information presented here was gathered from extensive fieldwork in a nationally known eating disorders treatment center based on the OA philosophy, participation in dozens of OA meetings, extensive readings of the OA literature, and interviews with OA members.

WHAT IS OVEREATER'S ANONYMOUS?

Please don't let any uncomfortable feelings or negative impressions you may have scare you away. Most of us felt the same way in the beginning. And yet, we soon found that practicing the OA twelve-step program of recovery was doing for us what we had never been able to do for ourselves. In time, we learned a whole new way of living. (Overeaters Anonymous 1993a)

Each year millions[4] of women[5] walk through the doors of their first Overeaters Anonymous meeting, seeking salvation. OA is a nonprofit organization founded to help those who suffer from compulsive eating. Although originally geared toward those who overeat, OA now seeks to help anyone who uses food compulsively—to satisfy emotional rather than physical hunger. This includes anorexics and bulimics, as well as compulsive eaters.

Founded in January 1960, OA is modeled on the structure and philosophy of Alcoholics Anonymous. The OA literature describes the organization as "a fellowship of men and women who meet to share their experience, strength, and hope with one another in order that they may solve their common problem and help those who still suffer from compulsive eating" (Overeaters Anonymous 1992). But OA (and other such daughter organizations of AA) do not only target particular addictions. Viewing addictions such as compulsive eating as "threefold illnesses" (physical, emotional, and spiritual), the OA program offers, as one member put it, "a code for living." The program philosophy provides a holistic framework for living and experiencing one's life.

At the heart of this framework are the twelve steps. These guidelines, which outline the core beliefs and values of Alcoholics Anonymous, have been adopted by groups such as OA to address different addictions. In each case, the "drug of choice" is substituted for the word "alcohol" in the twelve steps and throughout the AA literature, to make the program applicable to anything from heroin to gambling to sex. OA is no exception:

> The OA recovery program is identical with that of Alcoholics Anonymous. We use AA's twelve steps and twelve traditions, changing only the words "alcoholic" and "alcohol" to "food" and "compulsive overeater." (Overeaters Anonymous 1980:2)

Indeed, the "drug of choice" and particular addiction are only mentioned in steps one and twelve—the other ten steps contain moral and spiritual guidelines, and do not refer to any particular addiction. These steps are:

1.   We admitted we were powerless over food—that our lives had become unmanageable.
2.   Came to believe that a Power greater than ourselves could restore us to sanity.
3.   Made a decision to turn our will and our lives over to the care of God *as we understood Him.*
4.   Made a searching and fearless moral inventory of ourselves.
5.   Admitted to God, to ourselves, and to another human being the exact nature of our wrongs.
6.   Were entirely ready to have God remove all these defects of character.

7. Humbly asked Him to remove our shortcomings.

8. Made a list of all persons we had harmed, and became willing to make amends to them all.

9. Made direct amends to such people wherever possible, except when to do so would injure them or others.

10. Continued to take personal inventory and when we were wrong, promptly admitted it.

11. Sought through prayer and meditation to improve our conscious contact with God *as we understood Him,* praying only for knowledge of His will for us and the power to carry that out.

12. Having had a spiritual awakening as the result of these steps, we tried to carry this message to compulsive eaters and to practice these principles in all our affairs. (Overeaters Anonymous 1980:4, emphasis in original)

As we can see, the steps principally articulate a number of moral and spiritual propositions targeting the self and, more particularly, the relationship between the self and God. It is this stylization of the self in a particular way—to effect a particular relationship with God—that is believed to produce recovery.

FOOD AND EATING AS SIGNALS OF ONE'S SPIRITUAL STATE

The twelve steps are concretized articulations of broader propositions that underlie the program philosophy. In OA, accounts of one's history with food are used to represent one's relationship with God, both before entering the OA program and after finding recovery. The compulsive eater's relationship with food (whether she is "in her disease" and eating out of control, or successfully practicing her "abstinence") is used to signal the nature of her relationship with God—whose "power" is foregrounded.[6] The basic propositions that guide this evaluation of one's relationship to food simultaneously gauge one's spiritual state, one's relationship with one's Higher Power, and consequently one's degree of "health" or "disease."

Perhaps the most basic proposition of OA is that compulsive eating is undesirable. This belief underlies the entire program philosophy. It is taken as a given that compulsive eating is bad, that it makes one miserable, and that one should do anything to alleviate the compulsion or to prevent its return. This proposition is perhaps most explicitly stated in step one of the program: "We admitted that we were powerless over food—that our lives had become unmanageable." Compulsive eaters must admit and accept that they are powerless over food—that their lives have become unmanageable in the grip of their disease. This theme is further explicated in the personal stories presented in the OA literature and at OA meetings. Almost all of these stories contain a description of the "craziness" of compulsive overeating, and the destruction it has caused in the sufferer's life. The only way to arrest the disease, OA maintains, is to admit one's powerlessness over it and turn one's life and will over to a Higher Power of one's own choosing—the second step. This higher power may be God, Nature, the twelve-step group itself, the "force," or anything larger than the individual that is the most comfortable and manageable for her or him. The surrender must be complete (cf. Alcoholics Anonymous [1939] 1976:71). The literature of OA explicitly relates these beliefs:

> We believe that no amount of willpower or self-determination could have saved us. Times without number, our resolutions and plans were shattered as we saw our individual resources fail. So we honestly admitted to ourselves that we were powerless over food. This was the first step toward recovery. It followed that, if we had no power of our own, we needed a power outside ourselves to help us recover . . . the more total our surrender, the more fully realized our freedom from food obsession. (1980:3)

Often, this surrender is preceded by a point of desperation, of "hitting bottom," when the illusions that previously masked the illness from the individual no longer hold shape. (This was an essential element in Puritan conversion as well.) In her work on Alcoholics Anonymous, Cain maintains that this process of surrender demands the acceptance of the notion that the disease is part of one's self, that "alcoholism [or an eating disorder] is not something one *has*, but rather, an alcoholic [or compulsive eater, gambler, etc.] is what one is" (1991:214). The acceptance of this new identity means that one must accept a new and different perspective of one's life and problems. But more than a change of identity, AA and its daughter programs (like Overeaters Anonymous) change how one experiences and interprets life events (see Lester 1991).

OA also holds that compulsive eating is a disease, like alcoholism, which is progressive and incurable. From the personal stories presented in the OA literature and recounted at meetings, it seems that this fact is one of the most difficult for newcomers to OA to accept. OA prescribes that much of the pain and anguish involved in compulsive overeating stems from the misunderstanding that the disease can be controlled through willpower. To recover, the compulsive eater must accept the fact that her compulsion is a disease, like alcoholism, that cannot be controlled by sheer force of personal will. Then she must be willing to turn her personal control over to a Higher Power ("God" in the OA literature), and ask for that Higher Power's help. To recover, she must come to accept that she is not only powerless to control her compulsion today, but that she will never be able to control it, because it is a disease—uncontrollable by human means.

She must therefore look outside herself for redemption. These concepts are explicitly set forth in the twelve steps (steps two and three), but also run throughout personal OA stories.

OA holds that, unlike illnesses such as cancer and pneumonia, compulsive eating is primarily an emotional and spiritual disease. The person who eats compulsively is in a state of denial and lacks self-awareness. The OA literature states that "the disease of compulsive eating causes or contributes to illness on three levels—emotional, physical, and spiritual," and that "the basis of the program is spiritual" (1980:2). Specifically, compulsive eating is viewed as a technique of denial—of denying one's feelings, emotional awareness, and spiritual awareness. As one member stated, "OA teaches you to think, when you're stuffing your face, what feelings are you stuffing?" Compulsive eating is viewed as an impediment to complete self-awareness and actualization; therefore the person who is eating compulsively is by definition in a state of denial and lacks self-awareness. This self-awareness can be gained only through rigorous self-honesty about one's life and faults, and an admission of these shortcomings in front of God and the OA community. Once the self is humbled in this way, "true" self-awareness can be attained. It is the compulsive eater's "false" sense of personal power that impedes the development of the spiritual relationship between her self and God that will transform her life.

For example, one OA member (with whom I did the most interviewing) often used food stories as a flag to me, signaling her lack of self-awareness at particular points in her life. She discussed her experiences as a nun over twenty years ago, and briefly discussed why she had decided to leave the convent. When I asked her how she adjusted to convent life when she entered the nunnery at age eighteen, she replied:

> I guess I was resistant because I gained a lot of weight—I gained about fifty pounds. So I was resistant, but I didn't know it. You see, I didn't know. . . . I was just busy conforming. But there was another part of me that was going "you gotta' be nuts". . . . Food was my drug of choice, which I didn't know. But that was a very difficult thing for me, because I felt like such a fat pig, such a weak person, that I couldn't control the food, and yet the food was something that I needed to survive. But see, at that point, Overeater's Anonymous I don't think even existed—and if it did I wouldn't have gone anyway. I didn't know then that I couldn't stop it.

We can see here the ways in which compulsive eating is used to signal issues of self-awareness (or, more specifically, the *lack* of it), and how the question of power is implicated in this configuration. It is particularly revealing that she explicitly referred to her compulsive eating as a form of *resistance*, an assertion of personal will against a power greater that the self. I will return to this in more detail below.

As a correlate to the above proposition, OA also holds that recovering from the disease of compulsive eating must progress from the inside out, rather than from the outside in. In other words, the real "recovery" is emotional and spiritual. The physical recovery—losing weight—is not a focus of the program, although it usually occurs as a result. Recovering from the inside out is often a difficult notion for newcomers to accept. As one OA member noted, we are conditioned to seek "quick fixes" such as Jenny Craig, Slim Fast, and Weight Watchers, so the idea that one should focus on feelings rather than on weight often seems quite alien and frightening to newcomers. But this inner healing is held to be the core of the twelve-step program, rendering it applicable to a number of different addictions.

At the heart of this inner recovery is a reevaluation of one's life, a "searching and fearless moral inventory," as step four states. Recovery is therefore predicated on a reexamination of one's life and a reinterpretation of these events in the context of recovery (for example, viewing a broken marriage in terms of one's lack of self-awareness—"it was a sick relationship, but I didn't see that at the time"). The self is humbled—humbled before the disease, before God, and before one's sponsor (or program mentor), to whom the moral inventory is read. The self is continuously scrutinized for faults, and these faults are self-consciously exposed at every turn. In this way one works to maintain the abdication or personal power to God, and does not give in to the temptation of reclaiming that power and risking relapse.

The OA program maintains that true recovery must be based on rigorous self-honesty, both with oneself and with others. OA holds that the majority of pain in our lives comes from the denial of our feelings, a lack of self-awareness, and a lack of honesty, with ourselves and others. This holds true in areas of one's life other than compulsive eating. As discussed above, eating compulsively is viewed as a technique of denial, of "stuffing one's feelings." Thus, rigorous self- honesty ideally removes the impetus for compulsive eating. This self-honesty often demands that any actions, desires, or thoughts that are out of line with the "program" be confessed to the OA group and/or to one's sponsor as soon as possible, so that these desires do not lead one into temptation and relapse. Humiliation keeps the self humble.

THANK YOU FOR SHARING: THE PATH TO RECOVERY

And, I don't know, I sat there, and I kept taking notes, you know, taking notes of everything—you know, people just don't do that in OA meetings—but, I mean, I was sitting there just trying to really judge it. And, actually, they kept hitting the nail on the head. When people were getting up, sharing their stories, it was my story. (OA member, personal communication)

In addition to these basic understandings of addiction, the very structure of twelve-step programs sets this approach apart from more clinically based treatments. Specifically, the twelve-step philosophy centers on the telling and retelling of personal stories, individual accounts of how sufferers fell to the depths of their addictions and then, with the help of the program, clawed their way back to sanity. The OA philosophy reinforces this tradition, basing its program on the telling and retelling—in front of others—of one's diseased relationship with food. Indeed, the basic text for OA, which newcomers are encouraged to buy as an introduction to the OA philosophy and the OA way of life, contains nothing but personal stories (and a brief introduction and conclusion)—thirty conversion narratives recounting the experience of being a compulsive eater, and the "miracle" of finding recovery through OA (Overeaters Anonymous 1980). As one member explained it to me, personal stories comprise "ninety-five percent of the program," and she stressed that "the people who share get the most recovery."

Twelve-step meetings are built on these stories of salvation. The groups have no "leaders"—no one is "in charge." At each meeting, a person is selected (or, more often, volunteers) to guide the meeting by "sharing" her or his personal story with the group. This "sharing" may last anywhere from five minutes to the whole hour. Although the person "sharing" usually presents her or his whole story, containing a number of predictable elements (which I will discuss below), emphasis may be placed variously at the teller's discretion (on relapse, success, family history, etc.).

The purpose of sharing one's personal story, as it was explained to me by OA members, is to force one to take a hard, honest look at one's life-in-disease, to humble oneself enough to confess these behaviors to a group of relative strangers, and to begin the slow and painful process of dismantling the sick self so that a healthy self—a self-in-recovery—can emerge. In this way the OA personal story becomes an important tool for the encoding of beliefs about how the self should be stylized. This is important because the telling of the personal story both changes the teller's view of her own life—she both reorders her past experiences according to a particular model and adopts a frame for interpreting new experiences—and provides an interpretive model for newcomers to the program (Cain 1991; Eastland 1995).

Although the particular details of each story differ, there is indeed an identifiable structure to the stories, and they encode a number of specific propositions regarding compulsive eating and the "proper" relationship of the self to God (Cain 1991). The most prominent themes include the period in life when compulsive eating began or became salient; use of food to soothe emotional pain; denial that the compulsive eating poses a problem; hitting a "low point," often characterized by some sort of "craziness" (stealing, hiding in the bathroom and eating, vomiting several times a day, etc.); discovery that OA exists; first meeting (often followed by a period of vacillation or resistance to the program); acceptance of the program and a feeling of "coming home"; and how life has been transformed since finding OA. Each of these propositions enfolds complex moral evaluations communicated through such powerful cultural symbols as excess, control, sin, and abstinence. The question of power is pivotal in each of these elements. As one comes to realize that one's life is "out of control," and then offers up the self—totally and completely—to a Higher Power, the compulsion is lifted and one's life is transformed.

These elements arise from the core understandings of OA—some made explicit in both the literature and in meetings, others more implicitly conveyed through personal story narratives. Although many deal specifically with food and eating, others do not, and instead provide a more general interpretive frame for understanding one's life, actions, and emotions. All of them enfold beliefs about the "proper" relationship between the self and God (i.e., that self-will should be joyfully submissive to the will of the Lord), and link this relationship of power directly to one's degree of recovery.[7] In this way, these personal stories work to link the propositions of OA directly to the daily business of living, and serve as testimonials to how "working the steps" can affect a change not only in outward behavior, but, more importantly, in one's internal state of mental, emotional, and spiritual "health."

But we must remember that this movement of the self from illness to recovery does not take place in a vacuum. Not just any transformation is believed to produce recovery; not just any self is judged to be healthy. Rather, a very specific kind of internal journey in a very specific direction is understood to be necessary for liberation from addiction. To understand the cultural dimensions and implications of this change, I believe it is helpful to consider Foucault's notion of technologies of the self.

TECHNOLOGIES OF THE SELF

In the third volume of *The History of Sexuality* Foucault (1988c) turns away from a concern with apparatuses of domination, which did their work on bodies, and toward operations that looked inward—operations we perform on ourselves (see Lester 1996). Specifically, a "technology of the self" is an art of existence, a theoretical project, an ensemble of meaningful practices worked on the body, which both constitute and transform the self. It is "the relation of the self with self and the forming of oneself as subject" (Probyn 1993:121). But more than merely a collection of practices, the self is an "attitude," a way of thinking, feeling, and relating to contemporary society. It is the conscious and deliberate shaping of the self according to a particular philosophy of living, and through a given set of culturally meaningful bodily practices.

Technologies of the self, then, are two-pronged operations bridging theory (the self being sought and the justification for this ideal) and practice (the specific behaviors selected to aid the transformation of self). But we must remember that this self-project does not take place in a void. Notions of what kinds of selves are desirable (and which are not) and of what certain practices communicate to others about our internal states are laden with cultural significances. Technologies of the self, then, rest on the association of the moral and the practical. Foucault argues that one of the most important and successful techniques for building this association is confession.

PENITENCE, CONFESSION, AND THE STYLIZATION OF THE SELF

Although Foucault's earlier writings took up the question of how Christianity (and, specifically, traditional Catholic practices) worked upon the bodies and desires of its "objects," he later became interested in how such beliefs and practices constituted its *subjects*—how religious tenets were internalized and integrated into the everyday *experience* of the faithful, and how they, indeed, shaped this experience.

Foucault has argued that Christianity "is not only a salvation religion, it's a 'confessional religion'" (1988b:40). This essence lies in the fact that Christianity contains a set of truth obligations that set it apart from other religious traditions. Each person has the duty of self-knowledge, self-examination, and self-disclosure: "to know what is happening inside him [*sic*], to acknowledge faults, to recognize temptations, to locate desires, and everyone is obliged to disclose these things either to God or to others in the community and hence bear public or private witness against oneself" (ibid.). The significance of this, Foucault proposes, is that the purification of the soul is inextricably linked to knowledge of the self.

How is this self-knowledge acquired? The key, according to Foucault, is confession. Foucault has proposed that confession is "one of the West's most highly valued techniques for producing truth" (ibid.:59). He characterizes confessional discourse as that in which "the speaking subject is also the subject of the statement," and which takes place in the presence of an authority who "requires the confession, prescribes it and appreciates it, and intervenes in order to judge, punish, forgive, console, and reconcile" (ibid.). Confessional discourse, he maintains, "produces intrinsic modifications in the person who articulated it; it exonerates, redeems, and purifies him; it unburdens him of his wrongs, liberates him, and promises him salvation" (ibid.:61–62). Confession serves not only to absolve the sinner of her sin, but allows her to discern the "truth" about her self and soul, while simultaneously affirming her faith. While this process was first put forth by Foucault as a technology of domination, he later explored it as a technology of the self—a transformation of subjectivity.

Perhaps the most important feature of confessional discourse, according to Foucault, is that his self-revelation is predicated on self-destruction (1988a:43). The old self must be effaced. Once the self is eradicated through the process of confession, one takes on the identity of "penitent"—a particular model of the self set forth by the Church, which centers on the characteristics of humility and submission to the will of the Lord. This process, Foucault maintains, is an incisive one—the penitent "superimposes the truth about self by violent rupture and dissociation" (ibid.).

Foucault further proposes that confession and confessional discourse have extended into all aspects of Western society, that "we have . . . become a singularly confessing society. . . . [O]ne confesses one's crimes, one's sins, one's thoughts and desires, one's illnesses and troubles; one goes about telling, with the greatest precision, whatever is the most difficult to tell" (1988b:59). In this way, confession serves as a means of altering the self, both socially (by publicly declaring one's sins) and experientially—the penitent comes to actually *experience* the events in her life in a different way, according to the tenets of the Faith. The process of confession is one that simultaneously liberates the sinner and shapes her subjective understanding of herself.

Technologies of the self, then, can be described as projects that unite moral and/or spiritual principles with concrete daily practices through which individuals may actively strive to reshape their interior lives. One of the most powerful practices that facilitates this process is that of engaging in confessional discourse.

"LET GO AND LET GOD": OA AS A TECHNOLOGY OF THE SELF

All of this experience, knowledge, and help is augmented by a source of wisdom inside us that becomes more powerful as we recover from compulsive eating and develop our relationship with our Higher Power through prayer and meditation. This inner resource is our intuition. When we place our will and our lives in God's care in step three, we give God our intuition as well. Intuition is supposed to be God's direct line into our minds and hearts, but our problems and our self-will have interfered in this connection. As we work the steps, the interference begins to be removed, and intuition begins to function properly, helping us focus on God's will, both for our eating and for the living of our lives. (Overeaters Anonymous 1993c:22)

Inexperienced in this way of living, many of us have asked, "How do I reach this decision to turn my will and life over to a Higher Power? What exactly do I have to do?" It helps to understand that once we make this decision, our approach to all choices will be like our approach to food and eating choices. We will no longer simply do what we feel like doing or what we think we can get away with. Instead, we will earnestly seek to learn God's will for us, than we will act accordingly. We give up fear and indecision, knowing that if we are sincere, our Higher Power will give us the knowledge of our best course in life, along with the willingness and ability to follow that course, even when it seems difficult and uncomfortable. (ibid.:24)

Can we guarantee you this recovery? The answer is simple. If you will honestly face the truth about yourself and the illness; if you will keep coming back to meetings and talk and listen to other recovering compulsive overeaters; if you will read our literature and that of Alcoholics Anonymous with an open mind; and, most important, if you are willing to rely on a power greater than yourself for direction in your life, and to take the twelve steps to the best of your ability, we believe you can indeed join the ranks of those who recover. (Overeaters Anonymous 1980:2)

It's an interesting program, interesting program. It's one of those things that probably everybody should do it. I mean, not just for the weight, but for whatever it is. It's a wonderful code for living. . . . It's definitely changed the way I've thought about my life. (OA member, personal communication)

Each element of Foucault's technologies of the self finds clear expression in OA. As noted above, the explicit goal of Overeaters Anonymous, and other such programs built on the twelve steps, is to help sufferers escape from the clutches of a debilitating addiction through a program of spiritual enlightenment. The self is stylized in a particular relation to God (or other Higher Power)—a relationship that turns on the recognition of individual powerlessness and the complete surrender of self-will to a power outside the self. It is the breaking of the false sense of self, and an absolute and unquestioning surrender of one's life and will to God, that effects the alleviation of the compulsion, and will bring other miracles into one's life.

But research indicates that the influence of the twelve-step philosophy on members of recovery groups reaches beyond merely helping one to overcome an addictive behavior. The twelve-step "truths" are often assimilated into one's personal belief system, affecting not only interpretations of past life events, but the experience of new ones as well (cf. Blumberg 1991; Bufe 1991; Cain 1991; Galanter 1990; Kaminer 1992; Maxwell 1984; Robertson 1988; Robinson 1979; Rudy 1986; Rieff 1991). In this way a new self—and new subjectivities—are formed.

The *confessional* nature of sharing one's personal story as the centerpiece of the OA program gains new significance when viewed within the context of Foucault's approach. I suggest that this "sharing" of the personal story represents a form of confessional discourse, through which knowledge, truth, and meaning are negotiated, and which becomes the model for presenting and interpreting one's life events.[8]

Indeed, the confessional nature of "sharing" was discussed explicitly by one of my research subjects. In one of our interviews, she described to me two important "tools of the program": the "food history" and the "moral inventory":

> You do a food history. Because most of us, again, are in denial about our food history. We walk in to OA and say, "Well, yeah, I have this fifteen pounds I want to lose," or "I have this fifty pounds." But, that's all. Instead, you do a written food history, which is quite extensive. The written food history has you absolutely think back, from the very first time you can remember food problems. And most of us have ended up with pages and pages of notes of things we totally forgot about. But when we start to analyze it, it's incredible how much food has had a place in our lives. How much food has influenced us, how much food has ruled our lives: Thinking about food, eating too much, undereating, overeating, diets, every weight program, other abuse we've gone through—the exercise programs. And when you get through with it, it hits you. You read it to a sponsor,[9] you read it to someone. Which blows your mind. Because, again, you don't think about this stuff. You don't think about it until you write it down, and, you know, get a very thorough history. But most people are shocked when they look at the history and you think, "the wasted years!"

> Then step four is when you do a searching and moral inventory of your life. When you look back and you've written things—this may take a couple of months to do—searching and fearless moral inventory of your life. A lot of people are resistant, because we don't want to look at the bad parts of us. But the only way you can look at the—you can grow, is if you get rid of the stuff that you have inside. So it's an inventory that you work on: resentments, jealousies, hatefulness, you know, your own faults. You work on all of this. And being a Catholic, I can—it's easy. You know, confession. And then step five is when you actually read all of this to someone, to your sponsor. You read the whole thing—it's like going to confession. A cleansing.

It is particularly interesting that the food history and moral inventory are written down by members—made to be concrete and discrete artifacts—which are then analyzed with the assistance of a "sponsor." In other words, members are required not only to look back over their lives and to reevaluate past events, but this reevaluation is also presented to a "superior," who reacts to the new member's assessments, facilitating the reinterpretation of life events in accordance with program philosophy.[10]

The essence of the OA program, then, is that it is a program for self-(re)making. That is, compulsive eating as a disease is understood to infuse every aspect of one's life, not just those that pertain directly to food. Likewise, recovery from compulsive eating is seen to require a massive transformation of one's way of living and being. As one OA member explained to me, OA is different from other food-focused diet programs because OA demands "recovery from the inside out, rather than from the outside in." The program is, in short, a rather sophisticated technology of the self that is engaged by individuals consciously striving to reform their sick selves into healthy ones.

But what, we might ask, is wrong with this? What is so bad about injecting a moral or spiritual dimension to recovery, if it seems to help people not only conquer their addictions, but go on to lead more fulfilling, more productive lives? I would argue that it is not the moral/spiritual focus of the program per se that may become problematic, but rather that philosophies that work as technologies of the self, by relying on emotionally charged cultural practices, often reference complex meaning systems, and can communicate and reinforce beliefs that may not be explicitly endorsed by the program. At times, these may be perfectly in line with the aims of the program, but they may also reference cultural traditions and representations that actually work counter to the program's aims. This is what I propose is the case with Overeaters Anonymous in the areas of gender and power, two key concerns for women dealing with eating disorders.

(DIS)EMBODIED WOMAN: OA'S SELF THEORY AS A TECHNOLOGY OF GENDER

We had to admit that we had not acted sanely when we responded to our children's needs for attention by yelling at them, or when we were jealously possessive of our mates. . . . When we were around other people, we smiled and agreed when we really wanted to say no. Some of us were unable to stand up for ourselves in abusive relationships; we felt we deserved the abuse. . . . In all of life, as well as with the food, we were irrational, unbalanced, insane. If our willpower and determination couldn't change our unsuccessful way of living, what could? Clearly, a Power greater than ourselves had to be found if we were to be restored to sanity. (Overeaters Anonymous 1993c:12)

Just for Today I will be agreeable. I will look as well as I can, dress becomingly, talk low, act courteously, criticize not one bit, not find fault with anything, and not try to improve or regulate anybody except myself. (Overeaters Anonymous 1993b)

Although Foucault does not explicitly address gender in his discussions of technologies of the self, several feminists have argued that these self-projects are almost always simultaneously technologies of gender, in that in targeting one's subjective experiences of one's self these projects almost always make use of gendered categories that then work (usually implicitly) to inscribe and reinforce gendered distinctions. Probyn, for example, proposes that theories of the self have traditionally been divorced from theories of gender, with extremely problematic results:

> As an object, the self has been variously claimed and normally left in a neutered "natural" state, the sex of which is a barely concealed masculine one. And until very recently, when selves got spoken they were also taken as a-gendered although of course they were distinctly male. (1993:2)

De Lauretis makes a similar point in her discussion of technologies of gender, noting that theories that propose to be "gender-blind" (in the sense that they are theories of the self that do not specify a particular gender) indeed function as technologies of gender, as they ignore the differential constitution of female versus male subjectivities:

> Hence the paradox that mars Foucault's theory, as it does other contemporary, radical, but male-centered theories: in order to combat the social technology that produces sexuality and sexual oppression, these theories (and their respective politics) will deny gender. But to deny gender, first of all, is to deny the social relations of gender that constitute and validate the sexual oppression of women; and second, to deny gender is to remain "in ideology," an ideology which (not coincidentally if, of course, not intentionally) is manifestly self-serving to the male-gendered subject. (1987:15)

In other words, theories of the self that claim to be gender-neutral are not—and cannot be so. This makes them particularly dangerous: Although they appear to counter traditional gender assumptions, they instead inadvertently reinscribe them in a more covert way.

This, I propose, is the case with Overeaters Anonymous. It is significant that, although there is "no gender" in the OA twelve-step philosophy, the program is engaged by distinctly gendered beings (mostly women), dealing with particular problems tied up with questions of gender and power. Indeed, the only gendered reference to be found in the OA program philosophy and literature is in the representation of God, who is portrayed as unequivocally male, and to whom members are encouraged to surrender their selves and their will if they *truly* want recovery.[11] By ignoring the gendered component to compulsive eating, OA is not erasing gender, but rather communicating gendered issues in implicit ways.

This could be very problematic for women with eating disorders, which emerge out of conflicts about gender and how it relates to power. Specifically, eating disorders in women (over 90 percent of those who develop them are female) are largely held to evolve from struggles about autonomy and identity, bound up with cultural values concerning womanhood, female sexuality, and the female body (Lester 1996). When OA talks about power but not gender, only half of this equation is highlighted, leading to default/implicit associations that build on the very cultural concerns that have lead many women to develop eating disorders in the first place. Given this, it seems that women with food issues might engage the ideas set forth in the twelve-step philosophy (especially those turning on questions of surrender, power, and control) differently than men with food issues or men or women with other addictions (such as alcohol or gambling).

This may be particularly true, given that issues of the body are also absent from the twelve-step framework, apart from representing the body as somehow "diseased." Eating disorders first and foremost center on concerns about the body—more so than other addictions such as alcoholism or drug addiction. Although these addictions certainly involve the body, the body—as an object of concern—is not highlighted in these addictions as it is for the eating-disordered woman, where it is, indeed, the focus of all attention and energy.[12]

In the process of "recovery" the OA subject is disembodied. She is told that her disease is spiritual and emotional, not physical. While it is indeed crucial to deflect the eating-disordered woman's focus from her body to the issues that fuel her obsession with food, weight, and thinness, OA does not address the connection between emotional and spiritual distress and concerns about the body. Indeed, the "underlying" causes of compulsive eating are seen to be the same as for alcoholism, drug addiction, sex addiction, and the like—that is, a faulty relationship between the self and God. The question of why some individuals seek refuge in alcohol or heroin, and others seek it in food, is not addressed. This leaves out an essential part of recovery, and ignores many of the key issues implicated for those who develop compulsive eating. It is a common understanding in the literature on eating disorders that the use of food by eating-disordered women reflects particular concerns about the embodied self—concerns that are inextricably bound up with issues of gender, sexuality, and the female body. These concerns are ignored in OA. As the transplantation of the notion of "abstinence" from Alcoholics Anonymous to Overeaters Anonymous highlights (can one *truly* be "abstinent" from food?) the focus of the program is a reformulation of the *self*, not the dynamics implicated in particular addictions. But like the omission of gender from self theories, the postulation of a *disembodied* self is enormously problematic—especially, I would argue, for those women for whom the embodied self is indeed at the core of their distress.

The idea that women develop eating disorders as techniques of resisting dominant gender proscriptions is prominent in the literature on these illnesses (cf. Chernin 1985; Faludi 1991; Lester 1994; Orbach 1978, 1982, 1986; Wolf 1991). It would seem, then, that the values contained in the OA program implicating issues of gender, power, surrender, and the body would carry different significance for women with eating disorders versus individuals with other addictions. Specifically, I propose that the omission of gender and the body from the OA program for self-stylization serves to *reinscribe* traditional gender values and configurations onto the eating-disordered woman, as she is slowly convinced that her *resistance* to this gendering (represented as false belief in personal power) is indeed what caused her eating disorder in the first place (remember Christina's description of her compulsive eating as "resistance"). The OA program has a particular effect on this configuration. It preaches that when the compulsive eater reconciles herself to her own powerlessness, her drive to eat compulsively will diminish. In other words, when the desire to resist is squelched, there will no longer be any need to use food as a tool of rebellion.

Interestingly, OA has developed a distinctly "religious" ritualistic nature, as opposed to the "spiritual" foundation of Alcoholics Anonymous.[13] Specifically, OA relies much more heavily than AA on the rituals imbedded in its meetings, the different shades and degrees of food "abstinence," "confession" of transgressions, and, most notably, elaborate food plans with lists of "allowable" and "forbidden" foods (including, for example, all sugar, white flour, caffeine, and any other "binge foods" a person might have). This religiosity and focus on ritual in OA indicate the incongruity between the program philosophy and the participants' needs. Two possibilities point in this direction. First, the incongruity may represent a response to the incompatibility of the twelve steps of AA with the particular psychological issues involved in eating disorders. The focus on ritual would seem to become an avenue for exerting the control that one must abdicate through the practice of the twelve steps, and that is the central concern for those who develop food addictions. Second, the religiosity of OA effects a transformation of compulsive eating behaviors into a new "acceptable" form. Although this gives the illusion of recovery, it could be argued that the structure of OA—and its emphasis on forfeiting control over one's self and one's life—indeed perpetuates the concerns that are basic to the illnesses it is supposed to treat.

In short, the issues involved in eating disorders are mobilized emotively in OA, but without explicit attention to their interaction. The complex of relations regarding issues of gender, power, and control—and the moral judgments attached to them—is left primarily latent in the program. This leads, I suggest, to default associations that conform to (gendered) cultural norms about what constitutes health and normality for women. When the focus of the program is on power over gender, gender is left to conform to notions of power.

CONCLUSION

Overeaters Anonymous is a highly successful and well-intentioned program that has helped millions of people find relief from a debilitating and life-destroying addiction. It offers an alternative to expensive inpatient treatment or long- term psychotherapy. It is available in practically every town and city in the country, the only cost being a willingness to search for recovery in the community of fellow and sister sufferers. It should not be surprising, then, that OA has long been touted as the most practical and effective approach for the recovery from eating disorders. But is it?

This chapter argues that the process of recovery in OA is much more complex—and perhaps more problematic—than it first appears. I have suggested that the program banks on powerful cultural notions and practices that are selected precisely because of their moral/emotional purchase on people. The goal of participating in the program is not just to stop eating compulsively, but to transform one's life, to leave a "sick" self behind for a "healthy" self—a self-in-recovery. This new self enfolds particular qualities that are understood to indicate health—not just (or even primarily) of the body, but of the mind and the soul.

Many sufferers of compulsive eating are (quite understandably) willing to do anything that seems to work, without much caring about the "how" of the process. And when one is in the throes of an addiction, stopping the destructive behavior is, indeed, generally considered to be a necessary first step in the process of recovery. But in the long run, if recovery is to become a new way of life rather than a temporary period of sobriety from addiction, it is the "how" of this process that really counts. In the case of OA, the core of recovery is constituted by a conscious and deliberate reshaping of the self according to a specific set of cultural and moral propositions. Given this, we must think about the "how" of OA and what it means for people in recovery. Specifically, we need to consider more carefully the costs of this recovery for women with eating disorders.

It is not the argument of this chapter that the perpetuation of harmful, gendered conceptualizations of health is the "underlying" or "secret" goal of OA. Rather, I believe it to be a problematic consequence of the adoption of religious values for the treatment of alcoholism, and then a transplantation of these proscriptions to the arena of compulsive eating. We should remember that the twelve steps were first developed by a man struggling with the "vice" of alcoholism. He turned to what he found to be the most effective, and then sought to share his success with others (see Stafford 1991). Indeed, the program of Overeaters Anonymous does seem to help many people overcome their desire to eat compulsively. But, as I have suggested, this particular path to recovery is fraught with difficulties, and the cost of such "recovery" for eating-disordered women remains unclear. Specifically, the problem arises with the abstraction of a theory of self-stylization, which ignores the issues of gender and the body implicitly contained within in it.

A reexamination of the twelve-step approach to the treatment of eating disorders is needed. While the twelve-step philosophy in general has come under recent criticism from some corners for its implicit inscription of race, gender, and class values (cf. Bepko 1991; Hafner 1992; Rapping 1996; Riessman 1990; Rosenqvist 1991; Roth 1990; Sandoz 1996a, 1996b; Tallen 1990), the specific problems such an approach may produce for eating-disordered women deserve special attention. Although there have been a few notable steps in this direction (see, particularly, Hackney 1996; Hopwood 1995; Suler and Barthelomew 1986), none of these studies builds on extensive, long-term fieldwork in the OA culture or intensive interviewing of members, and none significantly explores the interactions among spirituality, food addiction, and notions of morality in fin-de-siècle American culture. An in-depth investigation of the effects religious narratives of empowerment might have for some women struggling with eating disorders is urgently needed, as the twelve-step approach is widely held to be the most effective means of treating eating disorders today.

NOTES

1.   For more feminist interpretations of eating disorders, see Brown and Jasper (1993), Dolan and Gitzinger (1994), Fallon, Katzman, and Wooley (1994), Hesse-Biber (1996), and Manlowe (1995).

2.   See Lester (1996, 1998) for a more complete discussion of these approaches.

3.   For recent works on OA see Hackney (1996), Hopwood (1995), and Suler and Barthelomew (1986). For works dealing with various aspects of the recovery movement more generally, see Browne (1994), Chalfant (1992), DuPont and McGovern (1994), Humphreys (1994), Kaminer (1992), Makela (1992), Maton (1989), Mercadante (1996), Nealon-Woods, Ferrari, and Jason (1995), Nowinski and Baker (1992), Ragge (1991), Rapping (1996), Reinarman (1995), Riessman (1990), Saulnier (1996), Simpson (1995), Tallen (1990), Tessina (1991), Wexler (1994), and Wuthnow (1994).

4.   Because OA is a voluntary organization predicated on the principle of confidentiality of its members, it is difficult to know exactly how many people are involved in the program. What we do know is the there are daily OA meetings in almost every city and small town in the United States, as well as in twenty-four countries from Japan to Mexico to New Zealand (Overeaters Anonymous 1996). It would seem reasonable to estimate, then, that the number of OA members reaches well into the millions.

5.   Although many men do attend OA, the membership is overwhelmingly female.

6. When one is "in the disease," this means that one is falsely relying on self-will. It is this "false" sense of personal power that is seen to fuel the compulsive behavior and impede recovery.

7. These propositions are drawn from Alcoholics Anonymous with, again, minor adjustments in the replacement of "food" for "alcohol." For example, "abstinence" for the alcoholic means not touching alcohol in any form, not even in candy or medicine. Thus, an alcoholic *drinker* is viewed as out of control or insane, as he or she is playing with fire and courting relapse. "Abstinence" for the compulsive eater is slightly different: "We are not a 'diet and calories' club. We do not endorse any particular plan of eating. We practice abstinence by staying away from all eating between planned meals and from all individual binge foods. Once we become abstinent, the preoccupation with food diminishes and in many cases leaves us entirely. We then find that, to deal with our inner turmoil, we have to have a new way of thinking, of acting on life rather then reacting to it—in essence, and new way of living" (Overeaters Anonymous 1980:2–3).

Therefore, the compulsive eater who eats between meals or eats her/his binge foods is—like the alcoholic who drinks— out of control or insane and headed for disaster. Despite adjustments such as this appropriate to the addiction addressed (drugs, sex, gambling, etc.), the basic philosophy of AA provides the foundation for all twelve-step groups of this sort.

8. It is beyond the scope of this chapter to detail the mechanisms through which truth and knowledge are constructed in twelve-step meetings through the telling of the personal story. Cain (1991) discusses this, and I direct the reader to this work for further discussion of these issues. Here I am more concerned with the window these stories may give us on the values encoded in beliefs about "healthy" and "sick" selves.

9. A sponsor is an OA member, with at least one year of "abstinence," who serves as a program mentor for newcomers. The bond between a member and her sponsor is often intensely emotional, as it is to the sponsor, to whom the newcomer looks for guidance and support during the OA transformation process. Interestingly, the newcomer is often referred to as the "baby," whom the sponsor helps to "acquire a state of humility so necessary for the practice of the twelve steps" (Overeaters Anonymous 1993a).

10. This is an explicit example of the role of confessional discourse in the twelve-step programs, as it directly parallels Foucault's description of the confessional narrative. The similarities between this and the Puritan confessional journal (an "account book" of one's sins, which helps to keep the self humble before God) are particularly striking.

11. The implication, of course, being that if they are *resistant* to such surrender, they must not want to recover—that perhaps they are "masochistic types" who enjoy the pain, suffering, and distress their addiction brings.

12. It would seem that the body is likely to be a central concern for those dealing with sex addiction as well, although with a different configuration of concerns than is found in individuals with food addiction.

13. For recent works on the spiritual foundations and articulations of the twelve-step philosophy see Chalfant (1992), Manlowe (1995), McNeill (1995), Nealon-Woods et al. (1995), Olitzky and Copans (1991), Sandoz (1996a, 1996b),

Schaler (1996), and Spalding and Metz (1997). See also Wuthnow (1994) for a discussion of the spiritual aspects of the small-group movement more generally.

REFERENCES

Alcoholics Anonymous, Inc. [1939] 1976. *Alcoholics Anonymous: The Story of How Many Thousands of Men and Women Have Recovered from Alcoholism*, 3rd edition. New York: Alcoholics Anonymous World Services.
Bepko, C., ed. 1991. *Feminism and Addiction*. Binghamton, NY: Haworth.
Bittner, E. 1980. *Popular Interest in Psychiatric Remedies: A Study in Social Control*. New York: Arno.
Blumberg, L. U. 1991. *Beware the First Drink!: The Washington Temperance Movement and Alcoholics Anonymous*. Seattle, WA: Glen Abbey.
Bordo, S. 1993. *Unbearable Weight: Feminism, Western Culture, and the Body*. Berkeley: University of California Press.
Broverman, I., J. G. Draguns, L. Phillips, and W. Caudill. 1970. "Sex Role Stereotypes and Clinical Judgments of Mental Health." *Journal of Consulting and Clinical Psychology* 34(1):1–7.
Brown, C., and K. Jasper, eds. 1993. *Consuming Passions: Feminist Approaches to Weight Preoccupation and Eating Disorders*. Toronto: Second Story.
Browne, B. R. 1994. "Really Not God: Secularization and Pragmatism in Gamblers Anonymous." *Journal of Gambling Studies* 10(3):247–60.
Bruch, H. 1973. *Eating Disorders*. New York: Basic Books.
———. 1978. *The Golden Cage: The Enigma of Anorexia Nervosa*. New York: Vintage.
———. 1988. *Conversations with Anorexics*, edited by D. Czyzewski and M. A. Suhr. New York: Basic Books.
Brumberg, J. J. 1989. *Fasting Girls: The History of Anorexia Nervosa*. Cambridge, MA: Harvard University Press.
Bufe, C. 1991. *Alcoholics Anonymous: Cult or Cure?* San Francisco: See Sharp.
Busfield, J. 1996. *Men, Women, and Madness: Understanding Gender and Mental Disorder*. New York: New York University Press.
Cain, C. 1991. "Personal Stories: Identity Acquisition and Self-Understanding in Alcoholics Anonymous." *Ethos* 19(2):210–53.
Caplan, P. J. 1985. *The Myth of Women's Masochism*. New York: Dutton.
Chalfant, H. P. 1992. "Stepping to Redemption: Twelve Step Groups as Implicit Religion." *Free Inquiry in Creative Sociology* 20(2):115–20.
Chernin, K. 1985. *The Hungry Self: Women, Eating and Identity*. New York: Times Books.
Chesler, P. 1989. *Women and Madness*. San Diego: Harcourt Brace Jovanovich.
Chin-Shong, E. T. 1968. *Rejection of the Mentally Ill: A Comparison with the Findings of Ethnic Prejudice*. Unpublished Ph.D. thesis, Columbia University, New York.
Coles, P. 1988. "Aspects of Perversion in Anorexic/Bulimic Disorders." *Psychoanalytic Psychotherapy* 3(2):137–47.
Crocetti, G. M., H. R. Spiro, and I. Siassi. 1974. *Contemporary Attitudes Toward Mental Illness*. Pittsburgh: University of Pittsburgh Press.
de Lauretis, T. 1987. *Technologies of Gender: Essays on Theory, Film and Fiction*. Bloomington: Indiana University Press.

Dolan, B., and I. Gitzinger. 1994. *Why Women? Gender Issues and Eating Disorders.* Atlantic Highlands, NJ: Athlone.

DuPont, R. L., and McGovern, J. P. 1994. *A Bridge to Recovery: An Introduction to 12-Step Programs.* Washington, DC: American Psychiatric Press.

Eastland, L. S. 1995. "Recovery as an Interactive Process: Explanation and Empowerment in 12-Step Programs." *Qualitative Health Research* 5(3):292–314.

Fallon, P., M. A. Katzman, and S. C. Wooley, eds. 1994. *Feminist Perspectives on Eating Disorders.* New York: Guilford.

Faludi, S. 1991. *Backlash: The Undeclared War Against American Women.* New York: Doubleday.

Fink, P. J., and A. Tasman, eds. 1992. *Stigma and Mental Illness.* Washington, DC: American Psychiatric Press.

Fleming, M., and R. Manvell. 1985. *Images of Madness: The Portrayal of Insanity in the Feature Film.* Rutherford, NJ: Fairleigh Dickinson University Press.

Foucault, M. 1988a. *Madness and Civilization: A History of Insanity in the Age of Reason,* translated by R. Howard. New York: Vintage.

———. 1988b. "Technologies of the Self." Pp. 16–49 in *Technologies of the Self,* edited by L. H. Martin, H. Gutman, and P. H. Hutton. Amherst: University of Massachusetts Press.

———. 1988c. *The History of Sexuality,* vol. 3, translated by R. Hurley. New York: Vintage.

Galanter, M. 1990. "Cults and Zealous Self-Help Movements: A Psychiatric Perspective." *American Journal of Psychiatry* 147(5):543–51.

Gamwell, L., and N. Tomes. 1995. *Madness in America: Cultural and Medical Perceptions of Mental Illness Before 1914.* Ithaca, NY: Cornell University Press.

Hackney, J. K. 1996. "Stairway to Heaven: Religious Expressions in an Overeaters Anonymous Group." Paper presented at the annual meetings of the American Sociological Association.

Hafner, S. 1992. *Nice Girls Don't Drink: Stories of Recovery.* New York: Bergin & Garvey.

Hesse-Biber, S. J. 1996. *Am I Thin Enough Yet? The Cult of Thinness and the Commercialization of Identity.* New York: Oxford University Press.

Hopwood, C. 1995. "My Discourse/My-Self: Therapy as Possibility (for Women Who Eat Compulsively)." *Feminist Review* 49: 66–82.

Humphreys, K. 1994. "Are Twelve Step Programs Appropriate for Disenfranchised Groups? Evidence from a Study of Post-treatment Mutual Help Involvement." *Prevention in Human Services* 11(1):165–79.

Kaminer, W. 1992. *I'm Dysfunctional, You're Dysfunctional: The Recovery Movement and Other Self-Help Fashions.* Reading, MA: Addison-Wesley.

Kirk, S. A., and H. Kutchins. 1992. *The Selling of DSM: The Rhetoric of Science in Psychiatry.* Hawthorne, NY: Aldine de Gruyter.

Lerman, H. 1996. *Pigeonholing Women's Misery: A History and Critical Analysis of the Psychodiagnosis of Women in the Twentieth Century.* New York: Basic Books.

Lester, R. J. 1991. "Confessional Discourse and the Personal Story: The Twelve-Step Framework and the Shaping of Life History Narratives." Unpublished paper, University of California, San Diego.

———. 1994. "Embodied Voices: Women's Food Asceticism and the Negotiation of Identity." *Ethos* 23(2):187–222.

———. 1996. "The (Dis)Embodied Self in Anorexia Nervosa." *Social Science and Medicine* 44(4):479–89.

———. 1998. "Like a Natural Woman: Celibacy and the Embodied Self in Anorexia Nervosa." In *Not Tonight: Anthropological Approaches to Sexual Celibacy*, edited by E. J. Sobo and S. Bell. Madison: University of Wisconsin Press (in press).

Levenkron, S. 1981. *The Best Little Girl in the World*. New York: Warner.

Maine, M. 1991. *Father Hunger: Fathers, Daughters and Food*. Carlsbad, CA: Gurze.

Makela, K. 1992. "Professional Twelve-Step Treatment and AA as a Social Movement." *Nordisk Alkohol Tidskrift* 9(4):185–97.

Manlowe, J. 1995. *Faith Born of Seduction: Sexual Trauma, Body Image, and Religion*. New York: New York University Press.

Maton, K. I. 1989. "Towards an Ecological Understanding of Mutual-help Groups: The Social Ecology of 'Fit.'" *American Journal of Community Psychology* 17(6):729–53.

Maxwell, M. A. 1984. *The Alcoholics Anonymous Experience: A Close-up View for Professionals*. New York: McGraw- Hill.

McNeill, J. J. 1995. *Freedom, Glorious Freedom: The Spiritual Journey to the Fullness of Life for Gays, Lesbians, and Everybody Else*. Boston: Beacon.

Mercadante, L. A. 1996. *Victims and Sinners: Spiritual Roots of Addiction and Recovery*. Louisville, KY: Westminster John Knox.

Mezzich, J. E., ed. 1996. *Culture and Psychiatric Diagnosis: A DSM-IV Perspective*. Washington, DC: American Psychiatric Press.

Mogul, S. L. 1989. "Sexuality, Pregnancy, and Parenting in Anorexia Nervosa." *Journal of the American Academy of Psychoanalysis* 17(1):65–88.

Nealon-Woods, M. A., J. R. Ferrari, and L. A. Jason. 1995. "Twelve-Step Program Use among Oxford House Residents: Spirituality or Social Support in Sobriety?" *Journal of Substance Abuse* 7(3):311–18.

Nowinski, J., and S. Baker. 1992. *The Twelve-step Facilitation Handbook: A Systematic Approach to Early Recovery from Alcoholism and Addiction*. New York: Lexington.

Olitzky, K. M., and S. A. Copans. 1991. *Twelve Jewish Steps to Recovery: A Personal Guide to Turning from Alcoholism and Other Addictions*. Woodstock, VT: Jewish Lights.

Orbach, S. 1978. *Fat Is a Feminist Issue*. New York: Berkeley.

———. 1982. *Fat Is a Feminist Issue II*. New York: Berkeley.

———. 1986. *Hunger Strike*. New York: W. W. Norton.

Overeaters Anonymous, Inc. 1980. *Overeaters Anonymous*. Torrance, CA: Author.

———. 1992. "A Program of Recovery." A pamphlet distributed by Overeaters Anonymous, Torrance, CA.

———. 1993a. "A Commitment to Abstinence." A pamphlet distributed by Overeaters Anonymous, Torrance, CA.

———. 1993b. "Just for Today." A pamphlet distributed by Overeaters Anonymous, Torrance, CA.

———. 1993c. *The Twelve Steps and Twelve Traditions of Overeaters Anonymous*. Torrance, CA: Author.

———. 1996. Overeaters Anonymous homepage, http://www.overeaters/org/www/home/htm.

Pfohl, S. J. 1978. *Predicting Dangerousness: The Social Construction of Psychiatric Reality*. Lexington, MA: Lexington.

Probyn, E. 1993. *Sexing the Self: Gendered Positions in Cultural Studies*. New York: Routledge.

Radden, J. 1985. *Madness and Reason*. Boston: Allen & Unwin.

Ragge, K. 1991. *More Revealed: A Critical Analysis of Alcoholics Anonymous and the Twelve Steps*. Henderson, NV: Alert.

Rapping, E. 1996. *The Culture of Recovery: Making Sense of the Self-Help Movement in Women's Lives*. Boston, MA: Beacon.

Reinarman, C. 1995. "The Twelve-Step Movement and Advanced Capitalist Culture: The Politics of Self-Control in Postmodernity." Pp. 90–109 in *Cultural Politics and Social Movements*, edited by M. Darnovsky, B. Epstein, and R. Flacks. Philadelphia: Temple University Press.

Rieff, D. 1991. "Victims All? Recovery, Co-dependency, and the Art of Blaming Somebody Else." *Harper's Magazine* 283(1697):49–56.

Riessman, F. 1990. "The New Self-Help Backlash." *Social Policy* 21(1):42–48.

Robertson, N. 1988. *Getting Better: Inside Alcoholics Anonymous*. New York: Morrow.

Robinson, D. 1979. *Talking Out of Alcoholism: The Self-Help Process of Alcoholics Anonymous*. Baltimore, MD: University Park.

Rosenqvist, P. 1991. "AA, Al-Anon and Gender." *Contemporary Drug Problems* 18(4):687–705.

Roth, P., ed. 1990. *Alcohol and Drugs Are Women's Issues*. Metuchen, NJ: Women's Action Alliance and Scarecrow Press.

Rudy, D. R. 1986. *Becoming an Alcoholic: Alcoholics Anonymous and the Reality of Alcoholism*. Carbondale: Southern Illinois University Press.

Sandoz, C. J. 1996a. "The Effect of Spiritual Experience on the AA Promises, Locus of Control and Family Dynamics in Recovery within Alcoholics Anonymous." *Journal of Ministry in Addiction and Recovery* 3(2):79–90.

———. 1996b. "The Interaction Effects of Gender with Recovering ACOA Alcoholics and Non-ACOA Alcoholics." *Alcoholism Treatment Quarterly* 14(2): 67–77.

Saulnier, C. F. 1996. "Images of the Twelve-Step Model, and Sex and Love Addiction in an Alcohol Intervention Group for Black Women." *Journal of Drug Issues* 26(1):95–123.

Schaler, J. A. 1996. "Spiritual Thinking in Addiction-Treatment Providers: The Spiritual Belief Scale (SBS)." *Alcoholism Treatment Quarterly* 14(3):7–33.

Schneider, J. A. 1995. "Eating Disorders, Addictions, and Unconscious Fantasy." *Bulletin of the Menninger Clinic* 59(2):177–90.

Seeman, M. V. 1995. *Gender and Psychopathology*. Washington, DC: American Psychiatric Press.

Simpson, M. D. 1995. *Surrender, Conversion and Empowerment in Alcoholics Anonymous*. Unpublished thesis, San Francisco Theological Seminary.

Spalding, A. D., and G. J. Metz. 1997. "Spirituality and Quality of Life in Alcoholics Anonymous." *Alcoholism Treatment Quarterly* 15(1):1–14.

Stafford, T. 1991. "The Hidden Gospel of the 12 Steps." *Christianity Today* 35(8):14–19.

Suler, J., and E. Barthelomew. 1986. "The Ideology of Overeaters Anonymous."
    Social Policy 16(4):48–53.
Tallen, B. S. 1990. "Twelve Step Programs: A Lesbian Feminist Critique." *NWSA*
    Journal 2(3):390–407.
Tessina, T. B. 1991. *The Real Thirteenth Step: Discovering Confidence, Self-reliance, and*
    Autonomy Beyond the 12-step Programs. New York: St. Martin's.
Wexler, P. 1994. "From Sociology to Individual Practice and Cultural Renewal."
    Kasvatus 25(4):354–63.
Wolf, N. 1991. *The Beauty Myth: How Images of Beauty Are Used Against Women.* New
    York: William Morrow.
Wuthnow, R. 1994. *Sharing the Journey: Support Groups and America's New Quest for*
    Community. New York: Free Press.
Zerbe, K. J. 1992. "Why Eating-Disordered Patients Resist Sex Therapy: A
    Response to Simpson and Ramberg." *Journal of Sex and Marital Therapy*
    18(1):55–64.
——— . 1993. "Whose Body Is It Anyway? Understanding and Treating the Psy-
    chosomatic Aspects of Eating Disorders." *Bulletin of the Menninger Clinic*
    57:191–97.

9

Fat World/Thin World

"Fat Busters," "Equivocators," "Fat Boosters," and the Social Construction of Obesity

KAREN HONEYCUTT

Do I feel more attractive [since losing weight]? God, yes. I look at myself in the mirror more—I catch myself glancing into one every time I pass it. And I used to avoid looking into big plate-glass windows in the past, because I didn't like my reflection, or was too scared to see what I really looked like. I don't mind seeing myself any more. (Jessica)

I went to Jenny Craig for several months. When I first started, I went to one of their group meetings, and the counselor asked if anyone had gone off the program that week. I looked around and no one was raising their hands, but I decided to be honest and raise mine. So I did and everyone turned and stared at me and started saying, "Was it worth it? Was it worth it?" They were all so mad at me for going off. But I know there were other women there who had too. I was just the only one brave enough to admit it. But I never did again. [laughs] (Laura)

Fat bodies are beautiful. I think all of you are just gorgeous. I saw you out in the pool yesterday, and the fat was billowing out around you, and I thought it was just wonderful. You've made me believe that I'm beautiful too. (Leslie)

While Jessica, Laura, and Leslie were or are all considered "over-weight"[1] by American standards, they dealt with this "problem" very differently. Jessica dieted and lost sixty-three pounds (she is a "Fat Buster," in the terms I am using in this chapter). Laura decided to try to stop dieting altogether and accept herself as she was, but did so on her own (she is an "Equivocator"). Leslie joined a national fat activist organization (and thus she is a "Fat Booster" in my classification scheme).

The experiences and outlooks of these three women seem to be three different responses to the same "master narrative" about weight in the United States. In this chapter I argue that the "alternative realities" that the women appear to be constructing for themselves are, in many ways, simply different surface-level responses to the same dominant notions of attractiveness.

THEORETICAL FRAMEWORK

Throughout this chapter I blend social constructionist theory, an interactionist perspective, and a cultural studies approach with an emphasis on ideology and audience reception.

Social Constructionist Theory

Is "obesity," presumably objectively defined, a problem in and of itself? A social constructionist perspective would argue that it is more fruitful and interesting to look at the *process* by which obesity has become regarded as a problem (Spector and Kitsuse 1977). In this chapter I do not begin with the assumption that obesity, or being fat, is a problem; rather, consistent with a social constructionist approach, I briefly examine the literature on obesity that demonstrates how it has been *defined* as such, and then I look at how different groups of women have responded to the definition and the process by which their positions are socially reinforced.

Interactionist Perspective

In this chapter I use a modified framework of symbolic interactionism. As enumerated by Ritzer (1992:348), a symbolic interactionist approach emphasizes that human thought is shaped by social interaction, that interaction is made possible by the meanings and symbols that people develop, and that people may change those meanings and symbols. Meanings are critically important to interactionists; as Herbert Blumer wrote, "The nature of an object . . . consists of the meaning that it has for the person for whom it is an object" (1969:11).

Two of the three groups of women that I studied participate in official organizations that reinforce the women's position (e.g., losing weight as being good or bad). In this chapter I show that for the women in those organizations, the meanings created as part of their membership were critical in their construction of fatness as a problem (or not a problem).

Cultural Studies Approach with an Emphasis on
Ideology and Audience Reception

Since I am interested in looking at weight—and especially the definition of *over*weight—as a cultural phenomenon, a cultural studies approach is fruitful. Douglas Kellner (1995:8–9) suggests a three-pronged approach to critical cultural studies: an analysis of the political economy of the production of culture; an analysis of texts, including the importance of ideology (hegemony theory); and an analysis of audience reception of those texts. For example, a cultural studies approach that focuses on political economy would emphasize that to understand a cultural product or outcome—like women's responses to certain constructions of beauty—it is necessary to understand the socioeconomic context in which it is created. Naomi Wolf's (1991:17) work on the diet industry would be included in this category. On the other hand, those writers who focus on ideology— "the terrain of ideas so centrally constitutive of our worldview that we fail to notice what they are" (Press 1991:15)—tend to conduct analyses of particular texts, showing how those texts contribute to (or less often, go against) the dominant ideology. These studies often use Antonio Gramsci's (1971) notion of hegemony theory, which explains how and why dominated people consent to rule by a few even when such rule is demonstrably against their own interests; in short, he focused on ideology (as opposed, for example, to coercion) to explain this consent. Jean Kilbourne's (1994) analysis of advertising falls into this category. Finally, theorists who look at audience reception argue that not all groups respond to dominant ideologies in the same way; for example, some groups attempt to construct counterhegemonic notions of fatness. Marcia Millman's (1980) study of fat people falls in this category.

Of course, these three approaches can be combined. In this chapter I begin with the contention that almost all the research and popular literature on obesity demonstrates an "ideology in action," and clearly the ideology in this case is that women can never be quite thin enough. Several authors (e.g., Chapkis 1986; Hesse-Biber 1996; Orbach 1978) have argued that the intense focus on thinness, particularly *women's* thinness, is extremely damaging to women. I examine why women in three different groups appear to react so differently to the same societal "messages"; in other words, why some women seem to "buy into" hegemonic notions of attractiveness more than others. Specifically, I analyze how many women construct their body size as problematic (or not) within a culture that has very narrowly defined boundaries of acceptance. Most interesting as a test of hegemony theory are those women for whom hegemonic notions appear to *fail*.

METHODS

Most of the data for this chapter come from in-depth qualitative interviews conducted between 1992 and 1998 with women in three groups: forty-six in the weight-loss group (the Fat Busters), nineteen in the nondieting, nonactivist group (the Equivocators), and twenty-one in the nondieting, activist group (the Fat Boosters). The interview data are supplemented by participant-observation at weight-loss meetings and fat-activist functions. Further, when appropriate I discuss documents the groups use to bolster their arguments.

THE MASTER NARRATIVE AND THREE RESPONSES

Study after study confirms that the "master narrative" about weight in the United States is overwhelmingly negative. The literature certainly shows a revulsion toward obesity and obese people that appears to run very deep. For example, English (1991) asserted that fat people are subjected to a unique and more intense form of stigmatization than other deviant groups because of the highly visible obese condition and the societal tendency to attribute personal responsibility to fat people for their condition. Garner and Wooley noted that the social stigma against the obese "is extraordinary in its magnitude and pervasiveness" (1991:729). Other studies have consistently found that overweight and obese individuals are considered unattractive, unpleasant, sexless, lazy, and poor workers (e.g., Clayson and Klassen 1989; Harris, Walters, and Waschull 1991; Hiller 1981, 1982; Rothblum, Miller, and Garbutt 1988). Studies have also found that even women who are not "overweight" by medical standards still consider themselves so and are obsessed with losing weight (e.g., Hesse-Biber 1991; Ogaitis, Chen, and Steelman 1988; Wadden, Stunkard, and Liebschutz 1988).

Given that the master narrative is so negative, how do women respond? This was the question I began with when I interviewed women in three different groups (see Table 9.1): those who dieted and lost weight (the Fat Busters); those who, while they were considered overweight, said they were "trying to accept themselves as they were" but were doing so on their own (the Equivocators); and those who joined a national fat activist organization, NAAFA, the National Association to Advance Fat Acceptance (the Fat Boosters).

This typology describes the three groups of women in terms of whether or not they accept the mainstream societal definition of beauty as being possible (i.e., whether or not they believe they *can* be thin) and whether or not they seem to take a "passive" or "active" stand. It highlights the

Table 9.1. Typology of Reactions of Overweight Women to Societal Discourse

	Passive	Active
Accept societal definition of beauty as being possible	Feel bad about oneself: "Thin is beautiful; I'm not working hard enough to lose weight; I have no will power; I am a failure; I am ugly" (nondieting, nonactivist group: the Equivocators)	Diet, lose weight: "Thin is beautiful and I can make myself thin" (weight-loss group: Fat Busters)
Reject societal definition of beauty as being possible	Feel bad about oneself: "I can't be thin, but how can I be happy with myself when everyone and everything around me tells me I'm ugly?" (nondieting, nonactivist group: the Equivocators)	Refuse to diet: "Fat is just a word; fat is not ugly" (nondieting, activist group: Fat Boosters)

importance of social interaction for taking an active stand; I will discuss this more later in this chapter.

The Equivocators are passive because, while they are unhappy about being fat, their most common *reaction* was simply to feel bad about themselves because of it. They were not currently dieting (so they were not actively trying to lose weight, which presumably would have made them feel better), nor did they join an organization like NAAFA that would have given them social support in their decision not to diet. Therefore, their decision was, by my terms, more passive than that of those in the weight-loss and fat-activist groups.

The Equivocators also were unusual in that they expressed both belief and disbelief that meeting a societal construction of beauty—that is, losing weight and becoming thin—was even possible. While the Fat Busters overwhelmingly believed that becoming thin *was* possible—after all, they had done it themselves—and the Fat Boosters overwhelmingly expressed a belief that becoming thin was *not* possible, usually because their own dieting experiences had (they argued) ultimately made them even fatter, the Equivocators were ambivalent. Some women in this category stated sadly that while they could *lose* weight, they could never keep it off; thus they seemed to believe what Fat Boosters believed. Other Equivocators expressed the belief that since they had lost weight in the past, they could again if only they tried harder—that is, they sounded very much like Fat Busters—but they were not up to dieting at this time. Interestingly, many

Equivocators expressed *both* sentiments; that is, at times during the interview they would speak wistfully of thin women but argue that thinness did not seem to be a realistic goal for themselves, while later in the interview they would admit that they had not given up entirely on being thin, they just weren't ready to diet *right now*. This ambivalence should not be surprising given the Equivocators' lack of social support. In comparison to Equivocators, some of the Fat Boosters may have been larger, but their group's antidiet stand sustained them in their decision not to change their body size.

Weight-Loss Group: Fat Busters

Between 1992 and 1997 I conducted interviews with forty-six women whom I call "Fat Busters." Thirty-two were white, while fourteen were women of color, mostly African-American. They ranged in age from nineteen to sixty-one. These women had lost from thirty to eighty pounds, mostly through conventional methods such as calorie-cutting and increasing exercise on one's own or through commercial programs like Jenny Craig, Nutri-System, or Weight Watchers. At the time of the interview they had kept the weight off for anywhere from six months to several years.

Before being interviewed, Fat Busters completed a four-page survey to elicit information about three areas. First was how their feelings about various things had changed (if at all) since they lost weight (e.g., "Since I lost weight . . . men pay more attention to me," " . . . I am more attractive," " . . . I pay more attention to my appearance"). Second was how they felt about their own attractiveness both before and after losing weight (e.g., "I used to secretly wonder what my significant other saw in me because I was heavy," "In the past, I have avoided going to reunions or to visit old friends because I was embarrassed about my weight"). Third was how they felt about other overweight people once they were thin (e.g., "I look at overweight people now and feel sorry for them," "If I can lose weight, anyone can," "Our society puts too much emphasis on weight"). The survey included both closed-ended items such as those just described, which were rated on a five-point Likert scale of "strongly disagree" to "strongly agree," and open-ended questions that asked respondents to discuss their weight-loss experience in more detail. In addition to data from the interviews and surveys, this section includes some discussion of weight-loss literature (e.g., handouts from weight loss group meetings) and weight-loss meetings.

Several themes emerged from my interviews with Fat Busters. First, when they were fat, these women were acutely aware of themselves as *being* fat. During the interviews, I asked when the women felt their "fatness" most strongly. While some were able to pinpoint times when they felt particularly aware of being overweight (and particularly vulnerable to being *noticed by* others as being overweight)—times such as walking down the street eating an ice cream cone, or waiting to buy high-calorie foods in the checkout line at the supermarket—for many women awareness of their overweight status seemed to be constant. Mindy and Carol were typical in this respect:

> It's hard to pinpoint times when I felt it more. I mean, it was just always *there*. I was always aware, no matter what I was doing, that I was really heavy. (Mindy)

> When was I aware of myself as being overweight? [laughs] When was I *not*? Even if I wasn't doing something connected with my weight, like even if I wasn't on a diet or trying on clothes, I was still always very conscious of being this humongous person. (Carol)

A second theme was a strong belief in their own power to control their weight—and, by extension, a strong belief in *others'* power to control *their* weight. Many Fat Busters voiced some disapproval of other people—usually women—who were overweight. The vast majority indicated either agreement or strong agreement with the statement on the survey, "If I can lose weight, anyone can." While medical research indicates a strong genetic component to obesity, those studies are not consistent with the recent weight loss experiences of the women in my study. That is, the women I interviewed seemed to be "success stories" that the medical studies imply are rarities. Thus, relying on their own recent experiences, many tended to judge others rather harshly:

> It's not easy [to lose weight], I'm not saying that. I'm just saying that even if there *is* some genetic factors involved, you can overcome them. *I* did. Just eat less and exercise more. (Mindy)

> I think there may be some genetic component to obesity. But all I'm saying is that if anyone did what I did, they would lose weight too. It was hard, but I did it. (Dana)

This belief in their own control was also constantly socially reinforced through interactions with others at meetings at weight-loss centers. For example, women who lost weight were awarded with applause and with ribbons for achieving certain milestones. In addition, women that I interviewed from one particular weight-loss center always used the phrase "When I lost *my* weight" rather than the more common usage, "When I lost weight." They did not seem to even be aware of this until I pointed it out and asked them about it. The literature available at meetings also reinforced their sense of control. For example, the fact that weight-loss "success stories" are prominently featured in such literature implicitly argues that *these* women, too, can lose weight if only they try hard enough.

A third theme was that weight loss was consistently equated with improved appearance—and more specifically, *feminine* appearance and attractiveness to men. In this way, weight loss can be seen as an accommodation of gender norms. Although many respondents mentioned health concerns as a reason for wanting to lose weight, when they spoke in more detail what they said more often than not equated weight loss with improved *appearance*. Thus notions of femininity, of being the "correct" weight to be attractive to the opposite sex, were very much a part of many women's weight loss narratives. More specifically, very few mentioned "feeling healthier" once they lost weight; rather, they were much more likely to say they "felt prettier."

Fourth, the women in my study saw their lives as having been significantly transformed with the weight loss. Specifically, they generally indicated on their surveys that they considered themselves more attractive, more assertive, more outgoing, happier, emotionally stronger, and sexier since losing weight. *All* the women interviewed mentioned in some form or another how their lives had changed for the better since they lost weight (although some emphasized more changes than others):

> I definitely feel more attractive, but it's a weird feeling. I was sitting in a bar with a girlfriend recently, and this man was staring at me, and all I could think was, do I look that awful? Is my lipstick on my teeth or something? Then I realized he was looking at me because he found me attractive. It was like, revelation! (Lynn)

Nondieting, Nonactivist Group: The Equivocators

In 1992 and 1993 I interviewed nineteen women who were not currently dieting and who in fact had responded to an ad for "women who are comfortable with their bodies despite being 'overweight' by conventional standards." I had intended that this group be a counterpoint to the women in the weight-loss group, but it did not work out this way. Most striking in the interviews was the fact that although these women had identified themselves as being "happy with themselves despite their weight," during the interviews most expressed strong dissatisfaction with their bodies. They tended to be ambivalent about the process of losing weight, equivocating on whether or not they even believed it was possible for them to do so. They thus became the nondieting, nonactivist group: the Equivocators. Sixteen were white, while two were African-American, and one was Hispanic. They ranged in age from twenty-one to forty-five.

Several themes emerged from my interviews with the Equivocators. First, many had been fat since childhood, and the feelings they expressed during interviews showed many common bonds:

It was awful being fat as a child. If I think I have it bad now, I just think back to then and realize how much better off I am. Kids would call me fatso all the time. They'd laugh when I got on the school bus because I couldn't walk down the aisle without touching the sides. (Marie)

It's hard being different in childhood. Sometimes I would look in the mirror and think, you're not that fat. Then I would look again and be repulsed. But I'm not sure if I really hated myself that much—I mean I always felt like I was a good person inside. Maybe I was just responding to other kids' views of me. (Donna)

Second, the Equivocators were ambivalent about their own ability to lose weight. All had attempted to lose weight many times. Sometimes they did, but they always gained it back. Even so, some still believed they could lose weight if they tried hard enough:

I *could* lose weight if I wanted to. I've done it enough in the past. I mean, I can't blame people for being disgusted [at my weight]. I'm disgusted with myself sometimes. (Donna)

Third, all of the Equivocators mentioned things they had given up because of their weight. The following are typical:

Sometimes I think about all the things I've given up and I just can't believe it. My tenth-year high-school reunion was last year and I would have loved to go, but there was no way I was going to let them see me this way. (Melissa)

In the past, I have avoided so many things. It's just crazy. It's like I think I don't deserve to do fun things, just because of my weight. But when I go on a diet and lose a few pounds, suddenly I deserve them. I deserve to be treated better when I'm thinner. I'm really trying to get over this. (Susan)

Overall, as I indicated in the typology of reactions earlier, the Equivocators seemed to have a passive response to societal constructions of beauty; that is, they often simply felt miserable about their size but did not get involved in a group that would help them either change their size or the way they *feel* about their size.

NonDieting, Activist Group: The Fat Boosters

Between 1996 and 1998 I interviewed twenty-one members of NAAFA, the national fat activist organization. All of those interviewed were fat (although not all members of the organization are). Thirteen respondents were white and eight were women of color, seven of whom were African-Americans. They ranged in age from twenty-one to sixty. I also conducted participant-observation at regional NAAFA functions and at the national convention in July/August 1997, and analyzed documents produced by the organization.

Probably the most important theme that emerged in the interviews with Fat Boosters can be summed up by the statement of one: "My weight is my weight and I have to learn to live with it." The official NAAFA policy is that fatness is largely genetically determined and thus beyond individuals' control; this is in stark contrast with the Fat Busters' belief that they can reshape their bodies through dieting. For the Fat Boosters, joining NAAFA meant constantly hearing that "diets don't work." This message is reinforced in a number of ways: through members wearing buttons with a red line through the word DIET, through the group's championing of National No-Diet Day, and through members' interactions with each other. An example of the latter occurred during a dinner at the 1997 national convention. When one woman remarked how good the (high-fat and high-calorie) food tasted and how much she loved to eat, another woman angrily retorted, "We're trying to get across the idea that we're not fat because we love to eat, and you're not helping."

A second theme that became clear in my interviews, observations, and document analysis of this group was that they were attempting to change their own—and sometimes society's—definition of "fatness." For example, this became clear during the welcoming breakfast at the 1997 NAAFA convention, when the speaker, Glenn Gaesser, author of *Big Fat Lies: The Truth about Your Weight and Your Health* (1996), argued—to wild applause—that "moderate obesity" could actually be *good* for a person.

Third, it was obvious that members gained a sense of empowerment through NAAFA, in particular through their interactions with other NAAFA members. For example, during a workshop at the 1997 convention, participants were encouraged to change their attributions about why people sometimes react negatively to them: "Don't automatically assume it's because of your weight," the group leader said; "maybe the person is just having a bad day." Leslie, who was quoted in the opening of this chapter, is another example who spoke of gaining more self-confidence as she spent time at the convention. The organization itself recognizes that interactions with other members is critical in maintaining self-confidence; and a popular workshop at the 1997 meeting was one that discussed strategies for "taking these good thoughts home with you."

THE MORE THINGS CHANGE, THE MORE THEY
STAY THE SAME . . .

My original intention was to examine *different* responses that women have to societal constructions of obesity. The more I worked on this project, however, the more problematic I found my original assumptions. While on the surface the women in this study appear to be reacting in ways vastly at odds with each other, on a deeper level the reactions seem more similar than I originally imagined.

First, the Fat Busters, the Equivocators, *and* the Fat Boosters in some ways define their identities *reactively*—i.e., in reaction to societal constructions that, I would argue, they are themselves perpetuating. The Fat Busters define themselves as "not-fat-any-more"; the weight-loss groups of which they were or are members are based on accommodating conventional notions about fatness. The Equivocators, with their expressed dissatisfaction with their bodies and their admission of how different they think their lives would be if they were thin, are similarly accepting of societal prejudices about obesity.

However, what might be less obvious is that the Fat Boosters also define their identities reactively: Their group *exists* because of the weight issue; it is salient in everything the group does and thus perpetuates a kind of us-versus-them (fat-versus-thin) mentality. For example, in a recent national NAAFA newsletter the editor expressed disdain at news and journal stories about people who had lost weight and kept it off. Other newsletter articles suggested that food restriction of any kind (other than that required for certain diseases like diabetes) is a "sellout." Similarly, a book reviewer expressed anger that the author had suggested that there was a correlation between what people eat and their size. In short, the intense, self-conscious, and *defensive* focus on weight is inescapable.

My second point, which is closely related to the first, is that all three groups in many ways do not *challenge* the "fat-is-ugly" bias. It is clear that the Fat Busters perpetuated conventional constructions. The very groups they joined are committed to helping women "get over" being fat. In interviews, their own antifat biases, which were in many cases socially reinforced by their participation in weight-loss groups, also came through clearly:

> I really feel sorry for them [overweight people], but on the other hand, I lost weight so I know they can too. . . . Did you ever notice who drinks diet sodas and eats diet food? Diet jello, diet lunches, diet everything. Fat people do. Thin people eat normal stuff. I look at fat people sometimes and think, why are you drinking a Diet Coke, who are you trying to kid? I know they stuff themselves later, because I used to myself. (Lisa)

> Sometimes when I see fat people I think, that's what I used to look like, and it really repulses me. (Mindy)

> I remember years ago when I was heavy, I saw a talk show on TV that had some overweight women on it saying they liked themselves heavy. One of them said when she goes to bars with her make-up on and her clothes perfect, all the men are looking at her, not at the size-10 woman next to her. I remember thinking, no way. I just knew that wasn't true. (Andrea)

Similarly, the Equivocators perpetuated societal constructions when they expressed dissatisfaction with their bodies and antifat attitudes of their own. For example:

> I can understand it when I'm sitting on BART [the subway system in the Bay Area] and no one wants to sit next to me because I spill over, I take more than my share of space. Anyone who sat next to me would have to really squeeze. (Diane)

Again, however, what isn't obvious is that the Fat Boosters also express conventional antifat biases. While they are ostensibly fighting *against* hegemonic constructions of attractiveness, they don't necessarily question the idea that "thin is beautiful"; rather, they argue that it's "not their fault" that they are fat and that they shouldn't be "blamed" for it. Admittedly, some—like Leslie, who was quoted in the opening to this chapter—truly do believe that "fat is beautiful too"; however, many others admit that if they had a choice, they would prefer to be thin themselves. While in some cases this may simply reflect a recognition that their lives would be easier (that is, they would be accepted more easily by members of society) if they were thin, in other cases I believe it reflects the same kind of "fat-is-ugly" belief that pervades mainstream society.

This underlying "there's-something-wrong-with-fat" view also comes out in one of the major items on NAAFA's platform: disseminating the view that whether or not one is fat is largely genetically determined, so fat people are not making a choice and, again, should not be "blamed" for their size. Rather than arguing, "I've chosen to be fat and so what? Fat is beautiful too"—which would obviously be quite a radical stand—the organization argues that their members' being fat is beyond their control, a substantially different argument, which implies a recognition that there is something inherently *wrong* with being fat. And since the organization also argues that fatness is not the huge health risk that the mainstream medical profession says it is, then what's wrong with being fat must be that it's ugly, unattractive, and deviant.[2]

Weight has an enormous impact on the everyday lives of women in all three groups. They are very aware of themselves as being "of a certain size," whether "average" or "fat," and this appears to be a large part of their identity. For example, the Fat Busters consistently indicated an intense fear of regaining their lost weight:

> If I started gaining the weight back—it's really hard to even think about. When I was dieting all the time, going up and down, I felt totally out of control. I think if I started to get heavy again I would just feel out of control again. (Lisa)

There's no way I'll ever gain the weight back. No way. [shaking her head violently] It was just too painful to be overweight. I don't know what I would do if I got that way again. (Cheryl)

Fat Busters also indicated that they were "careful" about what they ate, that they "watched" their diets, that they had "good" days (when they did not eat "bad" foods such as chocolate or ice cream) and "bad" days (when they strayed from what they thought were "good" eating habits). Again, Cheryl is a good example:

> Sometimes I think I should just be more relaxed about it, but then I remember what it was like to be fat and I can't [be more relaxed]. So I just read labels like crazy, and try to do extra exercise whenever I eat bad stuff. I just watch out all the time. [KH: Is this kind of vigilance tiring?] Yes. Yes. But I just figure it's the price I have to pay to stay skinny. (Cheryl)

Weight also had a large impact on the everyday lives of the Equivocators. As I mentioned earlier, several spoke sadly about things they had given up because of their weight, such as participating in activities they had enjoyed before they gained weight or seeing people who knew them when they were thinner. They clearly saw themselves differently at different weights, and recognized that other people saw them differently as well. Similarly, the Fat Boosters admitted that despite NAAFA's championing of the idea that "fat people should be able to do anything thin people do," some things they did at NAAFA functions—like wearing shorts or eating an ice cream cone in public—they simply would not do at home. (A few even mentioned that even though they did go swimming with other NAAFA members, they were still very aware of themselves as being "fat people" and very aware of others' reactions to them.) In other words, their group's call for the "normalization" of fatness has not had as large an impact on the women as they (or the group) would probably like.

Finally, women in the two groups who had formal ties to organizations (the weight-loss group and the fat-activist group) seemed to be very aware not only of their own weight, but also that of other women. For example, for many Fat Busters the fear of regaining weight manifested itself in constant surveillance of both themselves and other women. Dana is a prime example:

> I'm very aware of my size now, maybe more now than when I was overweight. I look at other women on the street and I think, I'm thinner than her, I'm a little bigger than her but she's got small bones, I'm about her size and she looks good so I must be OK too. And then I'll go eat my yogurt. (Dana [lost 30 pounds])

Even the Fat Boosters showed the same kind of surveillance. For example, in NAAFA a distinction is made between two weight categories: "midsize" and "supersize," for which the dividing line is size 48. Within the organization debates have raged over which group has more problems. Some supersize women say that midsize women, being closer to "average," don't understand how difficult it is to be supersize. Some midsize women have expressed jealousy because at some NAAFA social functions (such as dances), the supersize women seem to get the most attention from men. In addition, one NAAFA member told me, rather sheepishly, that she was able to go swimming at the national convention because she wasn't "the fattest woman here." While this might seem extreme, many of the women I spoke with did seem to be very aware of their size in comparison to that of other members.

CONCLUSION: HEGEMONY THEORY REVISITED

Defining their identities reactively; expressing antifat attitudes; the enormous impact that weight continues to have on their lives; and the surveillance of other women's bodies—what can be concluded from all of these? I argue that the intense preoccupation with weight—and negative judgments of perceived *over*weight—that the literature shows most American women have, regardless of size, is perhaps even more pronounced with women who either were or are overweight themselves. While this might not be surprising for Fat Busters and Equivocators, I did find it surprising for the Fat Boosters.

Early cultural studies work on "audience reception" tended to portray people as passive receptors who were indoctrinated into dominant ways of thinking through cultural products, e.g., the mass media. More recent work on audience reception, though, has reminded us that hegemony is never total; rather, individuals and groups can potentially make sense of dominant ideas in different ways (Croteau and Hoynes 1997). I originally embraced this "active audience" view, expecting to argue that in the case of fat women, not all of them simply passively accept mainstream society's view of them as being ugly and morally deviant. Rather, I expected to argue, many actively reject constructions and norms of beauty that devalue and exclude them. Certainly I have collected a great deal of data on Fat Boosters that would support this contention; NAAFA newsletters, in particular, consistently support a view of the world that includes "fat" in its definition of beauty.

However, as I detailed in the previous section, the women participating in this project seemed to accept, on many levels, the larger society's prejudice about their body size. Thus my original suppositions about the inherent distinctiveness of the women's reactions in the three groups were not supported. Instead, in this chapter I have shown that in many ways the Fat Busters, Equivocators, and Fat Boosters do not challenge conventional definitions of beauty, but bolster them, colluding in constructions that exclude large numbers of women.

ACKNOWLEDGMENTS

I would like to thank Renee Anspach, Karin Martin, Andy Modigliani, and members of the CRSO community at the University of Michigan for their helpful comments on this project.

NOTES

1. I put the word "overweight" in quotation marks to indicate that it is a social construction. In fact, there is no clear definition of words like "overweight" or "obese" in most of the literature; the words are often used as though their definition were obvious. This is not only imprecise but it also obscures the fact that weight status is culturally contingent (i.e., what is considered "overweight" in the United States might very well not be considered so in the Caribbean) and ahistorical (i.e., standards of "ideal" weight have changed over time).

Members of NAAFA prefer the word "fat"—despite, or maybe because of, the fact that it is so emotionally "loaded"—and argue that "overweight" has hidden implications: "Over whose weight?" they ask. I have tried to use the word *fat* simply as an adjective, especially when referring to respondents who are NAAFA members. (This was a bit jarring at first, given that it has such negative connotations in the United States.)

2. Note the parallel here between the size acceptance movement, of which NAAFA is a main proponent, and the gay rights movement. Of course, I understand that from a social movement perspective, to argue that something is not a "choice"—that one is born a certain way—makes political sense in that people are (presumably) less likely to blame someone for being gay or fat if it is not their "choice." However, my point here is that simply asking the question "Is it a choice?" implies at least two things: first, that there is a "hierarchy of sexual orientations" or a "hierarchy of body sizes" and that being straight or being thin is *inherently better* than being gay or being fat; and second, that given the choice, gay or fat people would prefer to be straight or thin. So while it may seem quite progressive and tolerant to say "Those poor people were born that way so we'll give them the same things (e.g., political rights, antidiscrimination protection) that everyone else gets," it doesn't necessarily mean that homosexuality or fatness is considered to be as "good" an "option" of sexual orientation or body size as heterosexuality or thinness. To me, a more interesting (and certainly more provocative) way to answer the question "Is it a choice?" is to say, "Well, maybe it is, but so what?"

REFERENCES

Blumer, H. 1969. *Symbolic Interactionism: Perspective and Method*. Englewood Cliffs, NJ: Prentice-Hall.

Chapkis, W. 1986. *Beauty Secrets: Women and the Politics of Appearance*. Boston: South End.

Clayson, D. E., and M. L. Klassen. 1989. "Perception of Attractiveness by Obesity and Hair Color." *Perceptual and Motor Skills* 68:199–202.

Croteau, D., and W. Hoynes. 1997. *Media/Society: Industries, Images, and Audiences*. Thousand Oaks, CA: Pine Forge.

English, C. 1991. "Food Is My Best Friend: Self-Justifications and Weight Loss Efforts." *Research in the Sociology of Health Care* 9:335–45.

Gaesser, G. A. 1996. *Big Fat Lies: The Truth about Your Weight and Your Health*. New York: Fawcett.

Garner, D. M., and S. C. Wooley. 1991. "Confronting the Failure of Behavioral and Dietary Treatments for Obesity." *Clinical Psychology Review* 11:729–80.

Gramsci, A. 1971. *Selections from the Prison Notebooks of Antonio Gramsci*, edited by G. Nowell-Smith and Q. Hoare. London: Lawrence and Wishart.

Harris, M. B., L. C. Walters, and S. Waschull. 1991. "Gender and Ethnic Differences in Obesity-Related Behaviors and Attitudes in a College Sample." *Journal of Applied Social Psychology* 21:1545–66.

Hesse-Biber, S. 1991. "Women, Weight, and Eating Disorders: A Socio-cultural and Political-economic Analysis." *Women's Studies International Forum* 14(3): 173–91.

———. 1996. *Am I Thin Enough Yet? The Cult of Thinness and the Commercialization of Identity*. New York: Oxford University Press.

Hiller, D. V. 1981. "The Salience of Overweight in Personality Characterization." *Journal of Psychology* 108(2):233–40.

———. 1982. "Overweight as Master Status: A Replication." *Journal of Psychology* 110(1):107–13.

Kellner, D. 1995. "Cultural Studies, Multiculturalism, and Media Culture." Pp. 5–17 in *Gender, Race, and Class in Media*, edited by Gail Dines and Jean M. Humez. Thousand Oaks, CA: Sage.

Kilbourne, J. 1994. "Still Killing Us Softly: Advertising and the Obsession with Thinness." Pp. 395–418 in *Feminist Perspectives on Eating Disorders*, edited by P. Fallon, M. A. Katzman, and S. C. Wooley. New York: Guilford.

Millman, M. 1980. *Such a Pretty Face: Being Fat in America*. New York: Berkley.

Ogaitis, S., T. T. L. Chen, and L. C. Steelman. 1986. "Social Location, Significant Others and Body Image among Adolescents." *Social Psychology Quarterly* 49(4):330–37.

Orbach, S. 1978. *Fat Is a Feminist Issue*. New York: Berkley.

Press, A. 1991. *Women Watching Television: Gender, Class, and Generation in the American Television Experience*. Philadelphia: University of Pennsylvania Press.

Ritzer, G. 1992. *Sociological Theory*, 3rd edition. New York: McGraw-Hill.

Rothblum, E. D., C. T. Miller, and B. Garbutt. 1988. "Stereotypes of Obese Female Job Applicants." *International Journal of Eating Disorders* 7:277–83.

Spector, M., and J. I. Kitsuse. 1977. *Constructing Social Problems*. Menlo Park, CA: Cummings.

Wadden, T. A., A. J. Stunkard, and J. Liebschutz. 1988. "Three-year Follow-up of the Treatment of Obesity by Very Low Calorie Diet, Behavior Therapy, and Their Combination." *Journal of Consulting and Clinical Psychology* 56:925–28.

Wolf, N. 1991. *The Beauty Myth: How Images of Beauty Are Used Against Women*. New York: Morrow.

10

Creating "Uniformity"

The Construction of Bodies in Women's Collegiate Cross Country

ELIZABETH RANSOM

INTRODUCTION

The horizons of an athlete's world can never stray far beyond her body. The course of an athletic career entails development of the ability to focus increasingly greater amounts of awareness on increasingly specific parts of the body. . . . The horizons of an intellectual's world lie at the edge of an ever-expanding cosmos of ideas that seems to recede further and further from the body. Athletes are very much in their bodies and, as a consequence, are usually very much within the systems that sustain those bodies. Intellectuals are forever trying to escape beyond bodies and the systems that sustain them . . . . The chasm between the detachment from the body that characterizes much social science and the limited focus on the body that characterizes sports is difficult to bridge. (Brownell 1995:7–8)

Bodies are vehicles for examining the values, attitudes, and perspectives of a society. Today, the high levels of eating disorders and disordered eating among female athletes reflect a society where approximately 90 percent of those with diagnosed cases of eating disorders are women.[1] The issue of eating disorders among athletes mirrors our society's dominant ideas about the proper construction of bodies and how these constructions differ, particularly by gender, race, and ethnicity.

Anthropologist Susan Brownell's (1995) quotation at the beginning of this chapter eloquently reveals the chasm between the ideological world of the academic and the practical world of the competitive athlete. Both natural and social scientists have taken an individual entities approach to studying athletes. They have discussed the athlete's body as a natural, biological fact, while ignoring the body as the context of social interaction. Callon and Law (1998:175) write, "[S]ometimes it is useful to talk of individual entities: to imagine that they are discrete objects in an environment. But it is equally appropriate to treat them as collective effects—as patterned networks." Only in the past ten years has a significant discussion occurred regarding bodies as "collective effects" constituted within patterned networks (Beardsworth and Keil 1997; Scott and Morgan 1993; Turner 1992). Athletes with eating disorders are not only the products of individual endeavors, but joint products of everyone who participates in the sports world.

This study demonstrates that competitive collegiate runners' bodies, and in turn, their experiences, are shaped by the patterned networks within which they are embedded. For example, food, equipment, clothing, and bodies not only represent extensions of human agency, but they also impact and shape the athlete's social environment. First, I provide a brief overview of the medicalization literature on eating disorders, followed by a review of the historical and sociological critique of sport as it applies to women's long distance running. This is followed by a explanation of my methods and finally a discussion of the findings. The embodied female cross-country runner is the center of my discussion. Finally, I attempt to build a comprehensive picture of the cooperating networks within which the athlete is embedded (Becker 1982).

THE MEDICALIZATION OF DEVIANCE

In the cross-country team environment, just as in the rest of society, individuals diagnosed with eating disorders are viewed as slightly different or deviant from the rest of the team. In recent years this deviance has been medicalized. The medicalization process follows the biomedical model used in our society, which views the body as a series of separate, but interdependent parts (Doyal 1995). Doyal explains, "Health is defined in individualistic ways—it is always individuals who become sick, rather than social, economic, or environmental factors which cause them to do so" (1979:35).

With the increase in genetic research, critical scientists and feminist scholars have criticized the extreme individualism implied by the biomedical model (Doyal 1979, 1995; Hubbard 1995; Lewontin 1991). Geneticist R. C. Lewontin (1991) notes that an announcement appears almost weekly in the press proclaiming a possible genetic cause of some human illness. This focus on genetics has entered into the debate on eating disorders. For example, a recent article in *Science* claims that researchers have found a hormone that may help regulate body weight (Gura 1996). At issue in locating eating disorders strictly within the individual is the diagnosis that women, since they are the vast majority of sufferers, are fundamentally different from and inferior to men (Bordo 1993).

Critics have identified both positive and negative aspects of the medicalization of deviance (Conrad and Schneider 1980). One negative aspect of the medicalization of eating disorders, of primary concern in this work, is the dislocation of the problem from society. One author argues that the deviant label leads to social isolation and public apathy, "lessening the likelihood that audiences will respond to eating disorders as social problems worth 'doing something' about" (Way 1995:91). Thus, medicalization can depoliticize an issue.

Another aspect of the medicalization of eating disorders is the implicit assumption of "normal eating," against which eating disorders are measured. Thus, a false dichotomy is constructed between "normal" and "abnormal" eating patterns. Much of the literature suggests this binary opposition (Hesse-Biber 1996). Instead, it can be argued that disordered eating among women, though physically bad for the body, has been the norm for years and therefore cannot be considered deviant behavior. Bordo (1993), Root (1990), and Thompson (1992) suggest that, due to different life experiences, some women reach the stage of eating disorders, while others remain in the realm of disordered eating and many move between the two. When viewing the interaction of women in sport, it is striking that women who have a nonconflicting interaction with food are atypical. The overall definition of what is "normal" becomes blurred.

Thus, the medicalization of eating disorders inhibits an analysis of the networks of people and other factors that contribute to the construction of eating disorders and disorderly eating among female cross-country runners. However, recent sociological analyses of the medicalization process have revealed new ways that sport is linked with and infiltrated by medicine. In this analysis, eating disorders can be seen as an outcome of a web of complex social issues combined with individual biologies and psychologies. The networks that operate within sport construct an environment prone to eating disorders and disordered eating.

NETWORKS IN THE CONTEXT OF SPORT

Each network relies on a set of conventions that creates and facilitates cooperating patterned networks. Becker (1982:32) writes, "a system of conventions gets embodied in equipment, materials, training, available facilities and sites, systems of notation, and the like, all of which must be changed if any one component is." In sport, as elsewhere in society, gender is a core division upon which conventions are shaped and implemented. Goffman (1977) notes that physical surroundings can be enlisted to aid in the display or affirmation of gender, for example, the daily construction of gender through toilet segregation. Goffman (1977:316) explains, "[T]oilet segregation is presented as a natural consequence of the difference between the sex-classes [sic], when in fact it is rather a means of honoring, if not producing this difference." In sport the social construction of gender can be seen at all levels, from philosophy and policy to the seemingly trivial level of rules, equipment, uniforms, and bodies (Cahn 1994).

Sports is an institution in which biology continues to be used to justify segregating men and women (Birrell and Cole 1994; Burton 1994; Eitzen 1996; Messner 1988). Messner (1988:198) argues that women's involvement in sport "represents a genuine quest by women for equality, control of their own bodies, and self-definition and as such it represents a challenge to the ideological basis of male domination." However, as male hegemony has increasingly been threatened, the socially constructed gender division in sport has not only been replicated, but heightened. What could be considered minimal biological differences are naturalized and maximized through the construction of gender within the institution of sport.

The gender divide in sport constructs our notions of what is feminine and what is masculine. What is most important, however, is to realize that what is labeled feminine in the sporting world is defined as "less than" masculine sport. For example, playing with a larger ball in softball and a smaller one in basketball, lowering the net in volleyball and the hurdles in track, and specifying different rules, such as no stealing of bases or smaller court dimensions.

The history of women's and men's long-distance running demonstrates how culturally constructed gender systems have been created and sustained and how they change over time (Cahn 1994). The marathon was added to the modern Olympic games to commemorate the legendary Greek solider Pheidippides, who collapsed and died after running from Marathon to Athens (total distance about 35 kilometers) in 490 B.C. to announce the Greek victory over the Persians. Prior to 1908 the distance of the marathon was not standardized; it varied from 40 to 43 kilometers. In 1908 Dorondo Pietri collapsed at the end of the Olympic Marathon in London and as Downes and MacKay (1996:13) describe, "did so much to capture the public's imagination that it effectively institutionalized the marathon's distance at the oddly chosen 26 miles 385 yards, which was used for that race from Windsor to London for no better reason than to give the Royal Family a better view of the finish line in the White City stadium."

Contrast this to the women running in the Olympics of 1928. Running was viewed as excessively masculine, due to the lack of elaborate rules and equipment, with theoretically potentially harmful effects for women.

If women participated there was the hypothesized potential for a woman to actually become a man. The director of New York State's Physical Education, Dr. Frederick R. Rogers, representing the dominant view at that time, argued that the requirements of sport were unnatural for female athletes. He claimed that track in particular would make women unfit for motherhood and would sacrifice their "health, physical beauty, and social attractiveness" (quoted in Cahn 1994:114). Therefore, when several female runners fell to the ground in physical and emotional exhaustion at the end of an 800-meter race in the 1928 Olympics, critics saw this as proof that women were unfit for strenuous competition. This culminated with the Olympic Congress banning all medium- to long-distance races for women and their consideration of banning women's events completely (Cahn 1994).

As of 1978, scientists were still arguing that due to their physiology, women could not run marathons.[2] Prior to the 1980s, there were no women's distance races in the Olympics (Lovett 1997). Today, marathon running has reemerged as a sport in which women can compete, and likewise, female competition in cross- country running has reemerged as a college sport.

Today, most women distance runners are seen as feminine, with most participants unaware of the controversial history of women's participation in running. The fact that the sport is now viewed as feminine allows us to see that notions of femininity and masculinity are not "natural" or timeless (Cahn 1994). But how did the sport of long-distance running become a more feminine activity? To answer this question, the focus needs to fall on the cooperative networks that construct the sport and the athletic bodies in the sport's environment.

METHODS OF DATA COLLECTION

The research for this study took place over approximately one and a half years, from August 1995 to December 1996. This incorporated two seasons of cross-country running, which occur in the fall of each year. In-depth interviews were conducted with two collegiate women's cross-country teams. Fifteen of twenty-one women were interviewed from one team, and all ten women from the second team were interviewed ($n = 25$). The interviews were designed to be semistructured, open-ended discussions. I asked similar questions of all the women, but the interview process allowed each woman to elaborate on the areas she felt were important. All interviews were tape-recorded and later transcribed.

In addition to in-depth interviews, participant-observation was conducted for two seasons with one of the teams. Participant-observations took place at practice times, while traveling to competition sites, and at cross-country meets. Due to the physical aspect of participating with a sports team, written field notes were never taken on site. Instead, they were written immediately following practice or, in the case of road trips, whenever the opportunity became available.

The women involved in this study were predominantly white, middle-class, heterosexuals. The homogeneous composition of the groups in terms of class and sexuality reflects the collegiate sporting population, which Birrell (1994) notes is not very diverse or supportive of diversity. Also, the specific sport of cross-country running provides for little racial and ethnic diversity. With the exception of some Southwestern and West Coast schools, and a few international runners, the participants are pre-dominantly white from European descent. However, it should be noted that while most of these athletes were homogeneous in race, class, and sex-uality, the viewpoints and perspectives of these women varied widely. Pseudonyms are used throughout to protect the identities of the female athletes.

Working from a grounded theory approach, this study began with no specific agenda or theoretical perspective. The issue of weight and women's bodies kept coming to the fore in my participant observations and interviews. Women's bodily awareness is perhaps the strongest thread that weaves through these women's lives. Most women in this study would not be clinically diagnosed with eating disorders; there is wide variation in behavior among the women in this study. I use the term "disordered eating" to reflect the varied and strained relationship these cross-country women (and most women in society) have with food.

COOPERATING NETWORKS

Food—Constructing Food and Bodies

Intercollegiate athletes spend large quantities of time around one another, with most, though not all, establishing the team as their dominant social group in college. The structure of the sporting world, particularly that of intercollegiate sports, creates an environment where the team becomes one of the primary foci of the individual athlete's world. Interaction among team members forms a crucial aspect of the female athlete's network that sociologists often overlook.

Within the team interaction process, food and the conventions of food form one location in the network. More than just utilitarian in scope (i.e., nourishment) food fulfills multiple purposes in society and in the sports environment, for example, the standard of serving the "best" food for special occasions. Cline explains, "[F]ood is part of the nurturing process throughout the world, but in different places it takes on special meanings. Each culture marks it own society with special foods and food rituals" (1990:47). Particular foods are believed to be performance enhancing for long-distance running, such as those comprising a high-carbohydrate, low-fat diet. In the 1970s it was believed that in the week before a race, a runner should "carbo-load." However, today nutritionists recognize that eating carbohydrates, such as pasta, the night before a race (that is shorter than sixty minutes in length) does not help and may actually hurt a runner's performance, due to excessive water retention (Deuster 1996). Nonetheless, there continues to be the ritualistic event of eating a spaghetti dinner the night prior to a race.

The sport also contributes to constructing long-distance runners' daily eating, which is different than their eating patterns for competition. For example, here is an exchange I witnessed between two women one afternoon after a tough workout. Megan announced, "I had the perfect lunch today. I had some rice and then an apple. It is just perfect with a little salt and pepper on the rice and then an apple is just right. I had a big breakfast this morning though. I pigged out! I had three bowls of cereal." After the other woman commented, Megan continued, "I only eat 500 calories before practice everyday."

The other woman questioned how Megan could eat three bowls of cereal and still only have eaten 500 calories. Megan responded that with Rice Chex cereal you can eat under 500 calories. The other woman questioned the serving portion, however, at which point Megan announced, "Exactly a cup per serving. I measure!"

What is important to note about Megan's lunch of rice and an apple, is that in the sport of running, particularly on the day of a hard workout, eating something light that will not stay in your stomach is desirable, due to the ill consequences that affect the athlete if she does not eat lightly and then has a strenuous workout. However, Megan, as with most women on the team, had not eaten a light lunch only because she did not want to feel sick during the workout. She constructs and determines the food she eats each day based on the number of calories as well as the number of fat grams, regardless of what she will be doing that particular day within running. She also viewed her diet as an accomplishment, as she proudly announced to her teammate how and of what she constructed it. In addition, Megan commented that her roommates, who are also on the team, get mad at her for measuring her cereal. Thus, food consumption may be seen as an extension of competition within the team.

As this example illustrates, food rituals for performance enhancement also intersect with other conventions, such as the gendering of certain foods. In Western societies there are a number of assumptions concerning the types of food men and women prefer. Foods that are known to be low in calories and therefore not likely to cause weight gain or foods that help in weight loss are generally labeled as feminine foods. Foods labeled as feminine include chocolates, pastries, cakes, white meat, fish, noodles, pasta, salads, and vegetables (Lupton 1996). Note that all these foods are viewed as delicate and/or sweet and light—the same metaphorical description used to describe traditional white, middle-class femininity in Western society. Hence, while a high-carbohydrate dinner the night before a race is standard for long-distance runners, there generally is a differentiation between genders in the type of high-carbohydrate dinner consumed, with the females more likely to order something containing no meat, little or no fat, and a smaller quantity.

Food gendering arises from society's extension of the gendered construction of bodies. Thus, bodies impact how we view food and, reciprocally, food impacts how we construct bodies. The gendered construction of women's food and bodies in college athletics also comes from others within the sports network. Gender checking in the Olympics is a process that assumes that all men are similar in size, strength, and skill, and therefore that all men are better than all women in sports (Lorber 1993).[3] A similar assumption is made regarding women's consumption of food. A coach at one of the institutions where I conducted interviews asked, "Why do women get the same amount of meal money as the men do?" The built-in assumption of this statement is that all women eat less than all men, and therefore should be given less money with which to eat. This ignores the vast variety of eating patterns among people and among sports, with almost every sport instituting a particular diet to "enhance" an athlete's performance. Here again, the way female athletes' bodies and the food they consume are constructed reveals the multiple intersections of networks within society.

Linked with food rituals and the gendering of foods is the concept that food maintains social order in society. In Western societies, meals are eaten three times a day, with particular foods consumed at each meal in a certain quantity and even in a certain order. Meals structure our days more than the clock (Cline 1990). Likewise, meals provide a central organizing structure on sports teams.

Almost every weekend of a female cross-country runner's life is spent on road trips with the team. On road trips (but not confined to them) everyone eats together at a specific time to allow for the proper diet and digestion of food before running. For example, on the morning of a meet the team gathers together at a designated time and location to eat breakfast. In addition, when traveling with a large group, often the most accessible food is fast food, and for women who are weight conscious, the ability to eat, but eat low-fat, proves to be a struggle.

Therefore, it should be no surprise that weight and food are regular topics of discussion. Sometimes these discussions involve the entire team, such as one occasion when the women were riding in a van together returning from the weekend's competition. Everyone in the van, with a few women leading the discussion, began to discuss the appropriate foods to eat. The best foods were defined as those that are low in fat. The discussion lasted for hours. On other occasions team members would engage in bets or competitions to see who could lose a designated number of pounds first or who could avoid eating particular types of food, such as chocolate.

Some of the women may have no interest or may not want to participate in the discussion, however. For example, one evening after the team had just finished a pre-race homemade spaghetti dinner, one woman, Annie, held up a bottle of oil and announced, "We almost used the entire bottle for making dinner." The room fell silent, at which point she said, "Just kidding." Simultaneously, another woman who had helped make dinner, but is not on the team, held up a 64-ounce crock of butter and loudly stated, "But we did use almost all of this on the garlic bread." Immediately, Annie and Megan began to tally the number of total fat grams everyone had consumed, proclaiming, "454 grams of fat—just in the butter!" These examples show the endless ways the women verbally construct interpretations of food, and in turn their bodies. It also reveals that even when some of the women are not actively involved in the conversation, they are still subjected to the conversations that construct meanings for the food they consume. In the above example, some of the women in the room may have had no desire to know how many fat grams were in the food they ate.

The women also engage in nonverbal constructions of food. Nonverbal cues include the interaction of the women sitting together at meals. All observe what others are eating and there is an awareness of the woman who chooses to pick everything (cheese, meat, etc.) off her salad, and then eat only the lettuce. Less extreme than this is simply the awareness of what others are eating. Essentially, there is a constant watch over what others are eating, with team members often commenting, "You are going to eat that?" Sometimes, other team members view what others are eating as approval to eat an item also. Thus, when another team member chooses to eat something considered unhealthy (i.e., fattening) she will talk others into splitting it with her or getting one too. Again, this point reiterates that the act of eating serves multiple functions. Eating can be viewed as both bonding time for team members and an extension of competition within the team.

The construction of women's food and their bodies creates a subculture within the team, to the extent that these endless discussions and comparisons of food seem "normal." Team members are unaware of or unable to see how others new to their environment or how outsiders might view this emphasis on food and bodies as excessive. Eva, a new person on the team exclaimed, "I never dealt with people who were so worried about their weight until we got here. . . . I've never seen so many people that were so fat conscious in my life." In turn, team members are unable to see the impact this subculture has on themselves, much like the proverbial fish that does not realize its environment is made up of water. For example, Mary spoke of her increasing awareness of fat grams in college, but when asked how she became aware of fat content in food, she responded as if it were just common sense: "Well, well just pictures. I mean like seeing pictures . . . my freshmen year in college. I mean I was a little chunk." Mary's observation of herself expresses an increased level of attention and awareness of her body and the food she consumes. The increased attention to her body can in part be attributed to the ways the sport is constructed for women.

Bodies—Femininity by Way of the Body

Since the 1970s, women have been given the contradictory messages of run for "beauty" and run for "self-liberation." These contradictory messages came from many sources, including businesses and the media, which saw opportunities for new markets with the surge in female athleticism. These messages also came from within the sports structure, with the continued debate between physical educators who believed athleticism would enhance women and their opportunities, and those who viewed women as fundamentally different and therefore in need of sports with different goals and objectives (Cahn 1994; Cooper 1995).

Like society, sport has provided opportunities for the advancement of women, but it has been fraught with reassertions of sexism. Women and society are involved in this reframing of sustaining and countering views of women in sport. Cooper writes, "Marathon running became an opportunity for women to explore their own physical limits of endurance and speed" (1995:70). Yet Cooper also notes that there were differing reasons for why men and women should take up running. Men who took up running were supposedly perceived as "contemplative, taciturn, vagabond philosophers," while women's running emphasized the health and cosmetic benefits (ibid.:69).

During the increasing popularity of running in the mid-1970s, runners became important to the corporate world as consumers. Cooper (1995) states that running was the most popular sport among upwardly mobile urbanites. Increasingly, women runners in the 1970s fit the image of the desirable consumer, particularly when female runners who were homemakers were "ascribed their husbands' status" (ibid.:67). So with the rise in popularity of long-distance running among women, corporate America saw the opportunity to turn a profit by packaging a feminine image in what traditionally had been considered a masculine sport.

Thus, the commodification of the female runner began to emerge as one convention within the sport of women's long- distance running. It should be noted that the audience to which the appeal of the popularity of long-distance running was directed was a predominantly white, upwardly mobile, middle-class constituency. Thus, the constructions of the ideal feminine beauty that extended from this movement were based on a long history of Western ideals of white femininity. Other attributes of this feminine ideal include a pale, frail, thin body, characteristics inherently contradictory to athletic endeavors (Seid 1994; Wooley 1994). Almost all the women interviewed made reference to the idea that skinny is beautiful. One woman, Bridget, recognized this normalizing message women receive in society. Speaking of a high school teammate who was recovering from an eating disorder, Bridget said, "I think she needed that extra vote of confidence so she had a reason to get back to where she needed to be, like she had somewhere to go. Some girls that don't have that extra outlet, *they want to be thin, they want to be beautiful,* and they have no one telling them to be anything but" (emphasis added).

Other women recognized this "thin is beautiful" message as a personal goal. In this respect, women participating in cross-country running, like most athletes, are participating for multiple reasons and with a variety of goals that arise from intersecting networks. One reason for participation is athletic achievement, but also with the extra incentive of obtaining the "perfect" body. For example, Lois stated,

> I think a lot of it has to do with the fact that now all the models are slim, perfect-figured people . . . so if you see that and you say, "Wow, she looks like that, I want to look like that too." And for me I mean I do that, you know, you see some beautiful girl in a beautiful dress in a magazine, you go wow that's really pretty.

Lois continues on to explain how college long-distance running is part of her way of obtaining this ideal. She states,

> Running is my way of, I mean, I like this more than anything because it forces me to stay in shape. And that's my goal— to stay in shape. . . . I'm not going to be fat, that's all I can say. I'll never have a gut. No, I'll run, no I'll run like a lot to keep in shape.

Another woman, Nancy, reveals how she feels involvement in sport should help her obtain this ideal beauty, but she sees herself falling short of the beauty standard. She states of her other team members:

> I think if they were to have my body they would maybe think like I do a little more, because I told them I'm dieting right now, and they try to talk me out of it. But now I have just come to realize I shouldn't have to diet. I'm just not going to diet anymore, and even though I care what my body looks like

to be beautiful and everything, but as long as I am running good I really don't. It is just my thighs and my butt, I know every girl says that, but I just want them to be tiny. I don't know I just want to have no thighs and no butt and some people do . . . ten pounds probably everyone wants to lose.

Note that Nancy emphasizes the difference between her body, her team-mates' bodies, and women in general.

While the form of the beauty/athlete contradiction has changed over the years, sport today is still considered to be the one domain where suc-cess infers a certain degree of innate masculinity. Several statements made by the women in the interviews reflect the dominant ideology, which views the sporting world as the symbol of the "natural" order of things, an order in which men, and what have been labeled male body parts (e.g. hor-mones, muscles, etc.), are considered better. One woman wondered if female athletes have more masculine hormones than women who are not as athletically talented. She stated, "I mean because I do notice a lot of girls who are very masculine looking are the good ones." Another woman, Kathleen said, "I just think a lot of men are just naturally built with that [athletic] body and they're not going to, you know, women gain weight."

Lorber (1993) illuminates how conventions of sport train women to meet different goals than men within the network. Men's bodies are con-structed to be powerful, while women's bodies are constructed to be sex-ual in the sporting world. Her main argument is that "Bodies differ in many ways physiologically, but they are completely transformed by social practices to fit into the salient categories of a society, the most pervasive of which are 'female and male'" (ibid.:569).

Messner proposes that, "Sport offers a normalizing equation for men: athleticism = masculinity = heterosexuality. For female athletes, the equa-tion has nearly always been more paradoxical: athleticism? femininity? heterosexuality?" (1996:225). What is missing, but yet implicit in this equa-tion is the athlete's body. Sport offers a normalizing equation for male ath-letic bodies. Athletic men are thought to have a physically fit body, which in its most generalized notion means a muscular, large build. In contrast, for women a physically fit body is much more paradoxical, in that she should be toned, but not too muscular, nor of too large a build.

Both Lorber (1993) and Messner (1997) argue that society assigns bod-ies to fixed categories, but they fail to discuss how these categories impose and transform bodies. As Lewontin states, "Organisms do not find the world in which they develop. They make it. Reciprocally, the internal forces are not autonomous, but act in response to the external" (1991:63). Asked if there has ever been a conflict between being a female and being an athlete, Lois states, "I think runners are feminine. I don't think basket-ball or softball is feminine. . . . I definitely think running is a very feminine sport. I mean look at all the girls on the team. . . . They all wear pretty hairdos and this and that, you know." In this response she mentions hairdos as a measure of femininity. In other parts of the interview Lois alludes to an emphasis on the actual body size and shape of the female athlete. If only hairdos distinguished her ideals of femininity, then women in basketball and softball could not be excluded from her ideal.

The actual physiological demands for an athlete to be successful in sports competition also need to be taken into account. Not just *any* body will do in the sporting world. There are specific bodies required of athletes, primarily physically fit bodies for competition. One bodily requirement of female athletes, particularly in the sports of running, gymnastics, and swimming, is low percentage of body fat. In turn, low body fat is associated with thinness. However, this is socially constructed, because low body fat does not always equate with thinness. Body builders are the best example of this. The goal of body builders is to have a very low percentage of body fat, yet have a large build.

Therefore, in women's cross-country running, thin is viewed as performance enhancing, but thin is also associated with traditional white feminine beauty. For example, the following conversation occurred in a joking manner, but nevertheless expresses a certain level of jealousy and admiration between one teammate and another, concerning body size. Linda, concerned about her eating habits, told another teammate, Courtney, that she felt she was eating too much chocolate. Courtney, with a rather disconnected reply stated, "That is why you are always cold, because you are so skinny. She [Linda] doesn't have any meat on her bones to keep her warm." Linda replied, "You can't call me skinny anymore compared to all the girls on the team." Courtney responded, "There are only two girls on the team skinnier than you." Linda argued there was a third woman who was skinnier, at which point Courtney replied that the third woman was not skinnier, just shorter.

Eva's perspective represents the overarching view that some runners directly mentioned, while others only mentioned it indirectly. Eva sees being an athlete and being feminine as never having been an issue because "[t]hey think of cross- country girls as *little skinny girls,* that run miles and miles, it's that stereotype, it's not like oh, those *masculine big girls*" (emphasis added). This example illustrates that every aspect of the athlete's appearance, including body size, runs the risk of gender assessment (Curry 1996).

Creating Uniformity

In the 1950s, individual female athletes created personal strategies for combating the incompatible images of being female and being an athlete. Some women "demonstrated femininity through the clothes they wore, their demeanor, or off-field interest" (Cahn 1994:5). Today ways to express femininity in the sport of long-distance running are through the body, the uniforms on the body, and the length of distance run. All three are smaller versions of the bigger "male" counterparts. The length of distance run in men's college races is 5 and 6.2 miles, while the women's distance is 3.1 and 3.72 miles.

Aside from a change in the type of fabric used, the men's uniform for cross-country running has changed very little over the past twenty-five years. The women's uniform, however, has been drastically modified (see Figures 10.1–10.4). Uniforms moved from tank tops and briefs to body-suits, to crop tops with briefs, with each change involving increasingly smaller and tighter uniforms. Today, women's cross-country uniforms and the bodies in those uniforms are shrinking, paradoxically during the era of increasing "gender equity."[4]

Many women commented that the briefs were a source of status and teams that wear the briefs are viewed as the better teams. This was true in the 1950s as well. Cahn, writing of female basketball players in the 1950s notes, "Uniforms were either an unquestioned part of the game or, more positively, a badge that symbolized team membership and advanced skill" (1994:103). In other words, performance is associated with and tied to the uniform, although there is no intrinsic link. Not surprisingly, given that the uniform is a symbol of status, very few of the women were critical of

Figure 10.1.   The tank top with briefs. Uniform first worn in the late 1980s.

Figure 10.2. Teams began to wear the one-piece body suit in the early 1990s.

Figure 10.3. The most recent innovation in women's uniform, the crop top with briefs.

Figure 10.4. Example of a male uniform in 1996. Men's uniforms have changed
    very little over the past fifty years.

it. While uniforms provide no direct improvement of performance, they
are another convention of sport that goes unquestioned by most athletes
(despite the fact that coaches, spectators, and parents have often debated
appropriate uniforms).[5] Cross country uniforms (see Figures 10.1–10.3)
presuppose a certain body type *and* our society imposes notions of what
this body should be.

It appears that women shape their bodies to fit the uniforms. Most of
the women interviewed, like much of society, viewed eating disorders as
strictly an individual, psychological issue (the body as private domain),
yet at the same time the sport and the required uniform make the women
highly aware of their bodies (the body becomes public domain). Almost all
of the women interviewed said they initially did not like the uniforms, but
most have grown to like them. While one could argue that the women just
got used to them, I argue that these women are shaping their bodies,
mostly by losing weight, to make for a better fit in the uniforms. They feel
more comfortable in the uniform and in their bodies as they lose weight.
Hence, Nancy's comment, "I lost weight but it was like a gross skinny,

but . . . um . . . I liked it. I mean I just liked it. I just felt so comfortable being skinny."

For a few of the women, body size is not an issue for them personally, and therefore they never felt adverse to the uniform. Eva, for example, reveals how the uniform is a status symbol, but also how the uniform presupposes a certain body:

> I love the butt-huggers. I convinced my high school team to get them because I saw the college kids wearing them, people in my state were wearing them, the good teams, like high-status teams that were traditionally good had them. . . . I mean, we had a *real skinny cross country team, so nobody complained*. People complained more in track, but not very many, but after one year doing it, it was just accepted. . . . Some people got continually used to them, because it's such a power/status thing. . . . Now on this team I know a lot of people don't like them, a lot of people feel self-conscious. I mean, *if I was in their body I might feel self-conscious too*, I don't know. (emphasis added)

Another runner, Kathleen, articulated very clearly how the body is on public display, particularly in the patriarchal environment of sport. She spoke of a discussion she had had with one of the coaches about new uniforms. She explained that the coach was going to order new uniforms that consisted of crop tops with briefs (see Figure 10.3). She asked how the coach could order them before getting the size of each athlete. Kathleen states, "He responded, 'The men don't complain.' I'm like 'Yeah, you all don't complain because you get to see girls' butts.' It's fine if you're a bean pole and you don't have any fat on your legs."

Note, however, that the women rarely identified the connection between their weight loss and their increasing satisfaction with the uniforms. Referring to her initial dislike of the uniforms, Veronica stated, "I vowed I was not going to go to a school that wore bun huggers. . . . I definitely would stand at the [starting] line and, you know, try to cover my butt and my legs but, I mean, I was less competitive then, too . . . but I don't think I was self-conscious because the uniforms were risque. I think it was just more my own thoughts about it."

The key point is that Veronica does not feel the uniforms have anything to do with the way she felt; it was just "all in her mind." However, her comments allude to how she has reshaped her body to fit the uniform. Consider a discussion she had with her coach, which she conveyed in our interview: "The coach never said anything about my weight, like my sophomore and junior year the coach said, 'You're really looking fit now. You used to have a little on your hips and butt—you know, I wouldn't have said anything—but now you look good.'" This exchange with the coach, as well as Kathleen's exchange, highlights one more way the body is made a social concern.

THE NATIONAL COLLEGIATE ATHLETIC ASSOCIATION'S TREATMENT OF THE ISSUE

A final aspect of the athlete's network needs to be discussed. The National Collegiate Athletic Association (NCAA) is the dominant governing body of most intercollegiate sports in the United States. The NCAA creates the policy and rules of intercollegiate sport and regulates the coaches and the athletes. The NCAA is a silent structure present in these women's daily lives, regulating their practice time, study hours, money allocation, and uniforms. Therefore, the implications of the NCAA's treatment of eating disorders both helps and hurts these women. The NCAA has taken a reactive position in dealing with eating disorders, and they have adopted the biomedical model for diagnosis and treatment.

As discussed previously, within sports it is generally assumed that a male athlete will have a muscular body, while a female athlete will have a toned, but petite body. Therefore, it should be no surprise that the NCAA faces problems associated with steroid usage among male athletes, and high rates of eating disorders among female athletes. This is evident in two advertisements produced by the NCAA in an attempt to address these two problems associated with athletes' bodies (Figures 10.5 and 10.6).

The advertisement in Figure 10.5 encourages men to avoid using steroids and shows a male lifting weights, with the caption, "Make muscle the old-fashioned way." The photo in the ad indicates that the male is clearly in control of the situation. He is holding a weight (which we assume by the flex of his arm is heavy) and he can at any moment decide to put down the weight, once again implying he has control over the situation.

Contrast this to the advertisement in Figure 10.6. This ad shows a woman sitting slumped on a scale with her right leg chained to it. The caption reads, "Don't Let Weight Control You," and then gives two lists of warning signs for anorexia nervosa and bulimia. The caption and the photo imply the woman's lack of control. If the words are not enough to emphasize her helplessness, she is *chained* to the scale and her posture tells us she is mentally and physically exhausted or fed up with trying to unchain herself—meaning she cannot do it alone. Also, note the list of warning signs. This list has been provided not only for the individual sufferer, but more importantly for those around her to be able to judge and decide if this person has a problem. Again this implies that women in sport are mentally inferior, weak, and lacking control.

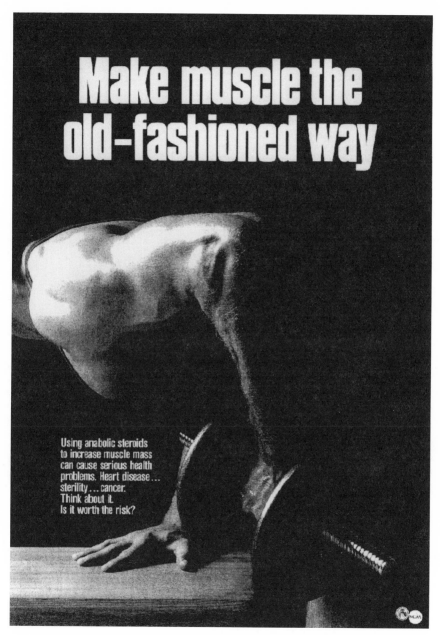

Figure 10.5. NCAA advertisement on steroid usage. From *NCAA News* 1996, vol. 33, p. 28. Reprinted with permission.

Figure 10.6. NCAA advertisement on eating disorders. From *NCAA News* 1996, vol. 33, p. 30. Reprinted with permission.

Finally, and most importantly, the woman in the ad is dressed in a pair of shorts and a T-shirt, not the standard uniform of female athletes in cross country, gymnastics, or swimming. These three sports, "appear to be the most affected by this phenomenon of eating disorders" (Blinde 1994:141).

Thus, while it is positive that the NCAA is dealing with the two issues of steroid use and eating disorders, its approach may be doing very little toward prevention. Both of these advertisements present the problems as strictly located within individuals, rather than addressing how intercollegiate sport produces an environment where steroid abuse and eating disorders are a part of the patterned networks that construct the environment of the athletes and the athletes' bodies.

CONCLUSIONS

If we place the embodied female athlete at the center of analysis of patterned networks, we can begin to understand the complex intersections of the body, sport, and society: why some male cross-country runners have disordered eating and eating disorders (thin for performance), but why more female runners have disordered eating and eating disorders (thin for performance and feminine identity).

This description of the various intersecting networks of food, sport, and bodies could be expanded to include many more intersections with other networks. However, this discussion has focused solely on the networks that are located closest to the embodied female athletes. All of these networks contribute to the construction of female cross-country runners' lives and in turn, contribute to the construction of their bodies. These patterned networks form a foundation for future analysis of the lives of intercollegiate female athletes.

My intent has been to demonstrate that collegiate runners' bodies and, in turn, their experiences are shaped by the patterned networks within which they are embedded. Food, physical bodies, and uniforms are points within cooperating networks, and all impact and are impacted by the social environment. Uniforms partially shape women's bodies and produce part of bodily and team collectivity, since nonuniform bodies have to fit into them. The particular type of uniform tends to promote eating disorders and disorderly eating by unduly emphasizing the differences between the actual and the ideal body type.

Discussing eating disorders and disorderly eating within a framework of cooperating networks provides for a better understanding than a strictly biological or psychological explanation. In the context of a sporting world constructed around false gender distinctions, a high level of disordered eating and eating disorders is the norm, not the exception.

Only by attempting to change the conventions of sport (and by extension society) will there be a decrease in disordered eating and eating disorders. However, changing the conventions of sport is an extremely difficult task, because conventions are "complexly interdependent systems, so that one small change may require a variety of other changes" (Becker 1982:35).

NOTES

1. A brief elaboration of the term "eating disorders" seems appropriate. Clinical eating disorders include bulimia and anorexia nervosa (Hsu 1990). A subclinical disorder, anorexia athletica, is the use of excessive amounts of exercise to "purge" the body of food consumed (Beals and Manore 1994). The term "disordered eaters" refers to individuals who have some of the characteristic traits of people with eating disorders, but do not have them all and therefore, would not fall under the clinical diagnosis.

2. It was not until 1972 that women were recognized as officially being allowed to participate in the Boston Marathon, although the first woman ran unofficially in 1966 (Falls 1977).

3. Gender checking is done by scraping cells from the interior wall of the woman's cheek to ensure that all competitors in women's Olympic sports are truly women. Gender checking is done to prevent men from passing as women and competing in women's sports.

4. "Psychologists and social researchers contend there has been a 30-year trend toward a feminine ideal of ever- increasing slenderness" (Way 1995:92).

5. Cahn (1994) provides a more in-depth historical discussion.

ACKNOWLEDGEMENTS

I would like to thank the Department of Sociology at Michigan State University. In particular, Lawrence Busch, Maxine Baca Zinn, Rita Gallin and Steve Gold who all offered critical feedback on previous drafts of this chapter. In addition, Heather Hotlzclaw, Mathew Kleiman, and Merideth Trahan all deserve thanks for their endless support.

REFERENCES

Beals, K. A., and M. M. Manore. 1994. "The Prevalence and Consequences of Sub-clinical Eating Disorders in Female Athletes." *International Journal of Sport Nutrition* 4(2):175–95.

Beardsworth, A., and T. Keil. 1997. *Sociology on the Menu: An Invitation to the Study of Food and Society*. New York: Routledge.

Becker, H. S. 1982. *Art Worlds*. Berkeley: University of California Press.

Birrell, S. 1994. "Is a Diamond Forever? Feminist Transformations of Sport." Pp. 221–44 in *Women, Sport, and Culture,* edited by S. Birrell and C. Cole. Champaign, IL: Human Kinetics.

Birrell, S., and C. L. Cole, eds. 1994. *Women, Sport, and Culture.* Champaign, IL: Human Kinetics.

Blinde, E. 1994. "Unequal Exchange and Exploitation in College Sport: The Case of the Female Athlete in Women, Sport and Culture." Pp. 135–48 in *Women, Sport, and Culture,* edited by S. Birrell and C. Cole. Champaign, IL: Human Kinetics.

Bordo, S. 1993. *Unbearable Weight: Feminism, Western Culture, and the Body.* Berkeley: University of California Press.

Brownell, S. 1995. *Training the Body in China: Sports in the Moral Order of the People's Republic of China.* Chicago: University of Chicago Press.

Burton, N. M. 1994. *The Stronger Women Get, The More Men Love Football: Sexism and the American Culture of Sports.* New York: Avon.

Cahn, S. 1994. *Coming On Strong: Gender and Sexuality in Twentieth-Century Women's Sport.* Cambridge, MA: Harvard University Press.

Callon, M., and J. Law. 1998. "After the Individual in Society: Lessons on Collectivity from Science, Technology and Society." *Canadian Journal of Sociology* 22:165–82.

Cline, S. 1990. *Just Desserts: Women and Food.* London: Andre Deutsch.

Conrad, P. and J. W. Schneider. 1980. *Deviance and Medicalization: From Badness to Sickness.* St. Louis, MO: C. V. Mosby.

Cooper, P. 1995. "Marathon Women and the Corporation." *Journal of Women's History* 7(14):62–81.

Curry, T. J. 1996. "Fraternal Bonding in the Locker Room." Pp. 79–96 in *Sport in Contemporary Society: An Anthology,* fifth edition, edited by S. D. Eitzen. New York: St. Martin's.

Deuster, P. A. 1996. *The Navy SEAL Nutrition Guide.* Upland, PA: DIANE.

Downes, S., and D. MacKay. 1996. *Running Scared: How Athletics Lost Its Innocence.* Edinburgh: Mainstream Publishers Project.

Doyal, L. 1979. *The Political Economy of Health.* London: Pluto.

———. 1995. *What Makes Women Sick: Gender and the Political Economy of Health.* New Brunswick, NJ: Rutgers University Press.

Eitzen, D. S. 1996. *Sport in Contemporary Society: An Anthology,* fifth edition. New York: St. Martin's.

Falls, J. 1977. *The Boston Marathon.* New York: Collier.

Goffman, E. 1977. *The Arrangement Between the Sexes.* Amsterdam: Elsevier Scientific.

Gura, T. 1996. "Obesity Shares Its Secrets." *Science* 275(5301):751–53.

Hesse-Biber, S. 1996. *Am I Thin Enough Yet? The Cult of Thinness and the Commercialization of Identity.* New York: Oxford University Press.

Hsu, L. K. G. 1990. *Eating Disorders.* New York: Guilford.

Hubbard, R. 1995. *Profitable Promises: Essays on Women, Science and Health.* Monroe, ME: Common Courage.

Lewontin, R. C. 1991. *Biology as Ideology: The Doctrine of DNA.* New York: Harper Perennial.

Lorber, J. 1993. "Believing Is Seeing: Biology as Ideology." *Gender and Society* 7(4):568–81.

Lovett, C. 1997. *Olympic Marathon: A Centennial History of the Games' Most Storied Race.* London: Praeger.

Lupton, D. 1996. "Sugar and Snails: The Gendering of Food and Food Preferences." Pp. 22–27 in *The Sociology of Food and Nutrition: Australian Perspectives,* edited by J. Germov and L. Williams. Newcastle: Australian Sociological Association.

Messner, M. A. 1988. "Sports and Male Domination: The Female Athlete as Contested Ideological Terrain." *Sociology of Sport Journal* 5:197–211.

———. 1996. "Studying Up On Sex." *Sociology of Sport Journal* 13(3):221–37.

———. 1997. "When Bodies Are Weapons." Pp. 146–50 in *Through the Prism of Difference: Readings on Sex and Gender,* edited by M. B. Zinn, P. Hondagneu-Sotelo, and M. A. Messner. Boston: Allyn and Bacon.

NCAA News. 1996. 33(38, October 28):6, 11.

Root, M. P. 1990. "Disordered Eating in Women of Color." *Sex Roles* 22(7/8):525–35.

Scott, S., and D. Morgan, eds. 1993. *Body Matters: Essays on the Sociology of the Body.* Washington, DC: Falmer.

Seid, R. P. 1994. "Too 'Close to the Bone': The Historical Context for Women's Obsession with Slenderness." Pp. 3–16 in *Feminist Perspectives on Eating Disorders,* edited by P. Fallon, M. A. Katzman, and S. C. Wooley. New York: Guilford.

Thompson, B. 1992. ""A Way Outa No Way": Eating Problems Among African-American, Latina, and White Women." *Gender and Society* 6(4):546–62.

Turner, B. S. 1992. "The Body Question: Recent Developments in Social Theory." Pp. 31–66 in *Regulating Bodies,* edited by B. S. Turner. London: Routledge.

Way, K. 1995. "Never Too Rich . . . Or Too Thin: The Role of Stigma in the Social Construction of Anorexia Nervosa." Pp. 91–116 in *Eating Agendas: Food and Nutrition as Social Problems,* edited by D. Maurer and J. Sobal. Hawthorne, NY: Aldine de Gruyter.

Wooley, O. W. 1994 " . . . And Man Created 'Woman': Representations of Women's Bodies in Western Culture." Pp. 3–16 in *Feminist Perspectives on Eating Disorders,* edited by P. Fallon, M. A. Katzman, and S. C. Wooley. New York: Guilford.

V

REINTERPRETING WEIGHT

11

Pounds of Flesh
Weight, Gender, and Body Images

THOMAS F. CASH and ROBIN E. ROY

We live in a culture and era that place considerable emphasis on the aesthetics of the human body. In recognition of this fact, social and behavioral scientists increasingly have investigated and discussed the influences of physical appearance on human development in the course of everyday life (Bull and Rumsey 1988; Cash and Pruzinsky 1990; Hatfield and Sprecher 1986; Jackson 1992). Within this voluminous literature is a body of knowledge regarding the psychosocial correlates and consequences of obesity. In this chapter, we will first examine how body weight, especially obesity, affects body image and psychological adjustment. We will consider the roles played by culture and gender in the socialization of the personal meanings of weight in body image development. Finally, we will articulate and evaluate extant interventions that aim to promote body acceptance and well-being among individuals with obesity.

UNDERSTANDING BODY IMAGES: DEFINITIONS AND DIMENSIONS

Conceptually distinct from objective or socially defined physical attributes (e.g., physical attractiveness, body weight, or somatotype), the psychological construct of body image has attracted substantial public and professional interest in recent years (Cash and Pruzinsky 1990; Fisher 1986; Thompson 1996). Although disparately defined over the course of the twentieth century, body image refers, most simply, to persons' highly subjective experiences of their own conditions of embodiment (Cash and Pruzinsky 1990).

One contemporary viewpoint regards body image as a perceptual representation of the body, particularly its size and shape. This somewhat narrow perspective has been greatly influenced by clinical researchers trying to understand the distorted perceptions held by patients with eating disorders, such as anorexia nervosa and bulimia nervosa. Assessment of the perceptual dimension of body image uses various body size estimation techniques, such as video imaging, to measure the accuracy or distortion of one's judgments (Cash and Deagle 1997; Thompson 1996).

A second prominent perspective defines body image as a psychological attitude toward one's own physical characteristics, especially one's appearance (Cash 1990; Pruzinsky and Cash 1990). Body image attitudes are evident in people's mostly conscious, body-related cognitions, emotions, and behaviors. Body image is not only a traitlike construct, consisting of relatively stable dispositions toward one's body, but it also reflects more fluid experiential states in specific situational contexts (Pruzinsky and Cash 1990). Researchers typically use self-report questionnaires to measure specific components or dimensions of body image attitudes—including evaluations of physical attributes, beliefs about the importance of one's appearance, resultant emotional reactions in actual life situations, and behaviors to manage one's appearance or one's own reactions to it. Frequently used attitudinal measures include the Body Cathexis Scale, the Body Shape Questionnaire, the Multidimensional Body-Self Relations Questionnaire, the Body Image Ideals Questionnaire, the Appearance Schemas Inventory, and the Situational Inventory of Body Image Dysphoria (Cash and Pruzinsky 1990; Thompson 1996).

BODY IMAGES: A GROWING DISCONTENT

Cumulative survey research has confirmed the growing displeasure with which people, especially women, regard their own physical appearance (Cash and Henry 1995; Cash, Winstead, and Janda 1986; Feingold and Mazzella 1998; Garner 1997). A recent meta-analysis of 222 body image studies from the past fifty years reveals continual increases in women's body dissatisfaction (Feingold and Mazzella 1998). Whereas the physical foci of individuals' discontent certainly involve diverse concerns, discontent with body weight and shape dominate these concerns. For example, Garner's (1997) large-sample survey of Americans in *Psychology Today* magazine revealed that 52 percent of men and 66 percent of women were dissatisfied with their weight. Discontent with the middle torso was reported by 63 percent of men and 71 percent of women. Lower-torso dissatisfaction was reported by 29 percent of men and 61 percent of women. Muscle tone was felt to be unacceptable to 45 percent of men and 57 percent of women.

Clearly, body acceptance is a sizable challenge to many people. However, to those whose bodies do not conform to societal prescriptions and proscriptions, the challenge may weigh more heavily in the quality of their daily lives.

Preoccupation with body weight and shape is linked to the increasingly prevalent problem of eating disorders as well as other psychological dysfunctions, such as depression, social anxiety, and sexual difficulties (Cash and Pruzinsky 1990; Cash and Grant 1996; Cash and Deagle 1997; Freedman 1986; Thompson 1996). Gaining weight is one of the most common provocations of negative body image feelings. Two-thirds of women and over one-third of men in Garner's survey cited weight gains diminishing body satisfaction (Garner 1997). In an attempt to assuage feelings of dissatisfaction with weight, many people diet and exercise habitually, even obsessively. Americans spend more money on the products and services for beauty and weight control than they do on social services or education (Rodin 1992). Of Americans surveyed in 1996, 84 percent of women and 58 percent of men reported that they have dieted to lose weight, and women were much more likely than men to have attempted weight control in the past year by inducing vomiting (6 vs. 1 percent), abusing laxatives (6 vs. 3 percent), or taking diet pills (12 vs. 6 percent) (Garner 1997). Moreover, 24 percent of women and 17 percent of men said they would trade more than three years of their life if they could be at their desired weight. While physical exercise can certainly promote health and fitness, exercising is often motivated by attempts to lose or control weight and to enhance attractiveness (Cash, Novy, and Grant 1994). For example, 40 percent of men and 60 percent of women have reported that at least half of their workout time is spent exercising to control weight (Garner 1997).

FAT IS (MOSTLY) A FEMININE ISSUE

When asked to evaluate photographs of themselves or view their nude bodies in the mirror, women voice more criticism and feel greater self-consciousness and distress than men do (Freedman 1986). Muth and Cash (1997) found that, relative to college men, college women had more negative body image evaluations, stronger cognitive and behavioral investments in their looks, and more frequent body image dysphoria in everyday life situations. A community survey of people from ten to seventy-nine years of age revealed that, across the life span, female respondents placed more importance on their appearance and had lower body esteem than did males (Pliner, Chaiken, and Flett 1990).

Weight dissatisfaction has different meanings for women and men. For women, it almost always means feeling overweight; for men, it may mean "too skinny" as well as "too fat" (e.g., Cash et al. 1986; Drewnowski and Yee 1987; Silberstein, Striegel-Moore, Timko, and Rodin 1988). Garner's (1997) survey found that 89 percent of American women surveyed wanted to lose weight and only 3 percent of body-dissatisfied women wanted to gain weight. In contrast, 22 percent of body-dissatisfied men wished to gain weight. At most weight levels, women are more likely to think they are overweight than men are (Cash et al. 1986). Whereas about one-fourth of average-weight men regard themselves as overweight, the majority of average-weight women perceive themselves as overweight (Cash and Hicks 1990).

African-American women may be more immune to the tyranny of the thin ideal than their Caucasian counterparts. Identification with one's cultural group is important in what is perceived as ideal (Fallon 1990); African-Americans often have less strict standards of acceptable weight. At even heavier weights, African-American women have a more positive body image and less anxiety about being or becoming fat than do whites (e.g., Akan and Grilo 1995; Rucker and Cash 1992). Rucker and Cash (1992) found that African-American college women perceived silhouette figures as less fat than white women's judgments. In a large-sample U.S. study of nine- and ten-year old girls, Brown, Schreiber, McMahon, Crawford, and Ghee (1995) observed substantially greater body satisfaction among black than white girls, especially at higher body weights. However, not all African-American women are unaffected by society's slender ideal. With greater education, affluence, and assimilation into Caucasian culture, African-American women may be more likely to fall prey to these cultural standards of thinness (Altabe 1996; Thomas and James 1988).

Weight is a concrete criterion by which many women measure their worth (Rodin, Silberstein, and Striegel-Moore 1985). All too often, a number on the scale dictates how a woman feels about herself. Body image is a core component of self-concept (Cash and Pruzinsky 1990; Fisher 1986; Kreuger 1986). If one cannot accept the body one lives in, it is difficult to accept the person who lives there.

CULTURAL MESSAGES AND MIRRORS

Recent decades have witnessed the growth of the commercial diet and cosmetic surgery industries and the proliferation of media messages to promote culturally exacting standards of physical attractiveness (Brownell 1991; Cash 1995; Freedman 1986; Rodin 1992). Many individuals in our culture are in search of the "perfect body," an intense pursuit resembling what Brownell (1991) refers to as a "feeding frenzy." As a culture, we have an insatiable desire for information, medicines, and diet and exercise programs that will help us become slimmer and more fit. The media facilitate and feed this desire. Magazines promise to show us how to boost our metabolism, tone our thighs and abdomens, and teach us exercises that will melt away pounds. On television, we see countless commercials for diet drinks and foods, slimming exercise equipment, and weight-loss programs. News reports tell us about the latest diet drugs and may eventually inform us of their associated health risks.

Never Too Rich or Too Thin

The media clearly accentuate physical appearance for women more than for men, placing particular emphasis on a thin, trim figure (Garner, Garfinkel, Schwartz, and Thompson 1980; Heinberg 1996; Wiseman, Gray, Mosimann, and Ahrens 1992; Wiseman, Gunning, and Gray 1993). Andersen and DiDomenico (1992), for example, document the number of diet articles and advertisements in the ten magazines most frequently read by women as compared to the ten magazines most frequently read by men. The study's results indicate that women's magazines contained ten times as many diet-related articles as men's magazines did, and that men's magazines contained more fitness-related articles and advertisements.

The current standard of female attractiveness, much like past ideals of beauty, is restrictive and difficult to attain. Women who are tall and very thin with small hips and waists, large breasts, European facial features, and wrinkle-free skin are heralded as beautiful by our culture (Smith 1996). When Garner (1997) asked survey respondents what shaped their body images during childhood and adolescence, the majority of women cited the media-managed, cultural theme that thinness equals happiness. The media promulgate this message that beauty, success, happiness, wealth, love, and sexuality come with slimness (Fallon 1990; Orbach 1982). The "perfect body" also symbolizes self-control—the result of hard work and delay of gratification, traits that are valued in our society (Brownell 1991).

If Only She Weren't So Fat

In addition to aspiration for the slim-and-fit body ideals is another "weight-watching" force: anxiety, antipathy, and avoidance of fatness. Being overweight or obese is highly stigmatized in our society. Early in life, children learn the negative stereotypes associated with "excessive" weight (Flannery-Schroeder and Chrisler 1996). Lerner and Gellert (1969) found that five- and six-year-old children reacted with an aversion to photographs of "chubby" children, with 86 percent of children reporting that they did not want to look like such children. Caskey and Felker (1971) found that girls in the first through fifth grades attributed favorable characteristics to an ectomorphic silhouette, describing this thin image as honest, happy, pretty, smart, kind, and helpful. In contrast, they perceived endomorphs as lazy, lonely, sloppy, ugly, mean, dirty, and stupid. The research literature leaves little doubt that the insidious stigma of obesity is evident even in childhood (DeJong and Kleck 1986; Jackson 1992).

Even among people who eschew sexism or racism, an antifat sentiment seems less socially abhorrent. Recent research on prejudice toward fat people identified three basic attitudinal components (Lewis, Cash, Jacobi, and Bubb-Lewis 1997): (1) disparagement and attribution of negative character traits, (2) perceptions of physical and romantic unattractiveness, and (3) assignment of responsibility or blame for fatness. The latter dimension may be a pivotal factor. The belief that body weight is a personally controllable condition, as opposed to one that is strongly biogenetically controlled, engenders more stigmatization of fat individuals (DeJong and Kleck 1986; Lewis et al. 1997). One's own anxiety about being or becoming fat is also modestly related to negative views toward fat people (Lewis et al. 1997). More importantly, there is little evidence that actual body size is associated with such social prejudice (Allison, Basile, and Yuker 1991; Crandall and Biernat 1990; Lewis et al. 1997). If being heavier does not mitigate against having antifat attitudes, it is no wonder that body acceptance is so difficult for "overweight" or obese people.

Fat Chances

Not only is a thin figure associated with favorable social attributions, it is also linked to a higher socioeconomic status. Especially among women, there is an inverse relationship between weight and socioeconomic status (Sobal 1995b). In general, obesity may impede opportunities for interpersonal success and for socioeconomic mobility (Gortmaker, Must, Perrin, Sobol, and Deitz 1993; Sobal 1995b). Stereotyping of obese or overweight individuals may adversely affect their vocational (Larkin and Pines 1979) and educational opportunities (Canning and Mayer 1966). They may be discriminated against in the search for housing (Karris 1977), be assisted less quickly by salespeople (Pauley 1989), and may even find that others are less compliant with their requests (Rodin and Slochower 1974; Steinberg and Birk 1983). Heavier women have been found to date less often, have less date or mate satisfaction, and experience more peer criticism than their average-weight counterparts (Stake and Lauer 1987). Stigmatization of the obese or overweight is so powerful that such organizations as the National Association to Advance Fat Acceptance have been established to provide advocacy and support (Sobal 1995a; see also Chapter 4 in this volume).

Unreal Ideals: Weighing Heavy on the Mind

Cultural exhortations to pursue thinness and avoid fatness are not readily dismissed. Recent research reveals the deleterious effects of exposure to the media images that reflect the thin, attractive standards of feminine beauty. Such exposure may lead individuals to judge others' appearance more harshly (e.g., Kenrick and Guttieres 1980; Martin and Kennedy 1993). It may also engender self-evaluative social comparisons. As a result, the person concludes that she "doesn't measure up" to these standards and experiences body image discontent and dysphoria (e.g., Cash, Cash, and Butters 1983; Heinberg and Thompson 1995; Irving 1990; Richins 1991; Stice and Shaw 1994). In fact, 43 percent of women who are very dissatisfied with their appearance state that they compare themselves with models in fashion magazines, and 47 percent of dissatisfied women state they carefully study the shapes of the models (Garner 1997). Not only does such investment in unrealistic ideals of beauty foster chronic body dissatisfaction, it can also lead to competition, envy, jealousy, and stereotyping among women (Cash, Roy, and Strachan 1997; Joseph 1985; Smith 1996).

As a result of the personal internalization of these images and expectations, further damage is done. Striving to reach unrealistic standards of beauty may make for chronic dissatisfaction with appearance. Higgins's (1987, 1989) self-discrepancy theory maintains that psychological distress occurs when people's beliefs about themselves are discrepant from who they would like to be or who others expect them to be. Disparity between one's self-perceived physical characteristics and one's personal physical ideals is a major component of body image dissatisfaction and distress (Cash and Pruzinsky 1990; Cash and Szymanski 1995; Szymanski and Cash 1995; Thompson 1996). The internalization of thin standards leads people of average to heavier body weights to feel that their bodies are unacceptably large and in need of slimming changes. In fact, Cash and Hicks (1990) found that average-weight persons who labeled themselves as overweight had a less satisfying body image and poorer psychological well-being than average-weight peers who labeled their weight as "normal." The researchers further compared overweight persons and those who were average weight but classified themselves as overweight. These comparisons indicated that the psychological differences between "being fat" versus "thinking fat" were minimal and when present they occurred mostly for women.

According to Cash's cognitive-social learning perspective (Cash 1995, 1996, 1997; Cash and Grant 1996), situations that accentuate and bring to mind these physical self-ideal discrepancies will precipitate negative body image cognitions and emotions, especially for persons who are highly psychologically invested in their physical appearance. Rather than experience such distress, these individuals have several coping options. They may attempt to modify their body to match the ideal (e.g., diet, exercise, liposuction). They may conceal the offending feature (e.g., wear the loose, dark "fat clothes"). They may avoid the situation (e.g., no dancing, no beaches, no aerobics classes). They may compensate by pursuing more attainable ideals on other valued dimensions of appearance (e.g., getting a new hair style or more fashionable clothes), personality (e.g., being more friendly), or competence (e.g., mastering Italian cooking or stock market trading). While these various strategies serve to manage distress in the short term, they do little to produce body acceptance. In fact, situational avoidance and body concealment only reinforce one's sense of physical unacceptability.

OBESITY, BODY IMAGES, AND PSYCHOPATHOLOGY

A traditional, psychoanalytic perspective often regards obesity as a symptom of some unconscious intrapsychic conflict or a self-protective, defense mechanism (see Fisher 1986). Thus, obesity is viewed as a consequence and not a cause of psychological disturbance. Longitudinal research, however, does not support the proposition that childhood obesity results from psychological or familial dysfunctions (e.g., Klesges, Haddock, Stein, M. Klesges, Eck, and Hanson 1992). It can be argued that this perspective merely reflects the cultural bias against obesity, whereby fat people are blamed by ascribing their physical condition to moral or psychological defects (DeJong and Kleck 1986; Lewis et al. 1997; Sobal 1995a). In contrast, a biosocial learning paradigm recognizes the biogenetic determinants of obesity and regards its associated social and personal adversities as predisposing psychological distress.

So is there a relationship between obesity and psychopathology? Research suggests that there is *not* increased psychopathology among obese individuals in the general population (O'Neil and Jarrell 1992; Striegel-Moore and Rodin 1986; Stunkard and Wadden 1992; Wadden and Stunkard 1985). In the most thorough examination of this question to date, Friedman and Brownell (1995) used both narrative-review and meta-analytic techniques to determine whether there is a relationship between obesity and psychopathology. They found no association between obesity and either depression or anxiety, although they noted that methodological shortcomings of some studies preclude firm conclusions. Whereas obesity was modestly but inconsistently negatively related to self-concept or self-esteem, it was more strongly negatively related to body image—a finding recently corroborated among children and adolescents (Mendelson, White, and Mendelson 1996). Recognizing the heterogeneity of the obese population, Friedman and Brownell (1995) found that obese individuals' efforts to lose weight may partly reflect motives derived from greater psychological distress. Indeed, the investigators' meta-analytic evidence indicates that treatment-seekers do display a higher prevalence of psychopathology. Cash (1993) confirmed this proposition with specific respect to body dissatisfaction among enrollees in a commercial very-low-calorie diet (VLCD) program compared with weight-matched controls.

Friedman and Brownell (1995) further stressed the need to identify risk factors that enable us to understand which obese individuals will experience negative psychological consequences. Gender is clearly one such risk factor. Relative to men, women are more likely to experience both social stigma and psychological impairment from obesity and are overwhelmingly more likely to seek weight-loss treatment (Brownell 1991; Rodin 1992; Wadden and Stunkard 1985). From their review, Friedman and Brownell argued that obese women may be more likely to experience body image disturbances, low self-concept, and pessimistic attributions. The authors pointed to other empirically supported factors that may predispose psychological suffering from obesity, namely, histories of dietary restraint and weight cycling, binge eating, and the receipt of weight-related teasing during one's youth. Such factors reflect enduring and failing struggles in one's relationship with one's body.

To these vulnerability dimensions, we would add the factor of psychological investment in appearance, especially maladaptive beliefs (i.e., self-schemas) related to physical appearance, weight, or shape (Cash 1996, 1997; Cash and Grant 1996; Cash and Labarge 1996). Cash (1993) observed that treatment-seekers were more invested in their appearance than were weight-matched controls. Having a body that one views disparagingly as discrepant from valued physical ideals that are central to one's sense of personal acceptability can compromise psychological well-being.

WEIGHT LOSS FOR BODY IMAGE CHANGE

How can the inherent psychosocial difficulties of obesity be addressed? How can fat people find contentment with their corporeal condition? Professionals' predominant perspective for body image change among fat people encourages body change. Practitioners routinely reply to such persons' complaints of body loathing by offering expertise in weight loss management. In effect, the clinician says to the client, "Of course you hate your fat body. If you lose weight you will be able to feel better about your looks and yourself." This communication echoes the well-absorbed societal messages about the futility of body acceptance without body change and implicitly reinforces the client's disparaging thoughts and feelings about being fat.

So does weight loss effectively improve body image? Surprisingly few weight-loss studies have incorporated systematic attitudinal assessments of body image—an unfortunate fact that reveals the presumed irrelevance of body image as a motive for and goal of weight loss (Cash 1994; Rosen

1996). Several investigations do confirm that greater body satisfaction may result from "successful" weight loss. Two studies indicated body image improvements among severely obese patients who lost considerable weight as the result of gastrointestinal surgery (Adami, Gandolfo, Campostano, Bauer, Cocchi, and Scopinaro 1994; Stunkard and Wadden 1992). In one prospective study of a commercial weight loss program, Cash (1994) found that those who completed the treatment reduced their weight by an average of 24 percent and reported substantial improvements in body satisfaction that reflected diminished discrepancies from their personal body-size ideals.

Similarly, in a large-sample, twenty-four-week clinical trial of a diet-and-exercise treatment of obesity that also incorporated body image sessions (based on Cash 1995), Foster, Wadden, and Vogt (1997) found that significant body image improvements accompanied the mean 19.4-kg weight reduction and that body image changes were not linearly related to weight loss. Nevertheless, both Cash (1994) and Foster et al. (1997) documented that the partial regaining of weight at follow-up produced a modest but significant erosion of the body image gains. Retrospective research further indicates that diminished body satisfaction is one of the most frequent "side effects" of regaining weight in obesity treatment programs (Kayman, Bruvold, and Stern 1990; Wadden, Stunkard, and Liebschutz 1988).

The prevalence of substantial weight regains in such programs, particularly the poor long-term maintenance of weight loss (e.g., Brownell 1992; Garner and Wooley 1991; Grilo 1996; Wadden 1993; Wilson 1994), calls into question the durability of their efficacy in promoting body acceptance. To the extent that these programs ignore the personal, psychosocial meanings of body weight, they may contribute to clients' maladaptive equation of fatness, failure, and body image disparagement. In their journey to control and alter their unacceptable bodies, they have acquired vulnerable, weight-based body images. Evincing a "phantom fat" phenomenon (Stunkard and Burt 1967; Stunkard and Mendelson 1967), the body images of average-weight but formerly overweight women are more similar to currently overweight women than to stable average-weight peers (Cash, Counts, and Huffine 1990). Indeed, obese people with more recurrent weight-loss dieting have a more negative body image (Foster et al. 1997).

NONDIETING BODY IMAGE INTERVENTIONS

An expert panel assembled by the National Institutes of Health recommended a shift from the traditional dieting treatments, concluding that "approaches that can produce health benefits independently of weight loss may be the best way to improve the physical and psychological health of Americans seeking to lose weight" (1992:947). There is an emerging perspective that appreciates the importance of body image in the provision of therapeutic assistance to people with obesity (Brownell 1991; Brownell and Rodin 1994; Brownell and Wadden 1991, 1992; Cash 1994; Foster et al. 1997; Rosen 1996; Rosen and Cash 1995). This viewpoint recognizes the necessity of addressing body image issues in their own right—whether as a component of weight-management interventions or as a needed therapeutic alternative to weight reduction, particularly for individuals who are poor candidates for weight-loss regimens. Body image change as an alternative to weight-loss treatment has sometimes been included as a psychoeducational facet of "undieting" programs that aim to eliminate unproductive, unhealthy eating and dieting behaviors. Other proponents regard body image change as a primary goal without encouraging or discouraging concurrent weight-loss goals (Rosen 1996; Rosen and Cash 1995).

Psychoeducational Efforts

Do antidieting or undieting interventions enhance body acceptance among obese women? Program evaluations by Ciliska (1990) and Polivy and Herman (1992) failed to demonstrate body image improvements. While Roughan, Seddon, and Vernon-Roberts (1990) did observe body image gains in such a program, their study was uncontrolled, weight loss occurred, and analyses did not distinguish between obese and nonobese participants.

Robinson and Bacon (1996) developed an interesting program to decrease self-stigmatizing and enhance well-being of fat women. This eight-session group treatment aims to help them understand the cultural and social origins of their negative body image attitudes, reduce self-blame for their weight, examine misconceptions about their eating behaviors, redefine the meaning of beauty, expand activities restricted by their body image, and respond more assertively to weight-based social maltreatment. Robinson and Bacon (1996) conducted an uncontrolled evaluation of their program with forty-seven clients and found improvements in participants' fear of fatness, lifestyle restrictions, depression, and self-esteem. However, because the authors neglected to assess concomitant changes in weight or body image per se, the program remains scientifically unvalidated vis-à-vis durable body image enhancement among fat persons.

Lewis, Blair, and Booth (1992) evaluated an eleven-session group therapy program that included bibliotherapy (i.e., the assignment of detailed, written handouts) to promote a more positive body image and eating/dieting self-efficacy among obese women. Results revealed significant gains in self-esteem, assertiveness, and eating self-efficacy, with reduced emotional eating among the twenty-four participants. On the body image assessment focusing only on perceived size, a small but reliable decrement occurred. However, because participants also lost weight (2.4 kg), one cannot conclude that the psychological changes were independent of weight loss and not a veridical reflection of body-size appraisals. Blair, Lewis, and Booth (1992) also investigated the efficacy of four bibliotherapeutic leaflets entitled *Feeling Good about Your Body and Yourself.* After a year, relative to untreated controls, twenty-seven women receiving bibliotherapy reported somewhat less emotional eating but no changes in self-esteem, self-efficacy, or perceived or actual body size. Thus, such minimal interventions are unlikely to improve body image in the absence of weight loss.

Cognitive-Behavioral Body Image Therapy

The most promising approach for body image improvement is a comprehensive cognitive-behavioral program that specifically targets body image for change (Cash 1995, 1996, 1997; Cash and Grant 1996; Rosen 1996; Rosen and Cash 1995). Rosen, Orosan, and Reiter (1995) conducted a controlled outcome study of this eight-session program derived in adaptation and use of Cash's (1991) audiocassette program. The fifty-one obese women were randomly assigned to group cognitive-behavioral body image therapy or to a no-treatment control condition. Sessions included information to understand personal body image development and to confront antifat stereotypes, techniques of desensitizing exposure to distressing body areas and situations, and cognitive restructuring to alter disparaging body image thoughts and overvaluation of appearance standards and beliefs. Focusing exclusively on body image, the program did not provide any assistance to alter eating or exercise behaviors.

Rosen et al.'s (1995) treatment impressively benefited body image and other facets of psychosocial well-being. In contrast to the unimproved control group, 70 percent of the treated clients shifted from a clinically dysfunctional to a normal body image. These changes, which were sustained over four months and generalized to gains in self-esteem and psychological adjustment, were unrelated to changes in body weight—consistent with findings for nonobese participants in cognitive-behavioral body image treatment (Butters and Cash 1987; Grant and Cash 1995: Lavallee and Cash 1997).

Scientific evidence further confirms this program's efficacy even when self-administered with little or no professional supervision (Cash and Lavallee 1997; Grant and Cash 1995; Lavallee and Cash 1997). The structured eight-step program is currently available as *The Body Image Workbook* (Cash 1997). Though generally effective for body image enhancement, further research must determine its utility as a self-help intervention specifically for obese persons. Similarly, while we may wish to applaud the numerous, emergent books promoting self-acceptance among fat people (e.g., Erdman 1995; Garrison 1993; Higgs 1993; Johnson 1995; Mayer 1993; Schroeder 1992; Shaw 1982; Young 1995), their promises must be empirically evaluated.

SUMMARY AND CONCLUSIONS

In this chapter, we have offered an overview of the research literature on obesity and body image, defined as attitudes about one's physical appearance. The evidence reveals that body weight and shape are strong determinants of body image. In the context of our culture, fat people and those who view themselves as fat, especially women, struggle to accept a body not readily accepted by their social world. In fact, the most reliable psychological difference between obese and nonobese people is that the former have more negative body image attitudes.

The dieting industry's weight-loss programs and products reflect the dominant paradigm of body acceptance through body change. However, we have argued that such programs provide rather tenuous and temporary solutions, as they perpetuate the problematic equation of body weight and body acceptance. Although educating people about the traps and dangers of dieting and urging them to "just say no" is certainly a worthwhile message, alone it is somewhat simplistic and usually fails to facilitate body acceptance. Alternatively, as we have discussed, helpful cognitive-behavioral programs are emerging based on the premises that a positive body image need not depend on one's body size and that one can learn to change one's body image.

We should all aspire to a kinder, gentler society in which the size or appearance of one's body is irrelevant to one's worth. Social and political actions to transform our appearance-biased society offer crucial counterinfluences in the service of this goal. As admirable and necessary as such macromodifications may be, people whose bodies do not afford societal and personal acceptability need and deserve more immediate help to enhance their experiences of embodied life. As Burgard and Lyons cogently captured in a quotation of one fat woman's experience:

> I'm tired of being Sisyphus and rolling the weight loss boulder up the hill and over. I'm accepting my body as having been the innocent victim of society's torment. I want to love it, not hate it. (1994:228)

REFERENCES

Adami, G. F., P. Gandolfo, A. Campostano, B. Bauer, F. Cocchi, and N. Scopinaro. 1994. "Eating Disorder Inventory in the Assessment of Psychosocial Status in the Obese Patients Prior to and at Long Term Following Biliopancreatic Diversion for Obesity." *International Journal of Eating Disorders* 15:265–275.

Akan, G. E., and C. M. Grilo. 1995. "Sociocultural Influences on Eating Attitudes and Behaviors, Body-image, and Psychological Functioning: A Comparison of African-American, Asian-American, and Caucasian College Women." *International Journal of Eating Disorders* 18:181–87.

Allison, D. B., V. C. Basile, and H. E. Yuker. 1991. "The Measurement of Attitudes Toward and Beliefs About Obese Persons." *International Journal of Eating Disorders* 10:599–607.

Altabe, M. N. 1996. "Issues in the Assessment and Treatment of Body Image Disturbance in Culturally Diverse Populations." Pp. 129–47 in *Body Image, Eating Disorders, and Obesity: A Practical Guide for Assessment and Treatment,* edited by J. K. Thompson. Washington, DC: American Psychological Association.

Andersen, A. E., and L. DiDomenico. 1992. "Diet vs. Shape Content of Popular Male and Female Magazines: A Dose-Response Relationship to the Incidence of Eating Disorders?" *International Journal of Eating Disorders* 11:283–87.

Blair, A. J., V. J. Lewis, and D. A. Booth. 1992. "Response to Leaflets About Eating and Shape by Women Concerned About Their Weight." *Behavioural Psychotherapy* 20:279–86.

Brown, K. M., G. B. Schreiber, R. P. McMahon, P. Crawford, and K. L. Ghee. 1995. "Maternal Influences on Body Satisfaction in Black and White Girls Aged 9 and 10: The NHLBI Growth and Health Study (NGHS)." *Annals of Behavioral Medicine* 17:213–20.

Brownell, K. D. 1991. "Dieting and the Search for the Perfect Body: Where Physiology and Culture Collide." *Behavior Therapy* 22:1–12.

———. 1992. "Relapse and the Treatment of Obesity." Pp. 437–45 in *The Treatment of Severe Obesity by Diet and Lifestyle Modification,* edited by T. A. Wadden and T. B. Van Itallie. New York: Guilford.

Brownell, K. D., and J. Rodin. 1994. "The Dieting Maelstrom: Is it Possible and Advisable to Lose Weight?" *American Psychologist* 49:781–91.

Brownell, K. D., and T. A. Wadden. 1991. "The Heterogeneity of Obesity: Fitting Treatments to Individuals." *Behavior Therapy* 22:153–77.

———. 1992. "Etiology And Treatment of Obesity: Understanding a Serious, Prevalent, and Refractory Disorder." *Journal of Consulting and Clinical Psychology* 60:505–17.

Bull, R., and N. Rumsey. 1988. *The Social Psychology of Facial Appearance.* New York: Springer-Verlag.

Burgard, D., and P. Lyons. 1994. "Alternatives In Obesity Treatment: Focusing on Health for Fat Women." Pp. 212–30 in *Feminist Perspectives on Eating Disorders,* edited by P. Fallon, M. A. Katzman, and S. C. Wooley. New York: Guilford.

Butters, J. W., and T. F. Cash. 1987. "Cognitive-Behavioral Treatment of Women's Body-Image Dissatisfaction." *Journal of Consulting and Clinical Psychology* 55:889–97.

Canning, H., and J. Mayer. 1966. "Obesity—Its Possible Effects on College Admissions." *New England Journal of Medicine* 275:1172–74.

Cash, T. F. 1990. "The Psychology of Physical Appearance: Aesthetics, Attributes, and Images." Pp. 51–79 in *Body Images: Development, Deviance, and Change*, edited by T. F. Cash and T. Pruzinsky. New York: Guilford.

———. 1991. *Body-Image Therapy: A Program for Self-Directed Change*. New York: Guilford.

———. 1993. "Body-Image Attitudes Among Obese Enrolles in a Commercial Weight-Loss Program." *Perceptual and Motor Skills* 77:1099–1103.

———. 1994. "Body Image and Weight Changes in a Multisite, Comprehensive Very-Low-Calorie Diet Program." *Behavior Therapy* 25:239–54.

———. 1995. *What Do You See When You Look in the Mirror?* New York: Bantam.

———. 1996. "The Treatment of Body Image Disturbances." Pp. 83–107 in *Body Image, Eating Disorders, And Obesity: An Integrative Guide For Assessment And Treatment*, edited by J. K. Thompson. Washington, DC: American Psychological Association.

———. 1997. *The Body Image Workbook: An Eight-Step Program for Learning to Like Your Looks*. Oakland, CA: New Harbinger.

Cash, T. F., D. W. Cash, and J. W. Butters. 1983. "'Mirror Mirror on the Wall?': Contrast Effects and Self- Evaluations of Physical Attractiveness." *Personality and Social Psychology Bulletin* 9:351–58.

Cash, T. F., B. Counts, and C. E. Huffine. 1990. "Current and Vestigial Effects of Overweight Among Women: Fear of Fat, Attitudinal Body Image, and Eating Behaviors." *Journal of Psychopathology and Behavioral Assessment* 12:157–67.

Cash, T. F., and E. A. Deagle. 1997. "The Nature and Extent Of Body-Image Disturbances in Anorexia Nervosa and Bulimia Nervosa: A Meta-Analysis." *International Journal of Eating Disorders* 22:107–25.

Cash, T. F., and J. Grant. 1996. "The Cognitive-Behavioral Treatment of Body-Image Disturbances." Pp. 567–614 in *Sourcebook of Psychological Treatment Manuals for Adult Disorders*, edited by V. Van Hasselt and M. Hersen. New York: Plenum.

Cash, T. F., and P. E. Henry. 1995. "Women's Body Images: The Results of a National Survey in the U.S.A." *Sex Roles* 33:19–28.

Cash, T. F., and K. L. Hicks. 1990. "Being Fat versus Thinking Fat: Relationships with Body Image, Eating Behavior, and Well-Being." *Cognitive Therapy and Research* 14:327–41.

Cash, T. F., and A. S. Labarge. 1996. "Development of the Appearance Schemas Inventory: A New Cognitive Body-Image Assessment." *Cognitive Therapy and Research* 20:37–50.

Cash, T. F., and D. M. Lavallee. 1997. "Cognitive-Behavioral Body-Image Therapy: Extended Evidence of the Efficacy of a Self-Directed Program." *Journal of Rational-Emotive and Cognitive-Behavior Therapy* 15:281–94.

Cash, T. F., P. Novy, and J. Grant. 1994. "Why Do Women Exercise? Factor Analysis and Further Validation of the Reasons for Exercise Inventory." *Perceptual and Motor Skills* 78:539–44.

Cash, T. F., and T. Pruzinsky, eds. 1990. *Body Images: Development, Deviance, and Change*. New York: Guilford.

Cash, T. F., R. E. Roy, and M. D. Strachan. 1997. "How Physical Appearance Affects Relations Among Women: Implications for Women's Body Images." Poster session presented at the annual meeting of the American Psychological Society, Washington, DC.

Cash, T. F., and M. L. Szymanski. 1995. "The Development and Validation of the Body-Image Ideals Questionnaire." *Journal of Personality Assessment* 64:466–77.

Cash, T. F., B. A. Winstead, and L. H. Janda. 1986. "The Great American Shape-Up." *Psychology Today* 19:30–37.

Caskey, S. R., and D. W. Felker. 1971. "Social Stereotyping of Female Body Image by Elementary School Age Girls." *Research Quarterly* 42:251–55.

Ciliska, D. 1990. *Beyond Dieting: Psychoeducational Interventions for Chronically Obese Women, a Nondieting Approach.* New York: Brunner/Mazel.

Crandall, C. S., and M. Biernat. 1990. "The Ideology of Anti-Fat Attitudes." *Journal of Applied Social Psychology* 20:227–43.

DeJong, W., and R. Kleck. 1986. "The Social Psychological Effects of Overweight." Pp. 65–87 in *Physical Appearance, Stigma, and Social Behavior: The Ontario Symposium,* volume 3, edited by C. P. Herman, M. P. Zanna, and E. T. Higgins. Hillsdale, NJ: Erlbaum.

Drewnowski, A., and D. K. Yee. 1987. "Men and Body Image: Are Males Satisfied with Their Body Weight?" *Psychosomatic Medicine* 49:626–34.

Erdman, C. 1995. *Nothing to Lose: A Guide to Sane Living in a Large Body.* San Francisco: Harper.

Fallon, A. E. 1990. "Culture in the Mirror: Sociocultural Determinants of Body Image." Pp. 80–109 in *Body Images: Development, Deviance, and Change,* edited by T. F. Cash and T. Pruzinsky. New York: Guilford.

Feingold, A., and R. Mazzella. 1998. "Gender Differences in Body Image Are Increasing." *Psychological Science* 9:190–95.

Fisher, S. 1986. *Development and Structure of the Body Image.* Hillsdale, NJ: Earlbaum.

Flannery-Schroeder, E. C., and J. C. Chrisler. 1996. "Body Esteem, Eating Attitudes, and Gender-Role Orientation in Three Age Groups of Children." *Current Psychology* 15:235–48.

Foster, G. D., T. A. Wadden, and R. A. Vogt. 1997. "Body Image in Obese Women Before, During, and After Weight Loss Treatment." *Health Psychology* 16:226–29.

Freedman, R. 1986. *Beauty Bound.* Lexington, MA: Lexington.

Friedman, M. A., and K. D. Brownell. 1995. "Psychological Correlates of Obesity: Moving to the Next Research Generation." *Psychological Bulletin* 117:3–20.

Garner, D. M. 1997. "The 1997 Body Image Survey Results." *Psychology Today* 30:30–44, 75–84.

Garner, D. M., and S. C. Wooley. 1991. "Confronting the Failure of Behavioral and Dietary Treatments for Obesity." *Clinical Psychology Review* 11:729–80.

Garner, D. M., P. E. Garfinkel, D. Schwartz, and M. Thompson. 1980. "Cultural Expectations of Thinness in Women." *Psychological Reports* 47:483–91.

Garrison, T. N. 1993. *Fed Up! A Woman's Guide to Freedom from the Diet/Weight Prison.* New York: Carrol & Graf.

Gortmaker, S. L., A. Must, J. M. Perrin, A. M. Sobol, and W. H. Deitz. 1993. "Social and Economic Consequences of Overweight in Adolescence and Young Adulthood." *New England Journal of Medicine* 329:1008–12.

Grant, J. R., and T. F. Cash. 1995. "Cognitive-Behavioral Body-Image Therapy: Comparative Efficacy of Group and Modest-Contact Treatments." *Behavior Therapy* 26:69–84.

Grilo, C. M. 1996. "Treatment of Obesity: An Integrative Model." Pp. 389–423 in *Body Image, Eating Disorders, and Obesity: An Integrative Guide for Assessment and Treatment,* edited by J. K. Thompson. Washington, DC: American Psychological Association.

Hatfield, E., and S. Sprecher. 1986. *Mirror Mirror: The Importance of Looks in Everyday Life.* Albany, NY: SUNY Press.

Heinberg, L. 1996. "Theories of Body Image Disturbance: Perceptual, Developmental, and Sociocultural Factors." Pp. 27–47 in *Body Image, Eating Disorders, and Obesity: An Integrative Guide for Assessment and Treatment,* edited by J. K. Thompson. Washington, DC: American Psychological Association.

Heinberg, L. J., and J. K. Thompson. 1995. "Body Image and Televised Images of Thinness And Attractiveness: A Controlled Laboratory Investigation." *Journal of Social and Clinical Psychology* 14:325–38.

Higgins, E. T. 1987. "Self-Discrepancy: A Theory Relating Self and Affect." *Psychological Review* 94:319–40.

———. 1989. "Self-Discrepancy Theory: What Patterns of Self-Beliefs Cause People to Suffer?" Pp. 93–136 in *Advances in Experimental Social Psychology,* edited by L. Berkowitz. New York: Academic.

Higgs, L. C. 1993. *One Size Fits All—And Other Fables.* Nashville: Thomas Nelson.

Irving, L. M. 1990. "Mirror Images: Effects of the Standard of Beauty on the Self- and Body-Esteem of Women Exhibiting Varying Levels of Bulimic Symptoms." *Journal of Social and Clinical Psychology* 9:230–42.

Jackson, L. A. 1992. *Physical Appearance and Gender: Sociobiological and Sociocultural Perspectives.* Albany: SUNY Press.

Johnson, C. A. 1995. *Self-Esteem Comes in All Sizes.* New York: Doubleday.

Joseph, R. 1985. "Competition Between Women." *Psychology, A Quarterly Journal of Human Behavior* 22:1–12.

Karris, L. 1977. "Prejudice Against Obese Renters." *Journal of Social Psychology* 101:159–60.

Kayman, S., W. Bruvold, and J. S. Stern. 1990. "Maintenance and Relapse After Weight Loss in Women: Behavioral Aspects." *American Journal of Clinical Nutrition* 52:800–7.

Kenrick, D. T., and S. E. Guttieres. 1980. "Contrast Effects and Judgments of Physical Attractiveness: When Beauty Becomes a Social Problem." *Journal of Personality and Social Psychology* 38:131–40.

Klesges, R. C., C. K. Haddock, R. J. Stein, L. M. Klesges, L. H. Eck, and C. L. Hanson. 1992. "Relationship between Psychosocial Functioning and Body Fat in Pre-School Children: A Longitudinal Investigation." *Journal of Consulting and Clinical Psychology* 55:872–76.

Kreuger, D. W. 1986. *Body Self and Psychological Self: Developmental and Clinical Integration in Disorders of the Self.* New York: Brunner/Mazel.

Larkin, J. C., and H. A. Pines. 1979. "No Fat Persons Need Apply: Experimental Studies of the Overweight Stereotype and Hiring Preference." *Sociology of Work and Occupations* 6:312–27.

Lavallee, D. M., and T. F. Cash. 1997. "The Comparative Efficacy of Two Cognitive Behavioral Self-Help Programs for a Negative Body Image." Poster presented to the Association for Advancement of Behavior Therapy, Miami Beach.

Lerner, R. M., and E. Gellert. 1969. "Body Build Identification, Preference, and Aversion in Children." *Developmental Psychology* 1:456–62.

Lewis, V. J., A. J. Blair, and D. A. Booth. 1992. "Outcome of Group Therapy for Body-Image Emotionality and Weight- Control Self-Efficacy." *Behavioural Psychotherapy* 20:155–65.

Lewis, R. J., T. F. Cash, L. Jacobi, and C. Bubb-Lewis. 1997. "Prejudice Toward Fat People: The Development and Validation of the Antifat Attitudes Test." *Obesity Research* 5:297–307.

Martin, M. C., and P. F. Kennedy. 1993. "Advertising and Social Comparison: Consequences for Female Preadolescents and Adolescents." *Psychology and Marketing* 10:513–30.

Mayer, K. 1993. *Real Women Don't Diet.* Silver Spring, MD: Bartleby.

Mendelson, B. K., D. R. White, and M. J. Mendelson. 1996. "Self-Esteem and Body Esteem: Effects of Gender, Age, and Weight." *Journal of Applied Developmental Psychology* 17:321–46.

Muth, J. L., and T. F. Cash. 1997. "Body-Image Attitudes: What Difference Does Gender Make?" *Journal of Applied Social Psychology* 27:1438–52.

National Institutes of Health, Technology Assessment Conference Panel. 1992. "Methods for Voluntary Weight Loss and Control." *Annals of Internal Medicine* 116:942–49.

O'Neil, P. M., and M. P. Jarrell. 1992. "Psychological Aspects of Obesity and Dieting." Pp. 252–70 in *Treatment of the Seriously Obese Patient,* edited by T. A. Wadden and T. B. Van Itallie. New York: Guilford.

Orbach, S. 1982. *Fat is a Feminist Issue II.* New York: Berkley.

Pauley, L. L. 1989. "Customer Weight as a Variable in Salespersons' Response Time." *Journal of Social Psychology* 129:713–14.

Pliner, P., S. Chaiken, and G. L. Flett. 1990. "Gender Difference in Concern with Body Weight and Physical Appearance over the Life Span." *Personality and Social Psychology Bulletin* 16:263–73.

Polivy, J., and C. P. Herman. 1992. "Undieting: A Program to Help People Stop Dieting." *International Journal of Eating Disorders* 11:261–68.

Pruzinsky, T., and T. F. Cash. 1990. "Integrative Themes in Body-Image Deviance, Development, and Change." Pp. 333–49 in *Body Images: Development, Deviance, and Change,* edited by T. F. Cash and T. Pruzinsky. New York: Guilford.

Richins, M. L. 1991. "Social Comparison and the Idealized Images of Advertising." *Journal of Consumer Research* 18:71–83.

Robinson, B. B. E., and J. G. Bacon. 1996. "The 'If Only I Were Thin . . . ' Treatment Program: Decreasing the Stigmatizing Effects of Fatness." *Professional Psychology: Research and Practice* 27:175–83.

Rodin, J. 1992. *Body Traps.* New York: William Morrow.

Rodin, J., L. R. Silberstein, and R. H. Striegel-Moore. 1985. "Women and Weight: A Normative Discontent." Pp. 267–307 in *Nebraska Symposium on Motivation: Psychology and Gender,* edited by T. B. Sonderegger. Lincoln: University of Nebraska Press.

Rodin, J., and J. Slochower. 1974. "Fat Chance for a Favor: Obese-Normal Differences in Compliance and Incidental Learning." *Journal of Personality and Social Psychology* 29:557–65.

Rosen, J. C. 1996. "Improving Body Image in Obesity." Pp. 425–40 in *Body Image, Eating Disorders, and Obesity: An Integrative Guide for Assessment and Treatment,* edited by J. K. Thompson. Washington, DC: American Psychological Association.

Rosen, J. C., and T. F. Cash. 1995. "Learning to Have a Better Body Image." *Weight Control Digest* 5:409, 412–16.

Rosen, J. C., P. Orosan, and J. Reiter. 1995. "Cognitive Behavior Therapy for Negative Body Image in Obese Women." *Behavior Therapy* 26:25–42.

Roughan, P., E. Seddon, and J. Vernon-Roberts. 1990. "Long-Term Psychological Effects of a Psychologically Based Group Programme for Women Preoccupied with Body Weight and Eating Behavior." *International Journal of Obesity* 14:135–47.

Rucker, C. E., and T. F. Cash. 1992. "Body Images, Body-Size Perceptions, and Eating Behaviors Among African-American and White College Women." *International Journal of Eating Disorders* 12:291–99.

Schroeder, C. R. 1992. *Fat is Not a Four-Letter Word*. Minneapolis, MN: Chronimed.

Shaw, C. 1982. *Come Out, Come Out, Wherever You Are*. Los Angeles: American R. R.

Silberstein, L. R., C. Striegel-Moore, C. Timko, and J. Rodin. 1988. "Behavioral and Psychological Implications of Body Dissatisfaction: Do Men and Women Differ?" *Sex Roles* 19:219–32.

Smith, C. A. 1996. "Women, Weight, and Body Image." Pp. 91–106 in *Lectures on the Psychology of Women,* edited by J. C. Chrisler, C. Golden, and P. D. Rozee. New York: McGraw-Hill.

Sobal, J. 1995a. "The Medicalization and Demedicalization of Obesity." Pp. 67–90 in *Eating Agendas: Food and Nutrition as Social Problems,* edited by D. Maurer and J. Sobal. Hawthorne, NY: Aldine de Gruyter.

———. 1995b. "Social Influences on Body Weight." Pp. 73–77 in *Eating Disorders and Obesity: A Comprehensive Handbook,* edited by K. D. Brownell and C. G. Fairburn. New York: Guilford.

Stake, J., and M. L. Lauer. 1987. "The Consequences of Being Overweight: A Controlled Study of Gender Differences." *Sex Roles* 17:31–47.

Steinberg, C. L., and J. M. Birk. 1983. "Weight and Compliance: Male-Female Differences." *Journal of General Psychology* 109:95–102.

Stice, E., and H. Shaw. 1994. "Adverse Effects of the Media Portrayed Thin-Ideal on Women and Linkages to Bulimic Symptomatology." *Journal of Social and Clinical Psychology* 13:288–308.

Striegel-Moore, R., and J. Rodin. 1986. "The Influence of Psychological Variables in Obesity." Pp. 99–121 in *Handbook of Eating Disorders: Physiology, Psychology, and Treatment of Obesity, Anorexia, and Bulimia,* edited by K. D. Brownell and J. P. Foreyt. New York: Basic Books.

Stunkard, A. J., and V. Burt. 1967. "Obesity and Body Image II. Age at Onset of Disturbances in the Body Image." *American Journal of Psychiatry* 123:1443–47.

228   Thomas F. Cash and Robin E. Roy

Stunkard, A. J., and M. Mendelson. 1967. "Obesity and Body Image I. Characteristics of Disturbances in the Body Image of Some Obese Persons." *American Journal of Psychiatry* 123:1296–1300.
Stunkard, A. J., and T. A. Wadden. 1992. "Psychological Aspects of Severe Obesity." *American Journal of Clinical Nutrition* 55:524S–532S.
Szymanski, M. L., and T. F. Cash. 1995. "Body-Image Disturbances and Self-Discrepancy Theory: Expansion of the Body-Image Ideals Questionnaire." *Journal of Clinical and Social Psychology* 14:134–46.
Thomas, V. G., and M. D. James. 1988. "Body Image, Dieting Tendencies, and Sex Role Traits In Urban Black Women." *Sex Roles* 18:523–29.
Thompson, J. K., ed. 1996. *Body Image, Eating Disorders, and Obesity: An Integrative Guide for Assessment and Treatment*. Washington, DC: American Psychological Association.
Wadden, T. A. 1993. "Treatment of Obesity by Moderate and Severe Caloric Restriction: Results of Clinical Research Trials." *Annals of Internal Medicine* 119: 688–693.
Wadden, T. A., and A. J. Stunkard. 1985. "Social and Psychological Consequences of Obesity." *Annals of Internal Medicine* 103:1062–67.
Wadden, T. A., A. J. Stunkard, and J. Liebschutz. 1988. "Three-Year Follow-Up of the Treatment of Obesity by Very Low Calorie Diet, Behavior Therapy, and Their Combination." *Journal of Consulting and Clinical Psychology* 56:925–28.
Wilson, G. T. 1994. "Behavioral Treatment of Obesity: Thirty Years and Counting." *Advances in Behaviour Research and Therapy* 16:31–75.
Wiseman, C. V., J. J. Gray, J. E. Mosimann, and A. H. Ahrens. 1992. "Cultural Expectations of Thinness in Women: An Update." *International Journal of Eating Disorders* 11:85–89.
Wiseman, C. V., F. M. Gunning, and J. J. Gray. 1993. "Increasing Pressure to Be Thin: 19 Years of Diet Products in Television Commercials." *Eating Disorders: The Journal of Treatment and Prevention* 1:52–61.
Young, M. E. 1995. *Diet Breaking: Having It All without Having to Diet*. London: Hodder/Headline.

12

Re-evaluating the Weight-Centered Approach toward Health
The Need for a Paradigm Shift

JEANINE C. COGAN

INTRODUCTION

In the United States today, people are literally dying to be thin through weight-loss drugs (e.g., from pulmonary hypertension after prolonged use of fen/phen), very low calorie diets, stomach stapling, rapid weight loss, diet-induced nutritional deficiency, weight fluctuation, and eating disorders. This invisible iatrogenic cause of death results from our cultural understanding of obesity as a serious health threat and the consequences of obesity treatment as necessary and having minimal side effects. In this chapter, I argue that the dominant interpretations of obesity and eating disorders are based on incomplete and imprecise information and are therefore responsible for promoting harmful attitudes toward our bodies and health. To make this argument, first I briefly describe the common cultural meanings of obesity and eating disorders. Second, I describe and critique the many ways that these cultural meanings are based on a selective attention to the research and the inability of researchers and the public to accept certain key findings. Last, I discuss a paradigm change that reflects a more comprehensive approach toward the promotion of good health and the prevention of eating problems.

RECOGNITION OF INTERDEPENDENCE

The prevailing approach toward obesity and eating disorders treats them as two distinct and unrelated problems. Until recently, obesity researchers typically worked within a vacuum, not considering how their ardent recommendations for weight loss contributed to the rise of body image issues, weight dissatisfaction, and eating disorders. Though a central symptom of both anorexia and bulimia is a "fear of fat," most treatment approaches for eating disorders did not adequately address the etiologic influence of a thinness-oriented culture. Yet in order to understand the current societal trends, such as the large proportion of certain populations suffering from body dissatisfaction and deaths related to the pursuit of thinness, the interdependence of obesity and eating disorders must be recognized. Thus, both are addressed simultaneously in this chapter.

The current understanding of and approach toward obesity and eating disorders have been socially constructed. According to social constructionist theory, that which we come to know as truth or that which we define as knowledge reflects the shared values, beliefs, and practices of a given culture (Bohan 1993). Though long-established constructs are viewed as neutral and definitive, they derive their meaning and significance from a value-based culture. Therefore, obesity and eating disorders are not objective and value-free categories; their definitions and meanings are culturally produced.

OUR SHARED MEANING OF OBESITY

The current dominant model of obesity identifies it as a serious health threat, with enormous economic costs to individuals and society, and therefore in need of elimination (Institute of Medicine 1995). The terms "overweight" and "obesity" are often used interchangeably. These terms, as they are most commonly used, are defined as being 20 percent over the ideal weight according to the Metropolitan Life Insurance Table (Hall and Havassy 1981). This definition of obesity is inaccurate, since obesity refers to body fatness (adiposity) rather than relative body weight (Brownell 1982). The Body Mass Index (BMI), computed by dividing weight by the square of height is considered an improvement over simply using weight because this figure accounts for height and is considered a reliable measure of relative body weight (Brownell 1982; Keys 1980). Individuals with BMIs greater than 30 are considered to be severely overweight, with an estimated 14 percent of men and women in the United States in this category (Institute of Medicine 1995).

Due to associated health risks, obesity is defined as a medical condition and is included in the International Classification of Diseases. Perhaps the most widely accepted theory of etiology for obesity is that it is self-induced through voluntary and controllable behaviors such as overeating. For this reason, psychological theories and techniques, especially concepts from behavioral psychology, are popular in the treatment of obesity (Cogan and Rothblum 1992). The standard treatment is a form of restrictive dieting with the goal of weight loss (ibid.). For many decades, psychologists, physicians, nutritionists, other health professionals, and the corporate world have assisted those considered obese (and most anyone else interested) with their weight loss efforts. The federal government has spent millions of dollars on public health campaigns and other initiatives (e.g., panels convened by the National Institutes of Health) addressing the problem of obesity in our nation. In short, our shared understanding of obesity is that it is a public health threat in need of treatment and prevention.

OUR SHARED MEANING OF EATING DISORDERS

Our dominant cultural understanding of eating disorders contrasts with that of obesity. A not uncommon scenario illustrates this point: A group of women sits sipping their morning coffee, when their discussion turns to eating disorders. One woman casually quips, "Oh, I wouldn't mind catching anorexia. Maybe then I would finally get rid of these saddle bags," and the other women giggle with empathy and recognition.

Although taken seriously by researchers, clinicians, and advocates directly addressing the problem, eating disorders are more commonly trivialized and glorified. They are perceived as quirky, self-centered afflictions that only strike the rich and famous and have not received overwhelming concern from the public. Eating disorders are classified as psychological disorders in the *Diagnostic Statistical Manual of Mental Disorders* (*DSM-V*) (American Psychiatric Association 1994), and are defined as anorexia nervosa, bulimia nervosa, and eating disorders not otherwise specified (e.g., bingeing without purging or binge eating disorder). The most widely used theories to explain the etiology of eating disorders are individually focused: the person (in most cases a female) with anorexia or bulimia has character flaws that need reparation, for example, the person is emotionally unbalanced, needy, a perfectionist, desires control, or has cognitive distortions. Therefore, the most popular forms of treatment for eating disorders have been cognitive behavioral therapy, psychopharmacological therapy, family-based therapy, psychotherapy, nutrition therapy, hospitalization, or some combination of these.

The prevalence rate of eating disorders is from 0.5 to 20 percent, depending on the strictness of criteria used for diagnosis and the population investigated (Shisslak, Crago, Neal, and Swain 1987). Thus, millions of people, mostly women and girls, suffer from eating disorders that are associated with such serious health risks as reproductive and cardiovascular problems, amenorrhea, hypothermia, renal complications, blood dysfunction, osteoporosis, and death (American Psychiatric Association 1994; Bliss and Branch 1960; Gandour 1984; Herzog and Copeland 1985). According to the DSM-IV, the long-term mortality rate of individuals hospitalized with anorexia is 10 percent (American Psychiatric Association 1994). In addition, according to a ten-year longitudinal study 5.6 percent of women with anorexia eventually died from anorexia-related complications (Herzog 1997). Although eating disorders affect many individuals and endanger health, they are not adequately addressed in typical training programs for nutritionists, dieticians, and physicians, nor are they defined as a public health issue.

LIMITATIONS OF THE SOCIALLY CONSTRUCTED DEFINITIONS OF OBESITY AND EATING DISORDERS

Our culturally shared meanings of obesity and eating disorders are incomplete and therefore problematic. Specifically, our definitions are based on a selective attention to research and an inability to accept certain key findings. Some findings are clearly accepted and publicized, while others are ignored and submerged as if the research were nonexistent. This has led to an incomplete understanding of obesity and eating disorders, as well as recommendations that may be harmful to people's overall health and well-being. In the following section, I discuss several examples of how research findings are selectively acknowledged and popularized.

Obesity as a Health Risk

Perhaps one of the clearest illustrations of a selective review of the research is evident in the report *Health Implications of Obesity* produced by the National Institutes of Health (1985). After reviewing the evidence, this panel of experts concluded that the research showed a strong positive association between obesity and mortality and recommended that persons 20 percent or more above the desirable weights in the Metropolitan Life Insurance Tables lose weight (ibid.).

Much other research, however, challenges this widely accepted finding (e.g., Andres 1980; Barrett-Connor 1985; Ernsberger and Haskew 1987; Fitzgerald 1981; Jarrett 1986; Keys et al. 1984; Mann 1974). My goal at this point is not to offer a comprehensive discussion of this literature since that has been done by other researchers (e.g., Berg 1995; Ernsberger and Haskew 1987; Garner and Wooley 1991), but rather to draw attention to the fact that rigorous epidemiological studies have yielded different results.

Keys (1980) and Keys et al. (1984) investigated the relationship between obesity and coronary heart disease as well as overall mortality in a thorough review of sixteen long-term prospective studies conducted in seven different countries in North America and Europe, and did not find a consistent linear relationship between weight and mortality or coronary heart disease. In fact, those people most likely to survive were somewhat above average weight.

According to a Norwegian epidemiological study that followed 1.8 million people for ten years, those in the lowest weight category were at highest risk for mortality. Women who were considered morbidly obese, weighing twice the weight of the proposed standards, had a higher chance of survival than women in the leanest weight category (Waaler 1984).

Similarly, data from the Pooling Project, which included the weighted average of mortality rates from the Framingham study, which began in 1948, the Chicago People's Gas study, which followed men for over fourteen years, the Albany study, the Tecumseh study, and the Chicago Western Electric study, found those on the extreme ends of the weight continuum were at greatest risk for mortality. Individuals in the lowest weight category were at highest risk, those in the highest weight category were slightly more likely to survive than the thinnest group, and those somewhat above average weight (25–35 percent) were at least risk of mortality (Ernsberger and Haskew 1987).

Findings that moderate obesity is associated with optimal health and extreme thinness with increased mortality, though available to the NIH panel, were not seriously considered in their final decisions and recommendations. The fourteen panel members were mostly obesity researchers (conducting funded weight loss programs), as well as a consultant from the Association of Life Insurance (life insurance companies charge higher premiums for heavier policyholders), and a corporate nutritionist representing the food industry (which makes huge profits from diet foods). The panel based its conclusions and recommendations mainly on data from the insurance industry and rejected epidemiological studies similar to those outlined for reasons that contradicted the facts. The panel claimed these studies were problematic because: the subject samples were too small, the follow-up periods were too short (no longer than ten years), and the samples were not representative of the U.S. population. Yet many of the studies had more than a thousand participants, used a longer than ten-year follow-up, and were no less representative of the population than the insurance company data that were class and race biased (Bennett and Gurin 1982).

This example suggests that only selective data were accepted, reviewed, and used as the basis for the panel's recommendations (Ernsberger and Haskew 1987). With full knowledge of these findings just cited, the NIH recommended to the public that anyone more than 20 percent overweight reduce their weight to insurance table standards. As Ancel Keys (1980) has noted about the field of obesity research, the complete inattention to opposing evidence in the popular conceptualization of obesity is striking.

Potential Health Benefits of Moderate Obesity

Since this controversial NIH report, more research has documented the health benefits of moderate overweight. In a review of the research, Troiano, Frongillo, Sobal, and Levitsky (1996) analyzed twenty-two longitudinal studies examining weight and all-cause mortality. Controlling for smoking and preexisting illness, they found that men with BMIs that correspond with being moderately overweight (24–27) were at lowest risk of death. Those below and above these BMIs were equally at risk for mortality. Interpreting their findings, the authors critique the scientific community for only drawing attention to the finding that severe overweight causes health risks while ignoring the risks of underweight. Interestingly, although it is currently the only meta-analysis on the health risks associated with overweight, this article has received little attention from the scientific community, the popular press, and federal agencies that make health policy decisions.

Similarly, this literature was extensively reviewed by Ernsberger and Haskew (1987), who presented more than eighty-five different studies as finding lower incidence of illness among those considered moderately obese. These studies were organized and presented in a table entitled, "Obesity is associated with a lowered incidence of . . . " followed by a list of thirty-three different health conditions (1987:18).

After Ernsberger and Haskew published this detailed review of the obesity literature in which they clearly challenged the dominant notion that any degree of obesity is hazardous to health, the response they were expecting from in the scientific community—which prizes contradictory findings and discourse as the hallmark of increasing knowledge—was not the response they received. Instead there was a distinct silence so noticeable that the message communicated was clear: if the findings do not support the current understanding of obesity then they do not exist. Yet debate and discussion are the expected and appropriate responses to controversial findings and further serve to educate both scientists and the public. By blankly ignoring this research, our comprehensive understanding of health risks, benefits, and treatment stagnates.

Failure of Restrictive Dieting for Long-Term Weight Loss

Albert Stunkard first addressed the inefficacy of dieting in a 1959 publication where he reported that less than 5 percent of dieters lost large amounts of weight and were able to maintain this weight (Stunkard and

McLaren-Hume 1959). After decades of research and dozens of critical reviews, leading obesity experts are reaching the same conclusion (Institute of Medicine 1995). Restrictive dieting has approximately a 95 percent failure rate for maintaining permanent long-term weight loss, defined as five years or more (Garner and Wooley 1991; Goodrick and Foreyt 1991; Kramer, Jeffery, Forster, and Snell 1989; Stunkard and McLaren-Hume 1959; Wilson 1994). As an expert panel of obesity researchers recently summarized, "[S]tudies paint a grim picture: those who complete weight-loss programs lose approximately 10 percent of their body weight, only to regain two-thirds of it back within a year and almost all of it back within 5 years" (Institute of Medicine 1995:1).

As Garner and Wooley (1991) explain, the lag in determining dieting's efficacy was in part due to the differing points at which researchers measured success. Most weight loss programs are successful at producing short-term weight loss maintained for a year (Miller, Koceja, and Hamilton 1997). As time passes, however, there is surprising consistency in the research: the initial weight lost is eventually regained and the longer the follow-up period, the more weight is regained.

Psychological Tolls of Weight Regain

Research conducted by my colleague Esther Rothblum and myself (1992) offers a profile of a typical weight-loss program, its efficacy, and participant experience. Analyzing a stratified random sample of fifty weight loss studies published in the *Psychological Abstracts* between 1980 and 1989, we found that the typical participant was a white, middle-class woman, who weighed 189.5 pounds before treatment and who lost 12.8 pounds during a 13-week fairly rigorous behavioral treatment program. At a 6.5-month follow-up she had regained 4.3 pounds. Treatment efficacy was not greatly improved when only the most successful treatment conditions were examined or when the studies conducted during the later part of the decade were compared with early studies.

These findings raise important questions about weight-loss programs. What does an approximate ten-pound weight loss ten months after the start of treatment for a woman weighing nearly 190 pounds mean? Is this weight loss worth the time, energy, and money she is spending? Since a very common reason for weight loss efforts is to improve appearance and physical comfort (Foster, Wadden, Vogt, and Brewer 1997), does this ten-pound loss achieve these goals? This weight loss will most likely not alter women's dissatisfaction with their weight (ibid.), which is associated with diminished self-efficacy, body image, mood, and self-esteem (Brownell, Foster, and Wadden 1996).

Since this ten-pound loss would be considered disappointing (Foster et al. 1997) and not meet the dieter's expectations (Goodrick, Raynaud, Pace, and Foreyt 1992), how does she experience not having her expectations met? Since she gained almost half of the weight back from the end of treatment to a 6.5-month follow-up, does she view herself as a failure? Research indicates she will most likely attribute this weight-loss failure to herself (Goodrick et al. 1992). How does this affect her self-esteem and psychological well-being? Since people considered obese are held responsible for their condition (Brownell 1982), does she internalize this weight gain as an indication of her own weaknesses and do others evaluate her similarly? Although most studies yield statistically significant results by comparing one treatment condition with another, this does not tell us whether the minimal amount of weight loss is of any personal significance to the participants. These are all critical questions worthy of serious consideration. The toll of continued failed weight loss attempts has ramifications for individuals' social and emotional health, yet this is rarely addressed by those advocating health improvement.

Consequences of Dieting

In addition to the psychological cost of weight regain, there are documented psychological and physical consequences of restrictive dieting. In a landmark study, Keys, Brozek, Henschel, Mickelson, and Taylor (1950) placed men with no preexisting food or body image issues on a diet, reducing their intake to 1600 calories daily for twenty-four weeks. During this dieting period, these men exhibited emotional outbursts and symptoms of depression, became preoccupied with food, and experienced episodes of binge eating.

Since this landmark study, other researchers have found that dieting through calorie restriction has adverse effects on cognitive performance (Green, Rogers, Elliman, and Gatenby 1994) and body image (Brunner et al. 1994; French et al. 1995a), is associated with negative mood (Laessle, Platte, Schweiger, and Pirke 1996), depression (Ross 1994), binge behavior (French et al. 1995b; Polivy and Herman 1985), and the onset of eating disorders (Griffiths and Farnill 1996; Patton 1992).

Physiologically, restrictive dieting is associated with nutritional deficiency (Berg 1995), lowered resting metabolic rate (Donahoe, Lin, Kirschenbaum, and Keesey 1984), menstrual irregularity (Montero, Bernis, Fernandez, and Castro 1996), and even death (Wadden, Blackburn, and Van Itallie 1990). In the 1970s, a number of popular very low calorie diets such as the Cambridge diet caused more than fifty deaths (Berg 1995). Although this created a brief concern, each case was handled quietly out of court, with documents sealed to the public, and there was no organized tracking system to document similar cases. Today we do not know the number of people dying from similar diets. The consequences of dieting are not widely discussed or recognized as worthy health concerns that compromise or threaten lives.

Potential Health Risks Associated with Weight Fluctuation

At least ten different studies document a relationship between weight fluctuation and increased mortality and/or other health risks (Berg 1995; Blair et al. 1993; Hamm, Shekelle, and Stamler 1989; Hanson et al. 1996; Brownell and Rodin 1994; Iribarren, Sharp, Burchfiel, and Petrovitch 1995; Lissner et al. 1989, 1991; Morris and Rimm 1992). According to the Gothenburg Prospective studies (Lissner et al. 1989), variability in body weight is a risk factor for coronary heart disease among men and for total mortality rates among both men and women. Lissner et al. (1991) found that weight fluctuation is correlated with higher rates of total mortality, morbidity due to coronary heart disease (CHD), and mortality due to CHD. This finding held true even after such other important factors as cigarette smoking, physical activity level, and cholesterol level were taken into account. The risk increased as the amount of weight fluctuation increased. According to the Western Electric Company study, after adjusting for other health risk factors such as cigarette smoking, alcohol consumption, weight, age, and blood pressure, a single cycle of weight gain and loss put men at a greater risk for death from CHD (Hamm et al. 1989). Finally, Blair, Shaten, Brownell, Collins, and Lissner (1993) found that weight fluctuation in men is associated with CHD, myocardial infarction, hypertension, and diabetes type II.

Although weight fluctuation may be dangerous, this information remains widely unknown to the public. Rather than calling for caution in promoting weight fluctuation through such methods as restrictive dieting, the scientific community and federal agencies have instead warned against abandoning weight-loss strategies prematurely. Several critical reviews about weight fluctuation acknowledge yet minimize the documented associated health risks (French et al. 1995b; Jeffery 1996; Muls, Kempen, Vansant, and Saris 1995; Williamson 1996).

After reviewing the data on weight fluctuation, a NIH Task Force on the Prevention and Treatment of Obesity (1994) published a widely publicized report with far-reaching implications, concluding that weight cycling is not harmful and obese individuals should not be deterred from weight-loss techniques. The panel of experts acknowledged the outlined research that weight fluctuation is associated with certain health risks and increased mortality, yet they argued the evidence was not sufficiently persuasive to override the potential benefits of moderate weight loss for obese individuals.

A common response is to disregard the risks of weight fluctuation since most studies did not determine whether the weight fluctuation was intentional or unintentional. Although this is an accurate assessment, some researchers have controlled for factors that would most likely cause unintentional weight loss, such as smoking or illness. Second, there is a strong relationship between dieting and weight fluctuation (Biener and Heaton 1995; Bild et al. 1996). However, this argument misses the point. If weight fluctuation is associated with health risks including increased mortality, why advocate methods that further perpetuate weight fluctuation? Engaging in such weight-loss efforts as restrictive dieting is not a logical, health-based strategy, given that almost all people eventually regain the lost weight.

Weight Fluctuation as a Confounding Variable in Obesity Research

Another compelling reason to seriously consider the literature on the health risks associated with weight fluctuation is that it calls into question all research finding a relationship between obesity and poor health that did not account for weight fluctuation. For example, the main studies used in the 1985 NIH report that concluded obesity was a health threat were conducted in the 1970s, and weight fluctuation was not considered [e.g., National Health and Nutrition Examination Survey (NHANES), 1971–1974; four large insurance studies from 1903–1979]. If weight fluctuation, however, is associated with some of the *very risk factors with which obesity has been associated*, such as coronary heart disease, hypertension, and overall mortality, then it cannot be confidently concluded that these increased risks were due to obesity and not weight fluctuation.

The Importance of Changing Other Risk Factors

An additional finding overshadowed by the disproportionate focus on dieting that has important implications for our understanding of attaining optimal health is research on physical fitness. According to Blair et al. (1995), changing one's level of physical fitness, *rather than changing the amount one weighs,* may prolong life. In this research, men who were unfit at the first assessment period and increased their physical fitness to become fit at the second assessment period decreased their risk of mortality by 44 percent. Improved physical fitness is associated with lower risk for cardiovascular disease and all-cause mortality, whereas changes in other risk factors such as weight loss are not associated with lower mortality rates. Thus, physical fitness, rather than eliminating obesity, may be the key to health. Clearly, this area is worthy of more attention.

The Role of Genetics and Biology in Determining Body Weight

Although some early studies pointed to the importance of genetics in the etiology of obesity (e.g., Borjeson 1976), the genetic influence is still not widely known. Obesity experts are concluding that the preponderance of data suggests genetics is a central determinant of obesity. The role of genetics has been examined through both twin and adoption studies with the consistent finding that genetic factors are important (Bouchard et al. 1990; Poehlman et al. 1986; Price, Cadoret, Stunkard, and Troughton 1987; Stunkard, Foch, and Hrubec 1986; Stunkard, Harris, Pedersen, and McClearn 1990; Stunkard, Sorensen, Hanis, Teasdale, Chakraborty, Schull, and Schulsinger 1986). For example, in a study examining the body weight of fraternal and identical twin pairs, Stunkard et al. (1990) found that twins were likely to be similar in body weight regardless of whether they were reared together or apart. This finding, in combination with the research on other biological determinants of body weight, such as differences in resting metabolic rates and individual set-points (for reviews, see Bennett and Gurin 1982; Garner and Wooley 1991), clearly suggests that body weight and size are not solely determined by individual behaviors and therefore are not easily changeable.

In addition, research on the eating habits of those considered obese and those considered normal weight challenges a fundamental tenet in the current obesity conceptualization. No consistent or marked difference in the eating habits between the obese and nonobese in style, amount, and content of consumption occurs in both self-report surveys and observational studies (Coates, Jeffery, and Wing 1978; Garner and Wooley 1991; Institute of Medicine 1995; Wing and Jeffery 1978; Wooley, Wooley, and Dyernforth 1979). A central belief about obesity is that it is self-induced through overindulgence, gluttony, and laziness, which allows us to blame the obese individual. Yet if people are obese in part due to genetic and biological factors, then holding them completely responsible for their "condition" is inaccurate and eliminates the rationale for our sense of justified hostility and fat discrimination.

Obesity Related Stigma and Its Consequences

In our current conceptualization of obesity the fat person is dehumanized, viewed with disdain, and negatively marked. Such obesity-related stigma leads to great pain and suffering for those who are targeted. A 1996 story in *USA Today* tells about a twelve-year-old boy, Samuel Graham, who took a rope and hung himself because he could no longer bear the teasing and taunting of his classmates about his "174 pounds on his 5-foot-4-inch-frame."

In his well-known analysis, Erving Goffman defined stigma as "an attribute that is deeply discrediting within a particular social interaction" (1963:3). Stigma is not inherent in any attribute itself, but instead emerges in social interactions in which the attribute is given meaning based on the participants' expectations and ideas. This interaction leads to a discrepancy between social expectations and reality. This discrepancy is in an unfavorable direction; the individual is perceived as different and, accurately or not, as unable to fulfill the role requirements of the "normals." This "undesired differentness" overshadows all of the person's other attributes, feelings, and experiences (ibid.:5). The stigmatizing attribute attains a master status, which overrides all of the individual's other qualities and serves to define the individual as an "other," an outsider, one who is not part of "normal" society.

Following this definition, obesity is clearly a stigma. Research on the attitudes toward those who are considered obese and the discrimination they face is remarkably consistent. Those considered obese, when compared to nonobese counterparts, are less likely to be accepted into elite colleges (Canning and Mayer 1966), less likely to be chosen by apartment owners as renters (Karris 1977), less likely to marry into a higher social economic class (Elder 1969), less likely to be chosen by their peers as friends (Harris, Harris, and Bochner 1982; Lerner and Gellert 1969), more likely to be economically downwardly mobile (Rothblum 1990), more likely to be discriminated against in their place of employment (Larkin and Pines 1979; Rothblum, Brand, Miller, and Oetjen 1990), and more likely to have such negative stereotypes as lazy, ugly, and gluttonous associated with them (Maddox, Black, and Lieberman 1968; Wooley et al. 1979). Children learn this stigma early. According to research with grade school samples, fatness is associated with such adjectives as stupid, dirty, mean, ugly, and sad (Wooley et al. 1979). Even health professionals fall prey to obesity-related stigma. For example, Blumberg and Mellis (1985) surveyed one hundred medical students and found they described moderately obese patients as being more awkward, ugly, lacking in self-control, depressed, weak, difficult to manage, and unsuccessful than average weight patients.

Yet obesity as a stigmatized status is not universal. According to cross-cultural research, many developing nations consider obesity a sign of status and wealth (Cassidy 1991; Rothblum 1990; Sobal 1991; Sobal and Stunkard 1989), do not evaluate thinness as the ideal image of health and beauty (Cogan, Bhalla, Sefa-Dedeh, and Rothblum 1996), and have lower rates of disordered eating and negative body image (Cogan et al. 1996; Furnham and Alibhai 1983; Raich, Rosen, Deus, Perez, Requena, and Gross 1992; Tiggemann and Rothblum 1988).

Obesity-related stigma is socially constructed: an outcome of the dominant approach toward obesity. Another understanding, incorporating

typically ignored research findings, such as the role of genetics in the etiology of obesity may greatly reduce if not eliminate this culturally created
problem.

The Danger of Antiobesity Drugs

The recent publicity about the diet drug fen/phen casts a shadow on its
notable popularity as the dream drug for weight loss. According to the
Mayo Clinic, fen/phen was responsible for heart valve complications
detected in twenty-four previously healthy women. Fen/phen is a combination drug of fenfluramine and phentramine which was widely prescribed by physicians to millions of Americans annually for weight loss,
though research documented the dangers associated with these two drugs
for decades (Levitsky 1997). Since the late 1970s, the FDA has received a
large number of complaints of adverse effects caused by the use of these
two drugs (Brown 1997). Phentramine has been linked to damage of the
heart and circulatory system and dozens of studies have linked fenfluramine to brain damage (for a review, see Levitsky 1997) and pulmonary
hypertension (e.g., Abenhaim et al. 1996; Gurtner 1985). A second antiobesity drug, Redux, was approved by the FDA in 1996 despite the strong
opposition of more than twenty-five neuroscientists who signed a letter
requesting the FDA seriously consider the substantial evidence that Redux
causes primary pulmonary hypertension and brain damage (Ernsberger
1997). These antiobesity drugs also have been associated with depression
(Toornvliet, Pijl, and Meinders 1994), sleep disturbance (Myers et al. 1993),
acute glaucoma (Denis, Charpentier, Berros, and Touameur 1995), and
pancreatitis (Thys, Schapira, Ghilain, Maisin, and Henrion 1994).

Nutri/System, a commercial weight-loss program that incorporated
the use of fen/phen as part of its prescribed regimen, responded to the
public announcement of the medical dangers by running a television
commercial with a spokesman dressed like a doctor claiming that it is a
proven fact that the risks of obesity outweigh the risks of medication. This
argument is commonly used to justify prescribing weight reduction drugs
despite their deleterious health effects. However, currently there are no
data to support the assumption that weight loss as a result of taking medications reduces one's risk of mortality.

Economic Costs of the Pursuit of Thinness

Whereas the economic costs of obesity are widely publicized to be more
than $39 billion a year (Colditz 1992), no comparable figures are readily
available on the economic cost of the pursuit of thinness. The economic
cost of a particular health issue is used as an indicator of its severity and
often motivates a government response, such as providing funding for

prevention, intervention, and treatment efforts. The costs associated with pursuing thinness would be enormous, including the costs of dieting (estimated to be over $30 billion a year); surgical treatments for obesity (such as gastric bypass surgery, which costs from $10,000 to 40,000 per procedure) and then treating the common serious complications of surgical treatments (e.g., wound problems, abscess, ulceration, vitamin deficiency, gallstone formation); antiobesity drugs (e.g., prescriptions for Redux in 1996 were estimated to cost $134 million) and then treating the complications from antiobesity drugs (e.g., primary pulmonary hypertension); treating the ill health effects of weight fluctuation (e.g., cardiovascular disease), treating individuals with eating disorders (e.g., therapy and hospitalization), and the lost productivity of employees who are dealing with all of the aforementioned problems. Without a comparable estimate of costs associated with thinness attainment, this issue is unlikely to receive the appropriate social and policy response.

Where Is Culture in Eating Disorders?

Whereas there is no one causal factor in the development of eating disorders, the values and norms of U.S. society teach individuals to be afraid of fat, to be concerned about their weight and appearance, and to strive toward attaining thinness (e.g., Berg 1997; Killen et al. 1996; Levine, Smolak, and Hayden 1994; Stormer and Thompson 1996; Shisslak et al. 1987; Striegel-Moore, Silberstein, and Rodin 1986). Although some researchers underscored the importance of sociocultural factors in the development of eating disorders decades ago (e.g., Wooley and Wooley 1979), this perspective has received minimal attention. For example, of more than three hundred studies that appeared in the *Psychological Abstracts* since 1990 that addressed treatment for individuals with eating disorders, few acknowledge the contributing role of socio-cultural factors.

The Role of Culture: Thinness Ideology.   In the United States the belief system that values and strives toward the attainment of thinness, seemingly at any cost, is pervasive. To illustrate this culturally entrenched thinness ideology, a comparison of the symptoms of anorexia with cultural messages and practices is informative. Consider the first diagnostic criterion: "Refusal to maintain body weight at or above a minimally normal weight for age and height. (e.g., weight loss leading to maintenance of body weight less than 85 percent of that expected . . .)" (American Psychiatric Association 1994:545). While this is considered a sign of "abnormal" behavior, the role models incessantly portrayed to girls and women are consistently 15 percent or more below ideal weight. Supermodel Kate Moss's gaunt and hollow look is a result of a weight that is more than 15 percent under her expected weight. Silverstein, Perdue, Peterson, and Kelly (1986) examined the body size of characters on the forty most watched television shows, and found that 69 percent of female characters received the thinnest possible ratings while only 5 percent of the female characters were rated as heavy. Not surprisingly then, exposure to the media is associated with increased body dissatisfaction for women (Irving 1990; Stice and Shaw 1994). Such cultural messages create an environment conducive to developing eating disorders. Indeed, women suffering from anorexia often remember the repeated compliments and praise they received for their weight loss and only when they became visibly skeletal was their behavior viewed as problematic.

Consider another symptom of anorexia: "Disturbance in the way in which one's body weight or shape is experienced, undue influence of body weight or shape on self-evaluation, or denial of the seriousness of the current low body weight" (American Psychiatric Association 1994:545). Individuals who view their body weight as central to how they evaluate themselves have a symptom of anorexia, yet society pressures people (especially women) to squeeze or stretch their bodies into a confining beauty/health expectation. People are told over and over again to be thin, to diet, and to lose weight. For example, Silverstein et al. (1986) compared the four most popular male magazines to the four most popular female magazines. In 48 issues they found 63 advertisements for diet foods in women's magazines compared with one ad in men's magazines. Articles dealing with body shape or size included 96 for women versus only 8 for men. The number of food-related advertisements was 1179 in women's magazines and 10 in men's. As the researchers concluded, "[T]he messages women receive and the aspects of life they must attend to are gender specific, including the message to stay in shape and be slim while at the same time thinking about food and cooking" (ibid.:526).

The rewards for attaining the beauty and health standard of thinness are not fabricated and only in the minds of self- centered individuals; beauty and thinness have objective consequences. In the dating arena, pretty women go out more often than unattractive women and attractive female dates are rated more positively by men than unattractive dates (Bar-Tal and Saxe 1976; Stake and Lauer 1987; Walster, Aronson, Abrahams, and Rottman 1971). Women's economic and workplace opportunities are influenced by their body size and appearance (Elder 1969; Wolf 1991).

These findings illustrate that anorexia, the most deviant of eating disorders, may not be so deviant from the values and practices of the society at large. The relentless pursuit of thinness, with all its detrimental effects, is largely a result of societal expectations rather than a reflection of individual irrationality and pathology. The symptoms of eating disorders are embedded in the fabric of U.S. culture.

A Call for a Paradigm Shift

The costs of our current social construction of obesity and eating disorders are great, with a host of iatrogenic problems and casualties. Those considered obese are blamed and judged for their "condition." Women of all sizes and shapes suffer from body hatred. Children are "afraid to eat" (Berg 1997) and afraid of being fat, teased, and taunted. Millions of Americans repeatedly and unsuccessfully diet, and internalize their failures to maintain weight loss. Anorexic teenage girls are at risk for adult osteoporosis and death. Many people are shunned and scrutinized by peers and strangers for not fitting the ideal body size. Families lose their daughters, sisters, or mothers to anorexia, and diet drug–related deaths.

Recognizing the limitations of the social construction of obesity and eating disorders and moving toward overcoming them is necessary to minimize and eventually eliminate casualties. While each issue addressed in this chapter poses a challenge to our current shared meanings of obesity and eating disorders, the many issues jointly point to the need for a new conceptualization. Similar critiques and suggestions for paradigm shifts have been raised by professionals across many disciplines for decades (e.g., Allon 1973, 1981; Bennett and Gurin 1982; Berg 1995, 1997; Ernsberger and Haskew 1987; Garner and Wooley 1991; Lyons 1997; Polivy and Herman 1992; Wooley et al. 1979). The main response to this criticism has been a notable lack of recognition, which is ultimately the most effective tool for maintaining the current paradigm. The time has come, however, to change our approach toward health.

How to Shift the Paradigm

Several strategies can be used to change the current paradigm that dominates thinking about weight and health. Three key approaches will be outlined in greater detail.

1. Parity and Accuracy in the Information Offered to the Public. Disproportionate attention has been paid to the risks of obesity, while the average person is unaware of the documented health threats associated with weight fluctuation, the role of genetics in determining body weight, the psychological consequences and high failure rates of restrictive dieting, the economic cost of the thinness pursuit, and the dynamics and consequences of obesity-related stigma. Without equal exposure in the research arena, the media world, and in public policy debates, important information is ignored and approaches to health stagnate.

Thorough and accurate information on these other issues needs to be made as public as information on the health risks of obesity. For example, in its role to protect consumers, the Federal Trade Commission (FTC) could easily be a leader in providing accurate information about the efficacy of dieting and potential risks of weight fluctuation. Currently, the FTC has investigated sixteen commercial weight-loss companies for deceptive and false claims regarding efficacy or safety information provided (Berg 1995). As both researchers (Institute of Medicine 1995) and advocacy groups (Center for Science in the Public Interest 1996) have recommended, protecting consumers from fraudulent and potentially dangerous weight-loss treatments could be accomplished by establishing federal guidelines for dieting companies; these guidelines could include such consumer information as the long-term efficacy of the programs, the potential risks of weight fluctuation, the time and cost of the programs, and the credentials of the weight-loss program staff.

2. Not Promoting Restrictive Dieting as the Blanket Response toward Optimal Health. The monolithic approach of determining health primarily through body weight is shortsighted and dangerous. When considering the health of individuals, other important, yet less easily measured determinants of health and wellness must be taken into account so that health-damaging strategies are not recommended. If restrictive dieting has a virtually nonexistent success rate in producing permanent long-term weight loss (Garner and Wooley 1991; Institute of Medicine 1995) yet is associated with the onset of eating disorders, negative mood, preoccupation with food and eating, and increased binge behavior, then restrictive dieting is not a successful health-based behavior. Rather than recommending people work toward a certain body weight, a more useful goal is to work toward good health.

3. Assessment of Health Based on Physical and Psychological States Rather Than Body Weight and Size. As a growing number of health professionals are advocating (Berg 1995; Ernsberger 1997; Garner and Wooley 1991; Lyons 1997; Polivy and Herman 1992), a more comprehensive model is necessary for the promotion of good health and the prevention of eating problems. Such a model would teach people the importance of interdependent health factors, including:

a. Positive body image: Positive body image is feeling comfortable in one's body; experiencing the body as pleasurable, strong and capable; experiencing the body as intimately part of one's essence rather than an enemy in need of strict control; and appreciating and nurturing the body (e.g., through massage and baths).

b. Eating well: Eating well includes nutritionally balancing one's diet and decreasing fat consumption as well as eating a variety of foods in moderation (not bingeing) and being familiar with how different foods affect energy, mood and thinking.

   c. Maintaining a healthy relationship with food: Maintaining a healthy relationship with food begins with removing "good" and "bad" food labels and not restricting oneself to only the "good" foods. Additionally, learning to eat when physically hungry is important, rather than responding mainly to external cues (e.g., feeling anxious, bored, or because it is noon). Finally, eating for the enjoyment of food: To appreciate its taste and texture is central, rather than worrying about the calories.

   d. Challenging obesity-related stigma: Not making negative attributions about self and others simply based on large body size challenges obesity-related stigma and minimizes the negative impact of such cognitions on one's sense of self. Doing so lets people eventually feel good in their bodies regardless of size. An important acknowledgment in challenging obesity-related stigma is that people come in all sizes (just as people come in all heights, hair textures, and skin tone).

   e. Building strong self-esteem: In order to build strong self-esteem, it is essential to appreciate a range of attributes rather than merely body size. We acknowledge and celebrate our accomplishments and appreciate the "small things," such as meaningful interactions with other people and feeling connected to nature. We treat ourselves (which includes our bodies) as we would treat others, with respect and dignity.

   f. Physical activity: Whereas physical activity improves mental and physical health, it is important to take pleasure in being physically active rather than feeling the pain and pressures of goal attainment motivated out of a desire to lose weight. A healthy attitude toward exercise is to do it for the enjoyment and to feel a sense of agency in one's body; to feel strong and able.

   Intervention programs that include the above outlined factors can improve health as defined more broadly. For example, Polivy and Herman (1992) found that a shift to such a model resulted in improved self-esteem, and lowered depression and eating problems among women in an intervention program.

CONCLUSION

   In view of the evidence, promoting health primarily through weight-loss efforts is a misdirected goal. We must shift away from treating obesity through weight loss and focus instead on promoting good health. While a seemingly logical and research-grounded conclusion, this challenges the very fabric of American values. Therefore, this shift will only fully occur once the thinness ideology is directly uncovered and challenged within the scientific community, the media, public folklore, and government agencies. We must continue to hold experts and officials accountable, asking them to explain the many discrepancies that emerge as outlined in this chapter. More than ten years ago, Ernsberger and Haskew (1987) warned that if the status quo on obesity treatment continued, the rate of eating disorders would soar. Indeed it has. The time has come to recognize and promote a comprehensive model of health and prevent another generation of children, women, and men from becoming new casualties of the current problem-ridden weight paradigm.

REFERENCES

Abenhaim, L., Moride, Y., Brenot, F., Rich, S., Benichou, J., Kurz, X., Higenbottam, T., Oakley, C., Wouters, E., Aubier, M., Simonneau, G., and Begaud, B. 1996. "Appetite-Suppressant Drugs and the Risk of Primary Pulmonary Hypertension. International Pulmonary Hypertension Study." *New England Journal of Medicine* 335:606–16.

Allon, N. 1973. "The Stigma of Overweight in Everyday Life." Pp. 83–102 in *Obesity in Perspective*, Volume 2, Part 2, edited by G. A. Bray. Washington, DC: U.S. Government Printing Office.

——— . 1981. "The Stigma of Overweight in Everyday Life." Pp. 130–74 in *Psychological Aspects of Obesity*, edited by B. J. Wolman. New York: Van Nostrand Reinhold.

American Psychiatric Association. 1994. *Diagnostic and Statistical Manual of Mental Disorders*, 4th ed. Washington, DC: Author.

Andres, R. 1980. "Effect of Obesity on Total Mortality." *International Journal of Obesity* 4:381–86.

Bar-Tal, D., and L. Saxe. 1976. "Physical Attractiveness and Its Relationship to Sex-Role Stereotyping." *Sex Roles* 2(2):123–33.

Barrett-Connor, E. L. 1985. "Obesity, Atherosclerosis, and Coronary Heart Disease." *Annals of Internal Medicine* 103:1010–19.

Bennett, W., and J. Gurin. 1982. *The Dieter's Dilemma*. New York: Basic Books.

Berg, F. M. 1995. *Health Risks of Weight Loss*, 3rd ed., Hettinger, ND: Healthy Weight Journal.

——— . 1997. *Afraid to Eat: Children and Teens in Weight Crises*. Hettinger, ND: Healthy Weight Journal.

Biener, L. and A. Heaton. 1995. "Women Dieters or Normal Weight: Their Motives, Goals, and Risks." *American Journal of Public Health* 85:714–17.

Bild, D. E., P. Sholinsky, D. E. Smith, C. E. Lewis, J. M. Hardin, and G. L. Burke. 1996. "Correlates and Predictors of Weight Loss in Young Adults: The CARDIA Study." *International Journal of Obesity* 20:47–55.

Blair, S. N., H. W. Kohl III, C. E. Barlow, R. S. Paffenbarger, Jr., L. W. Gibbons, and C. A. Macera. 1995. "Changes in Physical Fitness and All-cause Mortality. A Prospective Study of Healthy and Unhealthy Men." *Journal of the American Medical Association* 273:1093–98.

Blair, S. N., J. Shaten, K. Brownell, G. Collins, and L. Lissner. 1993. "Body Weight Change, All-Cause Mortality, and Cause-Specific Mortality in the Multiple Risk Factor Intervention Trial." *Annals of Internal Medicine* 119:749–757.

Bliss, E. L., and C. H. Branch. 1960. *Anorexia Nervosa: Its History, Psychology, and Biology.* New York: Paul B. Hoeber.

Blumberg, P., and L. P. Mellis. 1985. "Medical Students' Attitudes toward the Obese and the Morbidly Obese." *International Journal of Eating Disorders* 4: 169–75.

Bohan, J. S. 1993. "Regarding Gender: Essentialism, Constructionism, and Feminist Psychology." *Psychology of Women Quarterly* 17:5–21.

Borjeson, M. 1976. "The Aetiology of Obesity in Children. A Study of 101 Twin Pairs." *Acta Paediatr. Scandinavia* 65(3):279–87.

Bouchard, C., A. Tremblay, J. Despres, A. Nadeau, J. P. Lupien, G. Theriault, J. Dussault, S. Moorjani, S. Pinault, and G. Fournier. 1990. "The Response to Long-term Overfeeding in Identical Twins." *New England Journal of Medicine* 322:1477–82.

Brown, D. 1997. "Two Weight Loss Drugs Linked to Heart Valve Ills." *Washington Post,* 9 July, p. A01.

Brownell, K. D. 1982. "Obesity: Understanding and Treating a Serious, Prevalent, and Refractory Disorder." *Journal of Consulting and Clinical Psychology* 50:820–40.

Brownell, K. D., G. D. Foster, and T. A. Wadden. 1996. "Reasonable Weight: Theoretical and Empirical Support for a New Model of Treatment for Obesity." Unpublished manuscript.

Brownell, K. D., and J. Rodin. 1994. "The Dieting Maelstrom: Is It Possible and Advisable to Lose Weight?" *American Psychologist* 49:781–91.

Brunner, R. L., S. T. St. Jeor, B. J. Scott, G. D. Miller, T. P. Carmody, K. D. Brownell, and J. Foryet. 1994. "Dieting and Disordered Eating Correlates of Weight Fluctuation in Normal and Obese Adults." *Eating Disorders: The Journal of Treatment and Prevention* 2:341–56.

Canning, H., and J. Mayer. 1966. "Obesity: Its Possible Effects on College Acceptance." *New England Journal of Medicine* 275:1172–74.

Cassidy, C. M. 1991. "The Good Body: When Big Is Better." *Medical Anthropology* 13:181–213.

Center for Science in the Public Interest. 1996. *Petition for Proposed Rulemaking to Regulate the Commercial Weight-loss Program Industry.* Submitted to the United States Federal Trade Commission, Washington D.C.

Coates, T. J., R. W. Jeffery, and R. R. Wing. 1978. "The Relationship between Persons' Relative Body Weights and the Quality and Quantity of Food Stored in Their Homes." *Addictive Behaviors* 3:179–84.

Cogan, J. C., S. K. Bhalla, A. Sefa-Dedeh, and E. D. Rothblum. 1996. "A Comparison Study of United States and African Students on the Perceptions of Obesity and Thinness." *Journal of Cross-Cultural Psychology* 27:98–113.

Cogan, J. C., and E. D. Rothblum. 1992. "Outcomes of Weight-loss Programs." *Genetic, Social, and General Psychology Monographs* 118:385–415.

Colditz, G. A. 1992. "Economic Costs of Obesity." *American Journal of Clinical Nutrition* 55:503S–7S.

Denis, P., D. Charpentier, P. Berros, and S. Touameur. 1995. "Bilateral Acute Angle-closure Glaucoma after Dexfenfluramine Treatment." *Ophthalmolgica* 209: 223–24.

Donahoe, C. P., D. H. Lin, D. S. Kirschenbaum, and R. E. Keesey. 1984. "Metabolic Consequences of Dieting and Exercise in the Treatment of Obesity." *Journal of Consulting and Clinical Psychology* 52:827–36.

Elder, G. 1969. "Appearance and Education in Marriage Mobility." *American Sociological Review* 34:519–33.

Ernsberger, P. 1997. "Adverse Reactions to Dexfenfluramine." *Healthy Weight Journal* 11:13–18.

Ernsberger, P., and P. Haskew. 1987. "Health Implications of Obesity: An Alternative View." *Journal of Obesity and Weight Regulation* 6:58–137.

Fitzgerald, F. T. 1981. "The Problem of Obesity." *Annual Review of Medicine* 32: 221–31.

Foster, G. D., T. A. Wadden, R. A. Vogt, and G. Brewer. 1997. "What Is a Reasonable Weight Loss? Patients' Expectations and Evaluations of Obesity Treatment Outcomes." *Journal of Consulting and Clinical Psychology* 65:79–85.

French, S. A., R. W. Jeffery, A. R. Folsom, D. F. Williamson, and T. Byers. 1995a. "History of Intentional and Unintentional Weight Loss in a Population-based Sample of Women Aged 55 to 69 Years." *Obesity Research* 3:163–70.

French, S. A., M. Story, B. Downes, Resnick, M. D., and R. W. Blum. 1995b. "Frequent Dieting Among Adolescents: Psychosocial and Health Behavior Correlates." *American Journal of Public Health* 85:695–710.

Furnham, A., and N. Alibhai. 1983. "Cross-cultural Differences in the Perception of Female Body Shapes." *Psychological Medicine* 13:829–37.

Gandour, M. J. 1984. "Bulimia: Clinical Description, Assessment, Etiology, and Treatment." *International Journal of Eating Disorders* 3:3–38.

Garner, D. M., and S. C. Wooley. 1991. "Confronting the Failure of Behavioral and Dietary Treatments for Obesity." *Clinical Psychology Review* 11:729–80.

Goffman, E. 1963. *Stigma: Notes on the Management of Spoiled Identity*. Englewood Cliffs, NJ: Prentice-Hall.

Goodrich, G. K., and J. P. Foreyt. 1991. "Why Treatments for Obesity Don't Last." *Journal of the American Dietetic Association* 91:1243–47.

Goodrich, G. K., A. S. Raynaud, P. W. Pace, and J. P. Foreyt. 1992. "Outcome Attribution in a Very Low Calorie Diet Program." *International Journal of Eating Disorders* 12:117–20.

Green, M. W., P. J. Rogers, N. A. Elliman, and S. J. Gatenby. 1994. "Impairment of Cognitive Performance Associated with Dieting and High Levels of Dietary Restraint." *Physiology and Behavior* 55:447–52.

Griffiths, R., and D. Farnill. 1996. "Primary Prevention of Eating Disorders: An Update." *Journal of Family Studies* 2:179–91.

Gurtner, H. P. 1985. "Aminorex and Pulmonary Hypertension. A Review." *Cor Vasa* 27(2–3):160–71.

Hall, S. M., and B. Havassy. 1981. "The Obese Woman: Causes, Correlates, and Treatment." *Professional Psychology* 12:163–70.

Hamm, P., R. B. Shekelle, and J. Stamler. 1989. "Large Fluctuations in Body Weight during Young Adulthood and Twenty-five Year Risk of Coronary Death in Men." *American Journal of Epidemiology* 129:312–18.

Hanson, R. L., L. T. Jacobsson, D. R. McCance, K. M. Narayan, D. J. Pettit, P. H. Bennett, and W. C. Knowler. 1996. "Weight Fluctuation, Mortality and Vascular Disease in Pima Indians." *International Journal of Obesity* 20:463–71.

Harris, M. B., R. J. Harris, and S. Bochner. 1982. "Fat, Four-eyed, and Female: Stereotypes of Obesity, Glasses, and Gender." *Journal of Applied Social Psychology* 12:503–16.

Herzog, D. 1997. "The Prevalence and Consequences of Eating Disorders and the Importance of Early Detection." Paper presented at a congressional briefing co-sponsored by the Society for the Psychological Study of Social Issues and the American Psychological Association. Washington, D.C.

Herzog, D. B., and P. M. Copeland. 1985. "Eating Disorders." *New England Journal of Medicine* 313:295–303.

Institute of Medicine. 1995. *Weighing the Options: Criteria for Evaluating Weight-Management Programs.* Washington, DC: National Academy Press.

Iribarren, C., D. S. Sharp, C. M. Burchfiel, and H. Petrovitch. 1995. "Association of Weight Loss and Weight Fluctuation with Mortality among Japanese American Men." *New England Journal of Medicine* 333:686–92.

Irving, L. M. 1990. "Mirror Images: Effects of the Standard of Beauty on the Self- and Body Esteem of Women Exhibiting Various Levels of Bulimic Symptoms." *Journal of Social and Clinical Psychology* 9:230–42.

Jarrett, R. J. 1986. "Is There an Ideal Body Weight?" *British Medical Journal* 293:493–95.

Jeffery, R. W. 1996. "Does Weight Cycling Present a Health Risk?" *American Journal of Clinical Nutrition* 63:452S–55S.

Karris, L. 1977. "Prejudice Against Obese Renters." *Journal of Social Psychology* 101:159–60.

Keys, A. 1980. "Overweight, Obesity, Coronary Heart Disease and Mortality." *Nutrition Reviews* 38:297–307.

Keys, A., J. Brozek, A. Henschel, O. Mickelson, and H. Taylor. 1950. *The Biology of Human Starvation.* Minneapolis: University of Minnesota Press.

Keys, A., A. Menotti, C. Aravanis, H. Blackburn, B. S. Djordevic, R. Buzina, A. S. Dontas, F. Fidanza, M. J. Karvonen, N. Kimura, I. Mohacek, S. Nedeljkovic, V. Puddu, S. Punsar, H. L. Taylor, S. Conti, D. Kromhout, and H. Toshima. 1984. "The Seven Countries Study: 2,289 Deaths in 15 Years." *Preventive Medicine* 13:141–54.

Killen J. D., C. B. Taylor, C. Hayward, K. F. Haydel, D. M. Wilson, L. Hammer, H. Kraemer, A. Blair-Greiner, and D. Strachowski. 1996. "Weight Concerns Influence the Development of Eating Disorders: A 4-Year Prospective Study." *Journal of Consulting and Clinical Psychology* 64:936–40.

Kramer, F. M., R. W. Jeffery, J. L. Forster, and M. K. Snell. 1989. "Long-term Follow-up of Behavioral Treatment for Obesity: Patterns of Weight Regain among men and women." *International Journal of Obesity* 13:123–36.

Laessle, R. G., P. Platte, U. Schweiger, and K. M. Pirke. 1996. "Biological and Psychological Correlates of Intermittent Dieting Behavior in Young Women: A Model for Bulimia Nervosa." *Physiology and Behavior* 60:1–5.

Larkin, J. C., and H. A. Pines. 1979. "No Fat Persons Need Apply: Experimental Studies of the Overweight Stereotype and Hiring Preference." *Sociology of Work and Occupations* 6:312–27.

Lerner, R. M., and E. Gellert. 1969. "Body Build Identification, Preference and Aversion in Children." *Developmental Psychology* 1:256–62.

Levine, M. P., L. Smolak, and H. Hayden. 1994. "The Relation of Sociocultural Factors to Eating Attitudes and Behaviors among Middle School Girls." *Journal of Early Adolescence* 14:471–90.

Levitsky, D. 1997. "Diet Drugs Gain Popularity." *Healthy Weight Journal* 11:8–12.

Lissner, L., C. Bengtsson, L. Lapidus, B. Larsson, B. Bengtsson, and K. D. Brownell. 1989. "Body Weight Variability and Mortality in the Gothenburg Prospective Studies of Men and Women." Pp. 55–60 in *Obesity in Europe 88: Proceedings of the First European Conference on Obesity*, edited by P. Bjorntorp and B. Rossner. London: Libbey.

Lissner, L., P. Odell, R. D'Agostino, J. Stokes, B. Kreger, A. Belanger, and K. D. Brownell. 1991. "Variability in Body Weight And Health Outcomes in the Framingham Population." *New England Journal of Medicine* 324:1839–44.

Lyons, P. 1997. "Do No Harm: Focus on Health, Not Weight Loss." *Healthy Weight Journal* 11:87–88.

Maddox, G. L., K. Back, and V. Lieberman. 1968. "Overweight as Social Deviance and Disability." *Journal of Health and Social Behavior* 9:287–98.

Mann, G. V. 1974. "The Influence of Obesity on Health (Part I and Part II)." *New England Journal of Medicine* 291:178–85, 245–53.

Miller, W. C., D. M. Koceja, and E. J. Hamilton. 1997. "A Meta-Analysis of the Past 25 Years of Weight Loss Research Using Diet, Exercise or Diet Plus Exercise Intervention." *International Journal of Obesity* 21:941–47.

Montero, P., C. Bernis, V. Fernandez, and S. Castro. 1996. "Influence of Body Mass Index and Slimming Habits on Menstrual Pain and Cycle Irregularity." *Journal of Biosocial Science* 28:315–23.

Morris, R. D., and A. A. Rimm. 1992. "Long-term Weight Fluctuation and Non-insulin-dependent Diabetes Mellitus in White Women." *Annals of Epidemiology* 2:657–64.

Muls, E., K. Kempen, G. Vansant, and W. Saris. 1995. "Is Weight Cycling Detrimental to Health? A Review of the Literature in Humans." *International Journal of Obesity* 19:S46–50.

Myers, J. E., D. J. Buysse, M. E. Thase, J. Perel, J. M. Miewald, T. B. Cooper, D. J. Kupfer, and J. J. Mann. 1993. "The Effects of Fenfluramine on Sleep and Prolactin in Depressed Inpatients: A Comparison of Potential Indices of Brain Aerotonergic Responsivity." *Biological Psychiatry* 34(11):753–58.

National Institutes of Health, Consensus Development Conference Statement. 1985. "Health Implications of Obesity." *Annals of Internal Medicine* 103:1073–77.

NIH Task Force on the Prevention and Treatment of Obesity. 1994. "Weight Cycling." *Journal of the American Medical Association* 272:1196–1202.

Patton, G. 1992. "Eating Disorders: Antecedents, Evolution and Course. Special Section: Eating Disorders." *Annals of Medicine* 24:281–85.

Poehlman, E. T., A. Tremblay, J. P. Despres, E. Fontaine, L. Perusse, G. Theriault, and C. Bouchard. 1986. "Genotype- controlled Changes in Body Composition and Fat Morphology Following Overfeeding in Twins." *American Journal of Clinical Nutrition* 43:723–31.

Polivy, J., and C. P. Herman. 1992. "Undieting: A Program to Help People Stop Dieting." *International Journal of Eating Disorders* 11:261–68.

Price, R. A., R. J. Cadoret, A. J. Stunkard, and E. Troughton. 1987. "Genetic Contributions to Human Fatness: An Adoption Study." *American Journal of Psychiatry* 144:1003–8.

Raich, R. M., J. C. Rosen, J. Deus, O. Perez, A. Requena, and J. Gross. 1992. "Eating Disorder Symptoms among Adolescents in the United States and Spain: A Comparative Study." *International Journal of Eating Disorders* 11:63–72.

Ross, C. E. 1994. "Overweight and Depression." *Journal of Health and Social Behavior* 35:63–79.

Rothblum, E. D. 1990. "Women and Weight: Fad and Fiction." *Journal of Psychology* 124(4):5–24.

Rothblum, E. D., P. A. Brand, C. T. Miller, and H. A. Oetjen. 1990. "The Relationship between Obesity, Employment Discrimination, and Employment Related Victimization." *Journal of Vocational Behavior* 37:251–66.

Shisslak, C. M., M. Crago, M. E. Neal, and B. Swain. 1987. "Primary Prevention of Eating Disorders." *Journal of Consulting and Clinical Psychology* 55:660–67.

Silverstein, B., L. Perdue, B. Peterson, and E. Kelly. 1986. "The Role of the Mass Media in Promoting a Thin Standard of Bodily Attractiveness for Women." *Sex Roles* 14:519–32.

Sobal, J. 1991. "Obesity and Socioeconomic Status: A Framework for Examining Relationships between Physical and Social Variables." *Medical Anthropology* 13:231–47.

Sobal, J., and A.J. Stunkard. 1989. "Obesity and Socioeconomic Status: A Review of the Literature." *Psychological Bulletin* 105:260–75.

Stake, J., and M. L. Lauer. 1987. "The Consequences of Being Overweight: A Controlled Study of Gender Differences." *Sex Roles* 17:31–47.

Stice, E., and H. E. Shaw. 1994. "Adverse Effects of the Media Portrayed Thin-ideal on Women and Linkages to Bulimic Symptomatology." *Journal of Social and Clinical Psychology* 13:288–308.

Stormer, S. M., and J. K. Thompson. 1996. "Explanations of Body Image Disturbance: A Test of Maturational Status, Negative Verbal Commentary, Social Comparison, and Sociocultural Hypotheses." *International Journal of Eating Disorders* 19:193–202.

Striegel-Moore, R. H., L. R. Silberstein, and J. Rodin. 1986. "Toward an Understanding of Risk Factors for Bulimia." *American Psychologist* 41:246–63.

Stunkard, A. J., T. T. Foch, and Z. Hrubec. 1986. "A Twin Study of Human Obesity." *Journal of the American Medical Association* 256:51–54.

Stunkard, A. J., J. R. Harris, N. L. Pedersen, and G. E. McClearn. 1990. "The Body Mass Index of Twins Who Have Been Reared Apart." *New England Journal of Medicine* 322:1483–87.

Stunkard, A. J., and M. McLaren-Hume. 1959. "The Results of Treatment for Obesity." *Archives of Internal Medicine* 103:79–85.

Stunkard, A. J., T. L. Sorensen, C. Hanis, T. W. Teasdale, R. Chakraborty, W. J. Schull, and F. Schulsinger. 1986. "An Adoption Study of Human Obesity." *New England Journal of Medicine* 314:193–98.

Thys, F., M. Schapira, J. M. Ghilain, J. M. Maisin, and J. Henrion. 1994. "Acute Pancreatitis and Fenfluramine." *Gastroenterology and Clinical Biology* 18(4):385–86.

Tiggemann, M., and E. D. Rothblum. 1988. "Gender Differences in Social Consequences of Perceived Overweight in the United States and Australia." *Sex Roles* 18:75–86.

Toornvliet, A. C., H. Pijl, and A. E. Meinders. 1994. "Major Depression during Dexfenfluramine Treatment." *International Journal of Obesity* 18(9):650.

Troiano, R. P., E. A. Frongillo, Jr., J. Sobal, and D. A. Levitsky. 1996. "The Relationship between Body Weight and Mortality: A Quantitative Analysis of Combined Information from Existing Studies." *International Journal of Obesity* 20:63–75.

Waaler, H. T. 1984. "Height, Weight, and Mortality. The Norwegian Experience." *Acta Medica Scandinavia Supplement* 679:1–51.

Wadden, T. A., G. Blackburn, and T. Van Itallie. 1990. "Responsible and Irresponsible Use of VLCDs in the Treatment of Obesity." *Journal of the American Medical Association* 263:83–85.

Wadden, T. A., and A. J. Stunkard. 1985. "Social and Psychological Consequences of Obesity." *Annuals of Internal Medicine* 103:1062–67.

Walster, E., V. Aronson, D. Abrahams, and L. Rottman. 1971. "Importance of Physical Attractiveness in Dating Behavior." *Journal of Personality and Social Psychology* 4:508–16.

Williamson, D. F. 1996. "Weight Cycling and Mortality: How Do the Epidemiologists Explain the Role of Intentional Weight Loss?" *Journal of the American College of Nutrition* 15:6–13.

Wilson, G. T. 1994. "Behavioral Treatment of Obesity: Thirty Years and Counting." *Advances in Behaviour Research and Therapy* 16:31–75.

Wing, R. R., and R. W. Jeffery. 1978. "Differential Restaurant Patronage of Obese and Nonobese People." *Addictive Behaviors* 3:135–38.

Wolf, N. 1991. *The Beauty Myth: How Images of Beauty Are Used Against Women.* New York: William Morrow.

Wooley, S. C., and O. W. Wooley. 1979. "Obesity and Women: A Closer Look at the Facts." *Women Studies International Quarterly* 2:68–79.

Wooley, S. C., O. W. Wooley, and S. Dyernforth. 1979. "Theoretical, Practical, and Social Issues in Behavioral Treatments of Obesity." *Journal of Applied Behavior Analysis* 12:3–25.

Biographical Sketches of the Contributors

Caron Bove is a Research Associate in the Division of Nutritional Sciences at Cornell University. She holds a Ph.D. in Nutrition from Cornell University and an M.D. from the University of Vermont. She is currently studying the changing dietary and physical activity behaviors and body weight patterns of newlyweds. Her previous research has focused on the infant feeding behaviors of low-income women and on postpartum weight retention.

Thomas Cash is a Professor of Psychology at Old Dominion University in Norfolk, Virginia. A clinical and research psychologist for over twenty-five years, his professional work focuses on the psychology of physical appearance. His research has examined appearance stereotyping and discrimination, the prevalence and development of body image dysfunctions, and the conceptualization, assessment, and treatment of body image. He has published three books and over 125 scientific publications. His most recent book, *The Body Image Workbook* (1997), offers an empirically validated, cognitive-behavioral therapy for body image problems within a self-help modality.

Gwen Chapman is an Associate Professor in the School of Family and Nutritional Sciences at the University of British Columbia in Vancouver, Canada. She teaches undergraduate and graduate courses in human nutrition, nutrition research, and consumer aspects of foods. She obtained her doctorate in Nutritional Sciences from the University of Toronto and is a Registered Dietitian/Nutritionist. Her research explores how women's food practices and concerns are shaped by socially constructed notions about food, health, bodies, and social roles.

Jeanine C. Cogan is a social psychologist who is currently an American Psychological Association Congressional Science Fellow. Her research and policy work focuses on addressing sociocultural factors such as media messages and societal expectations that contribute to the development of body image issues and eating problems. She has presented her work at professional conferences, educational and professional organizations, and community groups, and is working with Congress and federal agencies to improve the response to and prevention of eating disorders as a public health issue.

Gina Cordell is a researcher at the University of Alabama, Tuscaloosa. She completed her master's degree in Sociology at the University of Memphis in 1997. Her research interests include body image, contemporary theory, and urban sociology.

Douglas Degher is a Professor of Sociology in the Department of Sociology and Social Work at Northern Arizona University, where he has been a member of the faculty since 1973. He received his Ph.D. in Sociology from Washington State University in 1974. His primary interests are in deviance theory and the sociology of sport. His most recent published work involves research on status assumption and identity change.

Susan Haworth-Hoeppner is a Visiting Assistant Professor at Oakland University and Coordinator of the Women's Studies program. She received her doctorate in Sociology in 1996 from Wayne State University, Detroit, Michigan. Her research interests involve the role of body image in the production of eating disorders.

Karen Honeycutt is a doctoral candidate in the Department of Sociology at the University of Michigan, Ann Arbor. Her dissertation is a qualitative exploration of three groups of women: those who have lost weight, those who are "fat activists" or are otherwise active in the size acceptance movement, and those who are fat and trying to accept themselves as they are but without the support of an organization. In addition to gender and body image, her research interests include social psychology, cultural studies and the mass media, race/ethnic relations, and issues of social class.

Gerald Hughes is a Professor of Sociology in the Department of Sociology and Social Work at Northern Arizona University, where he has been a member of the faculty since 1973. He received his Ph.D. in Sociology from The University of Arizona in 1979. His primary interests are Program Planning and Evaluation, Distance Education, and Deviance. His recent work has focused on the development of World Wide Web courses in Sociology. His most recent papers have focused on subcultural disengagement within the identity change process.

Leanne Joanisse is a doctoral candidate in Sociology at McMaster University in Hamilton, Ontario, Canada. Her master's thesis, which examined the microlevel management of obesity stigma, was obtained from

Concordia University in Montreal, Quebec, Canada. Her research interests include sociology of the body, medical sociology, weight-related anxieties and concerns, and women's health. The subject of her dissertation is the controversy surrounding gastric bypass surgery in the treatment of morbid obesity.

Rebecca J. Lester is currently a Visiting Assistant Professor in Religious Studies at the University of California, Riverside. She received her doctorate in anthropology from the University of California, San Diego, where her dissertation examined nationalist expressions of religious vocation in a Mexican convent. Her primary research interests are in mental health, religion, gender, and the body. Her past work on anorexia nervosa has been published in *Social Science and Medicine* and *Ethos,* and a chapter in the forthcoming book *Not Tonight: Anthropological Approaches to Sexual Celibacy,* edited by E. J. Sobo and S. Bell.

Donna Maurer is a John S. Knight Postdoctoral Fellow in the Writing Program at Cornell University. In 1997, she received her doctorate in sociology from Southern Illinois University-Carbondale, where she won the Outstanding Dissertation Award. She co-edited, with Jeffery Sobal, *Eating Agendas: Food and Nutrition as Social Problems* (1995). She is currently completing a book on the North American vegetarian movement.

Elizabeth Ransom is a doctoral candidate in Sociology at Michigan State University. Her research centers on transformations occurring in the global agrifood system, and she is presently examining South Africa and the changes in the agrifood system as that nation integrates into the global economy. She has a particular interest in how global changes are related to people's construction of their bodies in society, especially the construction of bodies as they differ by race/ethnicity and gender.

Barbara Rauschenbach is a Research Associate in the Division of Nutritional Sciences at Cornell University. She received her Ph.D. in Sociology from the University of Minnesota-Minneapolis. Her primary research interest is in the social aspects of nutrition. Her publications include analyses of the interrelationships between marriage and weight, descriptions of clients of private and public food programs, and the measurement of food insecurity and analysis of its social antecedents and nutritional consequences.

Carol Rambo Ronai is Assistant Professor of Sociology at the University of Memphis. Her research interests include the intersections of discourse, narrative practices, and interpretive theory. She recently edited

Everyday Sexism in the Third Millenium (with Barbara Zsembik and Joe R. Feagin), which explores how discursive constraint and narrative resistance play a part in the lives of adult survivors of childhood sexual abuse. Currently she is conducting life history interviews with adults who have experienced childhood sexual abuse.

Robin Roy received her undergraduate psychology degree from Connecticut College in 1996 and her masters in psychology from Old Dominion University in 1998. She is currently completing a doctorate in social psychology at the University of Vermont. Her research interests and publications examine women's issues, body image, and interpersonal processes.

Jeffery Sobal is a Sociologist who is an Associate Professor in the Division of Nutritional Sciences at Cornell University, where he teaches about social science analysis of food, eating, and nutrition. His research interests focus on social patterns of obesity, especially body weight and marriage, and the role of weight in society, particularly stigmatization of obese individuals and medicalization of obesity as a social problem. He also examines the food choice process and the food and nutrition system. He co-edited, with Donna Maurer, *Eating Agendas: Food and Nutrition as Social Problems* (1995).

Anthony Synnott is a Professor of Sociology at Concordia University in Montreal, who received his doctorate from London University. His principal research interests are in the body and the senses. He is the author of *The Body Social: Symbolism, Self and Society* (1993) and *Shadows: Issues and Social Problems in Canada* (1996), and he is co-author with Constance Classen and David Howes of *Aroma: The Cultural History of Smell* (1994).

Index

Accounts, 18, 22–24
Activism, 64
Aggression, physical, 62–63, 67
Alcoholics Anonymous (AA), 142, 144, 155–158
Anger, 61–62
Anorexia nervosa, 89–90, 139
Anorexic and nonanorexic categorical distinctions
    "feeling fat" and, 94–97, 105
    study of, 93–94
    thinness and, 97–102, 105
    viability of, 92–93
Antidieting interventions, 218–221
Antiobesity drugs, 241
Appearance management, 3
Assertion, verbal, 62, 67
Attractiveness, 31–32, 97–99
Audience reception, 178
Avoidance, 19–20

Biology, weight and, 239
Biomedical model, 184–185
Bodily perfection, pursuit of, 73
Body image
    abnormal, 5
    culture and, 209, 212–216
    definitions, 209–210
    dimensions, 209–210
    discontent with, growing, 210–211
    dissatisfaction with, 5, 91–97, 106
    eating disorders and, 89–90
    feminine issue of, 211–212
    media messages and, 212–216
    medical discourse on normal, 5, 90–91
    nondieting interventions and, 218–221

"normal," 5, 90–91
    obesity and, 216–217
    overweight women and, 34–35
    psychopathology and, 216–217
    research among nonclinical populations, 91
    satisfaction with, 5, 102–105
    thinness and, 97–102, 105
    weight loss for change in, 217–218
Body Mass Index (BMI), 230, 234

Cognitive-behavioral body image therapy, 220–221
College athletes, 6, 183–184 (see also Construction of bodies in women's collegiate cross country)
Compensation, 20–21
Competitive athletes, 6, 183–184 (see also Construction of bodies in women's collegiate cross country)
Compliance, 21–22
Compulsive eating, 140, 143–145, 153, 157
Confession, 149–150, 152
Construction of bodies in women's collegiate cross country
    cooperating networks, 188–200
    data collection methods, 187–188
    intersection of body, sport, and society and, 203–204
    medicalization of deviance and, 184–185
    NCAA and, 200–203
    networks in context of sport, 185–187, 203
    overview, 183–184
Contextual factors, 127–128

Cooperating networks
  bodies, 192–195
  food, 188–192
  uniformity and, creating, 195–200
Coping strategies
  accounts, 18, 22–24
  avoidance, 19–20
  compensation, 20–21
  compliance, 21–22
  overview, 11, 18–19, 25
  reaction formation, 20
Cultural studies approach, 167
Culture
  body image and, 209, 212–216
  eating disorders and, 139–141,
    242–244
  fatness and, 114–115
  health and fitness movements and,
    82
  social constructions of obesity and, 4
  thinness and, 114–115, 242–244
  weddings and weight and, 113–115
  weight and, 7

Deviance exemplars, 31–37, 44–45
Deviant identity, 12–13, 18
Dieting
  commercial programs, 170, 241
  consequences of, psychological and
    physical, 236–237
  discourse, 80–81
  drugs, 229
  failure of, 83, 234–235
  negative effects of, 83
  older ways of, 75–77
  shift from, 5
  weight loss and, long-term, 234–235
Discourses on eating for weight control
  circulation of, 84
  dieting, 80–81
  healthy-eating, 81–83
  nature of, 79–80
Discrimination, 12, 55–57
Discursive constraint, 30–31, 43–44
Dissatisfaction with body image, 5,
  91–97, 106
Distancing self from deviance, 37–40

Eating disorders (*see also* Interdependence of obesity and eating disorders)
  body image and, 89–90
  compulsive eating, 140, 143–145,
    153, 157
  culturally shared meaning of,
    231–232
  culture and, 139–141, 242–244
  feminist-cultural interpretation of,
    140
  medical discourse on, 5
  medicalization of, 185
  mental illness and, 139–141
  paradigm shift in, call for, 244–247
  technology of gender and, 153–
    156
Eating stories, common, 23–24
Eating for weight control
  circulation of discourses, 84
  constructions of newer versus older,
    84–85
  dieting discourse, 80–81
  healthy-eating discourse, 81–83
  nature of discourses, 79–80
  newer ways of, 77–79
  older ways of, 75–77
  overview, 73
  trend toward, 5
  women's stories, 74–79
Employment discrimination, 55–57
Enlightenment, 65–67
Equivocators, 172–173, 179
Excepting from deviance, 40–43
Excuses, 23, 40
Exploitation, 33–34

Fat Boosters, 169, 173–174, 179
Fat Busters, 169–172, 179
Fat continuum, personal, 37–38
"Fat" identity
  adopting, 12–18
  coping strategies, 18–25
  deviant careers and, 25
  as deviant identity, 12–13
  overview, 11–12
Fat power, 66

"Feeling fat," 94–97, 105
Fen/phen, 229, 241
Fighting stigma of obesity
    activism, 64
    aggression, physical, 62–63, 67
    anger, 61–62
    assertion, verbal, 62, 67
    enlightenment, 65–67
    fat power, 66
    flamboyance, 63–64
    internalization, 60–61
    overview, 59–60, 67–68
    reflective resistance, 67
    self-acceptance, 64–657, 67
Flamboyance, 63–64

Gender identity, 15–16
Genetics, 41–42, 239

Health
    overweight women and, 39–40
    stigma of obesity and, 49
Health and fitness movements, 82
Healthy-eating discourse, 81–83
Hegemony theory, 178–179
Humor, 35–37, 44

Identities (*see also* "Fat" identity)
    deviant, 12–13, 18
    gender, 15–16
    "spoiled," 12
    weight, 3–4
Identity change process
    external levels of, 14
    internal level of, 13–14
    new status, 17–18
    placing, 11, 16–17, 24–25
    public level of, 13
    recognizing, 15–16, 24–25
    status cues in, 11, 14, 25
Inaction in weight management, 123,
    126
Interactionist perspective, 166
Interdependence of obesity and eating
    disorders
    eating disorders and, culturally
        shared meaning of, 231–232

limitations of socially constructed
    definitions and, 232–247
obesity and, culturally shared mean-
    ing of, 230–231
overview, 229
recognition of, 229–230
Internalization, 60–61, 215
Isolation, 53–54

Justifications, 23

Laziness stereotype, 38–39
Life history interviews with over-
    weight women
    deviance exemplars, 31–37, 44–45
    distancing from deviance, 37–40
    excepting from deviance, 40–43
    sampling for, 29–30
Living obese
    employment discrimination, 55–57
    family, 52–53
    loneliness and isolation, 53–54
    medical profession, 57–58
    public harassment, 58–59
    romantic relationships, 54–55
    school, 53
Loneliness, 53–54
Loopholes, 40–43

Master status, 13
Media messages and body image,
    212–216
Medical discourse, 5, 90–91
Medical history, 41
Medical profession, 5, 49, 57–58
Medicalization
    of deviance, 184–185
    of eating disorders, 185
    of weight, 5
Mental illness, 139–141, 216–217

Narrative resistance, 30–31, 43–45
National Association to Advance Fat
    Acceptance (NAAFA), 168–169,
    173–178
National Collegiate Athletic Associa-
    tion (NCAA), 200–203

Networks in context of sport, 185–187,
    203
New status, 17–18
Nondieting, activist group, 173–174,
    179
Nondieting interventions, 218–221
Nondieting, nonactivist group,
    172–173, 179
"Normal" body build, 15, 17, 90–91
Not taking action in weight manage-
    ment, 123, 126

Obesity (see also Interdependence of
    obesity and eating disorders;
    Overweight women; Social con-
    structions of obesity; Stigma of
    obesity)
  body image and, 216–217
  consequences of, social, 12–13
  culturally shared meaning of,
    230–231
  discrimination and, 12
  drugs fighting, 241
  health benefits of moderate, 234
  as health risk, 232–234
  living with, 52–59
  medical profession and, 57–58
  paradigm shift in, call for, 244–247
  psychopathology and, 216–217
  risk factors, changing, 238
  "spoiled" identity and, 12
Occupational ideologies, 18
Overeaters Anonymous (OA)
  Alcoholics Anonymous and, 142,
    155–158
  confession and, 149–150, 152
  overview, 141–143, 157
  penitence and, 149–150
  recovery process, 146–148, 155,
    157–158
  spiritual state and, 141, 143–146
  stylization of self and, 141, 149–150
  technologies of self and, 6, 141,
    148–153, 155
  technology of gender and, 153–156
  twelve-step philosophy and,
    141–144, 157–158

Overweight women (see also Obesity)
  attractiveness and, 31–32
  body image and, 34–35
  discursive constraint and, 30–31,
    43–44
  exploitation and, 33–34
  fat continuum and, personal, 37–38
  genetics and, 41–42
  health and, 39–40
  humor and, 35–37, 44
  laziness and, 38–39
  life history interviews with, 29,
    31–43
  loopholes and, 40–43
  medical history and, 41
  narrative resistance and, 30–31,
    43–45
  negative view of, 29
  sexual desirability and, 32–33
  sloppiness and, 38–39
  socialization and, 42–43
  society and, 29, 43, 45–46
  weight loss and, 34–35

Paradigm shift, call for, 244–247
Penitence, 149–150
Personal attractiveness, 98–99
Physical attractiveness, 31–32, 97–98
Placing, 11, 16–17, 24–25
Postponing action in weight manage-
    ment, 123, 126
Psychoeducational efforts as nondiet-
    ing interventions, 219–220
Psychological profession, 5, 49–50
Psychopathology, 139–141, 216–217
Public harassment, 58–59

Reaction formation, 20
Recognizing, 15–16, 24–25
Recovery process in Overeaters
    Anonymous, 146–148, 155,
    157–158
Reflective resistance, 67
Romantic relationships, 54–55

Satisfaction with body image, 5,
    102–105

Self-acceptance, 64–65, 67
Self-esteem, 100–102
Self-evidentiality, 15–16
Sexual desirability, 12, 32–33
Sites of dissatisfaction, 103–104
Sizism, 50–51
Sloppiness stereotype, 38–39
Social constructionist theory, 166
Social constructions of obesity
  assumptions in, faulty, 174–178
  culture and, 4
  limitations of, 232–247
  master narrative and three
    responses, 168–174
  methods, 168
  theoretical framework, 166–167
Socialization, 42–43
Socializing, 127–128
Spiritual state in Overeaters Anony-
    mous, 141, 143–146
"Spoiled" identity, 12
Status cues, 11, 14, 25
Stereotypes, 12 (*see also specific types*)
Stigma, 240 (*see also* Stigma of obesity)
Stigma of obesity
  consequences of, psychological and
    social, 239–241
  fighting, 59–67
  health and, 49
  living with, 52–59
  managing, 4, 50–59
  medical researchers and, 49
  psychological researchers and, 49–
    50
  social consequences of, 12
  surviving, 68
Stress, 127–128
Stylization of self, 141, 149–150
Symbolic interactionist framework,
    18–24

Taking action in weight management,
    123–125
Techniques of neutralization, 18
Technologies of self, 6, 141, 148–153,
    155
Technology of gender, 153–156

Thinness
  anorexic and nonanorexic categori-
    cal distinctions and, 97–102, 105
  as asset, 105–106
  body image and, 97–102, 105
  culture and, 114–115
  economic costs of pursuit of, 242
  expectations of, 99–100
  personal attractiveness and, 98–99
  physical attractiveness and, 97–98
  self-esteem and, 100–102
Twelve-step philosophy, 141–144,
    157–158

Undieting interventions, 218–221
Uniformity, creating, 195–200
Unusual action in weight manage-
    ment, 123, 126–127

Vigilant action in weight management,
    123, 125

Weddings and weight
  construction of, 5, 116–118, 131–132
  culture and, 113–115
  definition of, 117–121
  interpretation of, 117–121
  management of weight before wed-
    dings, 121–129
  negotiation of weight before wed-
    dings, 121–129
  overview, 5, 113–114
  performance of weight and, 117,
    129–131
  presentation of weight and, 117,
    129–131
  society and, contemporary, 115–116
Weight (*see also* Obesity; Overweight
    women; Weight management)
  biology and, 239
  culture and, 7
  definitions of, 5
  fluctuation, 237–238
  genetics and, 239
  ideal, 230
  identities, 3–4
  medicalization of, 5

Weight (*continued*)
  redefining, 4–5
  reinterpreting, 7
Weight loss
  body image and, change in, 217–218
  dieting and long-term, 234–235
  drugs for, 229, 241
  overweight women and, 34–35
Weight management (*see also* Eating
    for weight control)
  contextual factors, 127–128
  inaction in, 123, 126
  newer ways of, 77–79
  not taking action in, 123, 126
  older ways of, 75–77
  ongoing process of, 4–5
  organization processes in, 6
  orientations, 123–127
  postponing action in, 123, 126
  reasons for, 3
  taking action in, 123–125
  unusual action in, 123, 126–127
  vigilant action in, 123, 125
  before weddings, 121–129
Weight regain, 235–236
Weight-loss group, 170–172, 179
Weight-related organizations, 6 (*see
    also specific types*)